Barbara Thériault
The Cop and the Sociologist

Culture and Social Practice

Barbara Thériault is Associate Professor of Sociology and Director of the Canadian Centre for German and European Studies at the University of Montreal. She holds a PhD from the Max Weber Centre for Cultural and Social Studies (University of Erfurt, Germany).

Barbara Thériault
The Cop and the Sociologist
Investigating Diversity in German Police Forces

[transcript]

Bibliographic information published by the Deutsche Nationalbibliothek
The Deutsche Nationalbibliothek lists this publication in the Deutsche Nationalbibliografie; detailed bibliographic data are available in the Internet at http://dnb.d-nb.de

© 2013 transcript Verlag, Bielefeld

All rights reserved. No part of this book may be reprinted or reproduced or utilized in any form or by any electronic, mechanical, or other means, now known or hereafter invented, including photocopying and recording, or in any information storage or retrieval system, without permission in writing from the publisher.

Cover layout: Kordula Röckenhaus, Bielefeld
Cover illustration: jaeschko / photocase.com
Layout and Typeset by Barbara Thériault
Printed by Majuskel Medienproduktion GmbH, Wetzlar
ISBN 978-3-8376-2310-9

à Noa Blanche

Contents

List of Illustrations | 13
Preface | 15

I. Max Weber, the Sociologist, and the Police Officer

Diversity. A Word Without Qualities | 23

Apprehending the Individual | 43

II. Dealing With Difference. Four Portraits and a Half

Inspector Piontek, or *Sorge um die Seele*
(The Empathetic Type) | 63

Inspector Bobkowski, or Liberalism
(The Principled Type) | 85

Criminal Inspector Schmitt and the Police Researcher
(The Opportunist Type and Its Mirror Image) | 111

Ms. Berger, or Social Change
(Diversity as Profession and Vocation) | 137

III. A Three-Dimensional Picture

The Details and the Overall Picture | 159

Diversity. A Word With Qualities | 177

Appendix | 197
Bibliography | 199
Index | 219

Detailed Contents

List of Illustrations | 13

Preface | 15

I. MAX WEBER, THE SOCIOLOGIST, AND THE POLICE OFFICER

Diversity. A Word Without Qualities | 23
1. From Officers from Post-Migration Backgrounds to Carriers of Diversity | 25
   1.1 Defining Diversity | 29
2. Constructing the Field | 32
   2.1 Entering and Narrowing the Field: Material, Methods, Approach | 32
   2.2 Leaving the Field: Ideal Types | 36
3. Division of the Book | 38
4. The Sociologist and the Cop | 41

Apprehending the Individual | 43
1. The Place of the Individual in Weber's Sociology | 45
   1.1 Individuals, Fictional and Real | 46
2. The Object of Typical Sociological Investigation: Motives (and not Intent) | 48
   2.1 Possible Slippages | 51
   2.2 Weber's Desertion | 53
3. The Consequences of Action, Fate, and the Return of the Individual | 56
4. Investigating the Motives of Action: A Proposition | 58

II. DEALING WITH DIFFERENCE. FOUR PORTRAITS AND A HALF

Inspector Piontek, or *Sorge um die Seele* (The Empathetic Type) | 63
1. Inspector Piontek:
   Recruiting Officers from Post-Migration Backgrounds | 64
   1.1 Shaping the Rules of Entry | 65
   1.2 Leading Recruitment Activities | 68
   1.3 Representing Recruits in the Selection Process | 71

"Sorge um die Seele": Pastoral Care of the Soul
(Excursus on the Guide) | 72

2. Investigating Motives | 75
   2.1 On Ideal Types | 75
   2.2 The Empathetic Type… | 76
   2.3 … And the Flesh-and-Blood Officers | 78
3. Consequences of Action, Tensions, and Dilemmas | 79

Forth in Berlin, Back in Hamburg (Excursus on the Recruits) | 82

Inspector Bobkowski, or Liberalism (The Principled Type) | 85
❏ *Boxed Text 1: "Politische Bildung"* | 85
1. The Political Education Teacher | 87
   1.1 Inspector Bobkowski | 87
   1.2 In the Orbit of Political Education | 90

Excursus: A Story Within a Story.
The Planned Bernhard Weiß Square | 92

2. Entangled History | 96
   2.1 Investigating Motives | 99
   2.2 Measures Taken in a Hostile Context… | 102
   2.3 … and Pertaining Dilemmas | 103
3. A Principled Type | 106
   3.1 Bobkowski Cross-Examined | 106
4. Epilogue | 108

**Criminal Inspector Schmitt and the Police Researcher
(The Opportunist Type and Its Mirror Image) | 111**
PART ONE: OPPORTUNISM AS MOTIVE | 112
1. Working in Human Resources: Criminal Inspector Schmitt | 112
    1.1 The Action Plan | 114
A Glance at the Netherlands | 116
    1.2 Consequences, Dilemmas, Motives | 119
Theoretical Excursus I (The Opportunist Type) | 123
PART TWO: REACTION TO OPPORTUNISM | 124
1. Studying Police Culture: The Researcher | 125
    ❑ *Boxed Text 2: Diversity Management* | 126
    A Much Repeated Anecdote | 127
    1.1 The Book | 129
    1.2 The Motives, Not the Consequences | 131
Theoretical Excursus II (The Opportunist's Mirror Image) | 132
    1.3 Back to the Individuals | 134
PART THREE: CONCLUSION | 135

**Ms. Berger, or Social Change
(Diversity as Profession and Vocation) | 137**
1. Diversity as a Profession and a Vocation | 139
2. One Case: Claudia Berger | 141
    2.1 Change as Leitmotif | 144
    2.2 An Early Exit | 146
3. The Enigma: The Specialist's Absence | 149
    1.1 The Specialists as Carrier Group | 149
    1.2 The Specialists' Ideas, or Spirit of Diversity | 150
4. Reactions to Ms. Berger | 152
5. Conclusion: Meeting Up Again in a Few Years | 154

III. A THREE-DIMENSIONAL PICTURE

The Details and the Overall Picture | 159
1. First Detail: The Actors' Striking Resemblance | 161
A Note on Representation ("Stellvertretung") | 162
    1.1 A Specific Trait of the Relation Toward Difference… | 165
    1.2 … But a Contested One (A Fictional Conversation) | 167
2. Second Detail: The Weimar Connection | 172
3. The Picture as a Whole | 174

Diversity. A Word With Qualities | 177
1. (Another) Spirit of Diversity | 178
    1.1 Making Sense of Actions: Motives, Orders, and Legitimacy | 178
    1.2 Specific Traits (Historical Individual) | 180
2. Something *bildungsbürgerlich* | 182
    2.1 On German Liberalism | 183
Excursus: A Literary Account of the German Liberal Individual | 183
3. Simmel, the Individual, and the Relation Toward Difference in the Forces | 186
    3.1 Individuation and De-Individuation | 186
    3.2 The Police as Secret Society | 188
    ❑ *Boxed Text 3: Cop Culture* | 189
4. Type of Causation | 193

Appendix | 197

Bibliography | 199

Index | 219

List of Illustrations

Figure 1:   The Individual and the Ideal Types | 19

Figure 2:   Poster of the *Nationaler Integrationsplan* | 26

Figure 3:   Poster made by the Hamburg Police Academy for placement in Turkish shops | 68

Figure 4:   *Für türkische Berliner stehen die Sterne besonders gut* | 91

Figure 5:   Photo of Bernhard Weiß with Daisy Grzesinski, Charlie Chaplin, Albert Grzesinski and Lotte Weiß in Berlin, 1931 | 96

Figure 6:   Simmel's Secret Society | 188

Preface

This study is about diversity in the German police forces. Researching and teaching in the context of German studies and classical sociology, police forces were not an obvious object of inquiry at first; yet, they proved to be an exciting and challenging one. For sociology and its practitioners, police forces present two aspects, the kind of investigative business we are in and the often tense value relation we entertain toward it. In a form of a dialogue with Max Weber, who in this way became an actor in the investigation, the research underlying this book was accompanied by an interrogation of the object and method of sociological investigation, its specificity and its limits and, in turn, the limits of the endeavor undertaken here and of sociological writings as a genre.

Working on the study, I spoke with police officers and my social science colleagues, reacting to the interest shown by some and the irritation expressed by others. My colleagues in Montreal noticed and sometimes raised their eyebrows at the "conservative" character of the object of my research. In a previous project, I focused my attention on the churches. The police officers at the center of this study are not unlike the "conservative revolutionaries" within Germany's churches after political change in the 1990s. With the passage of time, it occurred to me that I was always fascinated by a particular type of actor: people who could be referred to as progressive within "semi-totalizing" organizations. As such, much of the people I write about in this book could be described, in the words used by Wolfgang Engler when discussing intellectuals in the former GDR, as "heretic reformers" (1995: 148), that is people both loyal to and critical of the organization they belong to. Beyond the empirical question—How can the relationship toward cultural and ethnic difference in today's Germany be characterized and explained within an organization characterized by strong socialization and homogenizing principles?—, this type of actor points to the existential side of the same question: How is an individual to live in such an organization? Not surprisingly, the attitudes of the people I met while working on these projects were often marked by ambivalence: they sometimes promoted change and at other times resisted the changes they had themselves sometimes helped to bring about.

The first project was carried out at the Max Weber Center for Advanced Social and Cultural Studies at the University of Erfurt; the second one originated in the Weber group at the Canadian Centre for German and European Studies and at the Department of Sociology of the University of Montreal as well as at the Section in Comparative Social and Cultural Anthropology at the European Viadrina University in Frankfurt (Oder). The writings of Max Weber constituted a starting point to the present project: while the book does not claim to offer a thoroughly new reading of his sociology, it brings it to fruition for the purpose of an empirical study, appropriating what is more a method and a "spirit" than a general theory. This meant thinking, working, and writing with and through ideal types, and sometimes subverting them. If references to Weber might appear to some as old-fashioned, they stand in close vicinity to what have recently been referred to in France as the sociologies of the individual (Martuccelli and de Singly 2009; Martuccelli 2010).

Working within such a frame brings specific theories and methods, but also an intellectual and existential sensibility for the individual, one also shared by novelists. Along the maturation process of this study, I have benefited from reading novelists such as Milan Kundera and Thomas Mann. They allowed me to better understand Weber's sociology and what they share: the study of motives and their conflicts, the question of sincerity as well as the chasm between intention and consequences and the often paradoxical effect of action.

As the photo below alludes to, both the construction of the types and the analysis move from the real individuals to the sociological types and back. Focusing on these two dimensions involved hanging on to description and theorization. The results are four portraits that are meant to represent and account for as many possible answers to the empirical question I raise on the relations toward cultural and ethnic difference in today's Germany. Throughout the chapters, the portraits refer to one another, completing and throwing light on each other. Toward the end, I integrate and interpret them by looking back on the police forces as organizations and pointing to a particular "spirit of diversity."

While writing the book, I gave up the idea of inserting a conventional review of the literature and a heavy discussion of theories at the beginning of the book. Apart from chapter one on Weberian sociology, which may appear too light for some and too bulky for others, both reviews as well as discussions on theories, methods, and themes are built into the chapters; often, they feed on concrete situations, characters, and problems encountered during the course of the research. This way of writing, which departed from sociology as I had practiced it so far, contributed, I hope, to a smooth approach to sociological language; it also proved to be somewhat of an existential necessity.

I would like to express my gratitude to the men and women behind Inspectors Bobkowski, Piontek, Schwarz, Winter, and Schmitt as well as to Ms. Berger and their colleagues for their time and generosity in sharing their experiences with me. My colleagues at the European Viadrina University in Frankfurt (Oder) who, while I spent a year on a Humboldt fellowship in 2006-2007 and beyond, were a great source of inspiration in preparing and writing this study. I especially want to thank Werner Schiffauer, Frank Peter, Alexandra Schwell, and Schirin Amir-Moazami for their insights. The Weber group—and its offshoots—at the Canadian Centre for German and European Studies at the University of Montreal, which aimed at revisiting classical writers of sociology for empirical purposes was a stimulating place to be. My colleagues at the Department of Sociology of the same institution: Valérie Amiraux, Sirma Bilge, Danielle Juteau and the late Gilles Houle as well as Ferdinand Sutterlüty who spent some time among us in 2011 are thanked. I am grateful to Thomas Beschorner for making me talk about one particular group for whom diversity is both a profession and a vocation, those I refer to as the specialists; this was an important step toward better distinguishing the ideal types I was constructing. My thanks also go to Anna Georgiev and Marcel Thériault for their more than technical support. I feel lucky to have met Johannes Weiß, for he was a great source of inspiration, first as an author and then as a friend. I am perhaps most indebted to my first readers, Rosalie Dion, Thomas Schmidt-Lux, and Kevin Hébert for commenting on the chapters at their various stages.

This book and some articles, which preceded it, were made possible thanks to grants by the Canadian Social Sciences and Humanities Research Council and the German Humboldt Foundation. I would like to thank *German Politics and Society* for permission to reproduce material from which they hold copyright: "Inquiring into Diversity. The Case of Berlin Police Inspector Bobkowski" (2009, 27[4]: 72-91) presented some of the material from chapter three ("Inspector Bobkowski, or Liberalism [The Principled Type]"). The preliminary ideas underlying chapter one ("Apprehending the Individual") were published in *Sociologie et sociétés* in 2009 under the title "Max Weber, le sociologue, et le policier: appréhender l'individu" (42[1]: 55-70).

Montreal, 6 March 2013

Figure 1: The Individual and the Ideal Types

Photo © Amélie Losier. All rights reserved

I. Max Weber, the Sociologist, and the Police Officer

Diversity. A Word Without Qualities

In one of his books sociologist Jean-Claude Kaufmann (2008 [1996]: 35-37) evokes the vagaries of a research project. Reflecting on his own experience as a researcher, he notes that a particular questioning is at times at the origin of a project while at others, it is a field of research that imposes itself, with the research question only emerging later. The research underlying this book began with the interrogation: How can the relation to (cultural and ethnic) difference in today's Germany be characterized and explained? For in this respect, Germany is not any country: in comparison to its Western European neighbors, it has often been described as hostile to difference. In their study of schools in four different national settings in the mid 1990s, Schiffauer and his colleagues (2004 [2002]) show that each case embodies a distinct variant of how ethnic and cultural difference is framed: Britain and the Netherlands are self-declared multicultural nation-states while France is the promoter of individual equality; Germany, however, lacks such positive assignments. The German situation as depicted, though, is marked neither by the absence of difference nor by the lack of people who contribute to its acknowledgement and who are sometimes dedicated to its promotion. This aspect of the German situation was of particular concern to me and called for more development; however, I had, at first, no particular fieldwork in mind.

Time passed. One day I was pondering over the treatment of difference in Germany while riding Montreal's subway, and I could not help noticing a poster. Entitled "The police are after you. University graduates! Yes you, Jamel, Maria, Kim, Maimouna. Your skills are wanted by the SPVM [Montreal's Police Department]." The poster invited members of visible minorities holding university degrees to join the police. Could police forces make up a privileged object of inquiry for the relation toward difference?

After all, police forces have, on the one hand, time and time again been condemned for their brutality toward minorities (Amnesty International 2004). On the other hand, they have also attempted to improve their relations with these communities and establish ethnically-based recruitment policies (Brodeur 2003; Holdaway 1991). Just like the school, which was the object of previous investigations, the police forces are a state institution. This seemed important as the recent debates touching upon issues of difference in Germany had emerged *within* state institutions (Tietze 2001: 182-183). Unlike the headscarf affair in France and other European countries, teachers—not pupils—have been at the center stage of debates in Germany.[1]

I set out to explore the police situation in Germany. To my surprise, I discovered that the Conference of Ministers and Senators of the Interior had granted permission in 1993 for recruiting candidates of "foreign origin" (*ausländischer Herkunft*) to join police departments. The ministers had used a derogatory clause in the civil service law (*Beamtengesetz*) to grant foreigners living in Germany access to the police profession; "when the hiring of a civil servant," the exception rule stipulates, "constitutes an urgent professional necessity." This recommendation is founded in a special clause for academic staff, which detracts from the principle according to which only Germans, as defined in Article 116 of the Basic Law, can be made civil servants. While confirming the rule of homogeneity and the principle of equality, the conceded exception represented an important change in a long tradition linking citizenship with the civil service (*Beamtentum*): German citizenship was no longer considered a prerequisite to become a police officer nor a synonym to civil service.

Sounding out this permission first took me to Hamburg to meet Inspector Piontek, a police inspector who was in charge of recruitment of candidates of foreign origins (*ausländische Herkunft*). As it turned out, what had started as the granting of a permission, an exception rule to the civil service law to hire nonnationals, had cautiously turned into the promotion of candidates from post-migration backgrounds. At the beginning, applicants of "foreign origin" (*ausländischer Herkunft*) were sought; later, recruitment

---

[1] The "Ludin case," a German teacher of Afghan descent who fought the federal state of Baden-Wurttemberg to wear a hijab in class, is a telling and much debated example (Mahlmann 2003).

efforts focused on candidates from post-migration backgrounds (*mit Migrationshintergrund*). The latter category is much more encompassing as it also includes repatriates and children of immigrants who were born in Germany and who may or may not be—German citizens. After my first visits in Hamburg, my curiosity was definitely aroused and I took to exploring other cases where similar initiatives had been called into being. Apart from similar recruitment initiatives, teaching, in-house training, counseling, and the commemoration of the past provided examples to examine the relation toward difference. Because police matters in Germany fall under the legislative power of the individual federal states, this took me to different police departments across the country. Surprise, frustration, enigmas, and discoveries ensued, until I realized that I had found my fieldwork.

1. From Officers from Post-Migration Backgrounds to Carriers of Diversity

I soon learned that one aspect, the initiatives to recruit officers from post-migration backgrounds, had raised much interest since their inception. Not only police research and newspaper articles, but also crime movies (Ertener 2007), novels (Arjouni 1987; Zaimoglu 2003) and stand-up comedy routines have dealt with them.[2] The interest they raised and the attention they received may be related to a certain feeling of incongruity they provoked at the time: considering the reputation and history of the police forces toward minorities, these new recruitment efforts and the sight of uniformed officers from visible minorities created a dissonance. The titles of magazine articles reporting on the initiatives to recruit candidates from post-migration backgrounds or publicizing them—just as the aforementioned publicity of the Montreal Police Department—often played on the oddness that may emerge from the juxtaposition of words like citizenship, civil service, uniform, crime and the images often associated with them (see the poster of a public awareness campaign below). Typically, the articles and advertise-

---

2 I refer to Murat Topal, a stand-up comedian and former Berlin police officer of mixed Turkish and German origins. See his CDs *Polizeiruf Topal, Getürkte Fälle. Ein Cop packt aus* and *Tschüssi Copski! Ein Cop packt ein* as well as his books (2008, 2010).

ments surrounding those initiatives relied on various wordplays derived from police language, to stress how an outsider has become an insider: "the police are looking for you," "taken down to the station," "Under physical surveillance," "the police are hunting down at full speed young people from post-migration backgrounds" (*Die Polizei fahndet auf Hochtouren nach Nachwuchs mit Migrationshintergrund*).[3]

Attempting to subvert prevailing representations of the police forces: this poster of the *Nationaler Integrationsplan*, a federal campaign to promote dialogue and integration, could be seen all over Germany in the Fall of 2007.

Figure 2: "Security is not an issue of origin"

Poster reproduced with the permission of the Federal Office for Migration and Refugees.

---

3   The phrases are taken from police advertisement campaigns in Montreal and in Lower-Saxony.

Commenting on journalism, sociologist Erving Goffman advises his students to draw on the example set by its practitioners. Journalists, the sociologist notes, turn to good account "exceptions to expected consistency among setting, appearance and manner." These exceptions, he adds, "provide the piquancy and glamour of many careers and the salable appeal of many magazine articles" (Goffman 1969 [1959]: 22). Reviewing the several studies dealing with recruitment initiatives that have been published in recent years, it would seem that police researchers have taken up Goffman's advice. Usually focusing on the experience of police officers from post-migration backgrounds (Franzke 1999; Blom 2005; Hunold 2008; Gauthier 2011), those studies accentuate, in the words of Patricia Hill Collins (1999 [1991]), their status as "outsiders within." They deal more specifically with the pressures the officers are submitted to—especially in regard to the lurking threat of double loyalty toward an ethnic group and the police forces—and, often, with what is seen as the token character of their recruitment. The researchers go on either to point out that the recruitments have not met, on the quantitative level, the goals set by police officials and politicians (Behr 2006: 124; Hunold *et al*. 2010) or to question, on a more practical level, whether the presence of officers from post-migration backgrounds actually brings a new quality to policing and police culture (Bornewasser 2009).[4]

The striking character of the initiatives to recruit officers from post-migration backgrounds and the "outsider within" status of the officers also caught my attention. However, the effect of exception and the playing on words lost their appeal to me before the fieldwork was completed and long before any results had been published. With the passage of time—

---

4 Politicians in several states have talked about a 10 percent goal. A 20 percent goal was even set in Hamburg, see "Ausbildungs-Aktion: Multikulti im Staatsdienst," *Hamburger Abendblatt*, 7 November 2006. Although there are no official statistics available for all federal states, about one percent of police officers are reported to be nonnationals. There are a higher percentage of police officers from post-migration backgrounds, although their overall numbers remain small. Hunold (2010: 138) counts less than two percent in 2009; however, police internal documents used for this study indicate that some 8 to 10 percent of police trainees recruited in 2009 in several federal states were from post-migration backgrounds.

unavoidable in the context of a long-term research project—the effect of evoked associations had gradually waned, threatening to turn into clichés.[5] The recruited officers from post-migration backgrounds also reacted, as we will see later in this book, to the attempts to portray them as outsiders within or as "strange species" (*Exoten*): they sometimes resisted being treated as different, criticizing the advertisement campaigns and the language use, and often turned them into derision.

Whereas the piquancy of seeing a member of a visible minority donning a uniform gradually faded away, some other aspects of the police forces emerged, which proved challenging and particularly worth looking into: the resistance to change within the forces, the confrontation with another investigating profession, that is sociology, and the rather tense value relation between police officers and sociologists to which the title of the book alludes to. Most importantly, it quickly appeared that the police officers from German backgrounds who have called the aforementioned recruitment initiatives—and other initiatives which I was to discover—into being, who have put them into practice and shaped them, turned out to be most instructive on the relation toward difference in the police; even more so than the officers from post-migration backgrounds who first struck attention. As the result of their work, these officers have contributed—wittingly or not—to the recognition of difference within police forces at the practical level; they have conferred it with a particular spirit. I refer to these people as "carriers of diversity." The more I understood about them, the more details caught my eyes, which were calling for explanations—the religious character of some events they organized, their dilettantism, the recurrent allusions to the Weimar Republic not to mention the insistence on linguistic competencies. These officers are at the center of the present study.

---

5 Something similar also happened with allusions to sociological language. Authors and commentators frequently draw upon Georg Simmel's definition of the stranger. Articles, which originality tends to decrease as their number increases, are for example entitled "*Polizei und Fremde. Ergebnisse des Forschungsprojektes der Polizei-Führungsakademie,*" "*Die Polizei und das Fremde,*" "*Ein 'Exot' im Dienst des Gesetzes.*" I cannot but remember the three speakers who were invited to pronounce a welcome address to the participants at a police conference in 2007. All alluded to Simmel's stranger, the situation becoming each time increasingly awkward.

1.1 Defining Diversity

Diversity is a "travelling concept" (Lehmkuhl and McFalls 2012: 4). Whereas the word has been characterized by different conceptions, it is *today* often charged with one particular meaning. At the time I was just starting this project, fellow sociologists in Germany insisted I should look into the management literature on diversity and regard it as something essential. Just pronouncing the word diversity (*Vielfalt*) when making a phone call to a police department, I was inevitably directed toward police management and people responsible for seminars on gender mainstreaming or personal policies. Later, the German colleague who had invited me to give a talk based on the material of this study in her class kept talking about my work on "diversity management" in the police. Politely I remarked that I wished not to limit myself to the management-inflected meaning of diversity and adopt a broader perspective, but it made no difference. The fact is that in its current usage in the literature and in German police forces, diversity is an imported concept—incidentally used in English or in new German as *Diversität*, but not in its literal translation as *Vielfalt*. It is generally associated with efforts on the management level to make greater use of personal competences, as "the 'positive' effects of cultural plurality and competence for private companies and public service delivery" (Faist 2009: 177). If I am well aware and concerned with this inflected meaning, I do not limit myself to it.[6] Diversity, as I understand it in this book, corresponds to *a relation to difference at a particular time*.

What is today referred to as diversity is rooted in different initiatives characterized by different and changing incentives. Let us take the example of special employment measures. Before becoming the object of scholarly and media attention, these measure were responses to tragic events. Indeed, tense relations between police officers and marginalized groups and, ultimately, police scandals have often triggered ethnically-based recruitment measures.[7] In Germany, both the 1993 exception rule of the Conference of

---

6   When I use diversity in quotation marks in the following chapters I refer to this widely used meaning in the police forces and social sciences; when I put it in italics it indicates the actors' use of the English word.

7   As a result of brutal incidents involving police officers in England, the USA, Canada and Ireland, ethnically-based recruiting policies and educational pro-

Ministers and Senators of the Interior and initiatives in Berlin in the 1980s were grounded in pragmatic police concerns, such as infiltrating criminal groups and milieus. However, in the midst of flashes of xenophobic violence at the beginning of the 1990s, following criticism from Amnesty International and police scandals (Behr 2006: 33-35), concern was also expressed toward racism in the police force; a report on racism in the police forces was commissioned and submitted in 1995 (Bornewasser *et al.* 1996; see also Bornewasser 2009: 16). After 2001, security issues came back to the fore while the intercultural opening of the civil service was officially announced both at the state and federal states levels. What is today designated under the label of diversity actually ranges—according to the stakes, the actors involved, and the contexts—from security issues, antiracism and, more recently, management and issues of organizational efficiency to the promotion of difference within the police forces and the incorporation of minorities into the workforce.[8] The timing is important: issues are framed in a particular context, which provide them with a vocabulary.

The question of differences at the core of the present book and its implications are obviously nothing new; however, they appear to us today as something "culturally significant." Like issues related to social classes in the 1960s, ethnic and cultural differences have been placed high on the social science agenda and are bestowed with political urgency. This urgency should be understood as a direct consequence of the new status acquired by some differences in our eye—the eye of both the actors and the researchers (*qua* researchers and citizens)—as our connection and relation to the object undergoes significant modifications.

What then is this relation to difference within German police forces today? And how does it influence practices? To answer this question is the very aim of this study; as such, it cannot be defined from the start. For the time being, diversity within German police forces today must remain a word without qualities; the definition will take shape in the process of researching and will gain consistency as I tell the story. "It lies in the nature of the study," Weber writes at the beginning of his *Protestant Ethic*, "that no conceptual definition can be given at the beginning" (2007 [1904/1905]:

---

grams were called for (see notably the prominent and much talked Macpherson report on the London Metropolitan police [1999]).

8   For similar findings on the French army, see Bertossi (2013).

13). Diversity in Germany today is not unlike the spirit of capitalism in Weber's *Protestant Ethic*: it is a "historical individual," or "a complex of elements associated in historical reality which we unite into a conceptual whole from the standpoint of their cultural significance" (Weber 2007 [1904/1905]: 12). As in Weber's essay, the aim of the research underlying this book was not "to grasp historical reality in abstract general formulae, but in a concrete genetic sets of relation, which are inevitably of a specifically unique and individual character" (2007 [1904/1905]: 14). This specifically unique and individual character of diversity in the German police forces today or, in other words, its qualities will appear to the fullest toward the end of the study.

Inquiring into diversity within the police implies taking into account official discourses and what the actors have to say about them, but also observing those who (have to) deal with difference in their daily work. As such, the construction of the "field of diversity" in Germany will not always correspond to the actors' definitions; for it reveals itself through the gaze of the sociologist who has the time to mull over these questions and is attentive to everyday interactions. Faced with the various meanings conferred on diversity, this study attempts to make sense of what we have before our eyes and to describe and explain a phenomenon that has gained urgency today. To draw once again on Weber, this means being attentive to the actors who have to do with difference, the motives underlying their action, and their culturally embedded significance (Weber 1978a [1921]: 8) while working with ideal types.

Just as the construction of the field of diversity in Germany will not always correspond to the actors' definitions, it will not match to existing definitions in the academic literature. This has to do with the theoretical and contextual standpoints from which one can frame and conduct such a study.[9] The standpoint from which I investigate diversity in German police forces is admittedly not the only one from which it can be analyzed. What applies to the essay previously mentioned does so equally here: "Other standpoints would, for this [the spirit of capitalism] as for every historical phenomenon, yield other characteristics as essential ones" (Weber 2007

---

9 In the academic literature on the police, diversity is generally linked to gender, migration background, and sexual orientation (van Ewijk 2012; Dudek 2009; Dudek and Raczynsky 2002).

[1904/1905]: 14). Weber adds: "The result is that it is by no means necessary to understand by the spirit of capitalism only what it will come to mean to *us* for the purpose of our analysis" (2007 [1904/1905]: 14). The passage responds to potential criticism as to the arbitrary character of ideal types (see Gerhardt 1986) and, before all, attests to the importance of the particular points of view from which the analysis is conducted. Studies related to the case at hand put the police forces in a different light. For example, in Jérémie Gauthier's comparison between police forces in Paris and Berlin he carried out at the time I was researching this book, the German case appears accommodating to police officers from post-migration backgrounds (2012: 270, 2011: 467). This result echoes comments I received when presenting the current study in Poland, but would find little resonance within the German context alone or glancing at the Canadian case.

In the process of migrating from a political, medial, and internal police problem to a sociological one, the object of inquiry allowing the grasping of the relation toward difference gained contours. Yet I still had to construct the field and undertake the research. With the methods employed, and the interpretive approach underlying the study in mind, in the following section, I describe this process, what Glaser and Strauss refer to as theoretical sampling: "the process of data collection for generating theory whereby the analyst jointly collects, codes, and analyzes his data and decides what data to collect next and where to find them, in order to develop his theory as it emerges" (2008 [1967]: 45).

2. CONSTRUCTING THE FIELD

2.1 Entering and Narrowing the Field: Material, Methods, and Approach

How did I proceed concretely? I started with the most obvious. The first step was to become familiar with the literature documenting police initiatives launched in the 1990s (for an overview of the first initiatives, see Leiprecht 2002 and, for later ones, see Hunold *et al.* 2010), reading the newspaper and magazine articles that have been published in their wake and meeting with experts. Before going to Germany, I did preliminary fieldwork in Montreal, one of Canada's metropolises. I conducted six interviews with people in charge of recruitment, equal opportunity programs, and community policing, went on night shift patrols with officers in one neighborhood known for the large presence of ethnic minorities, attended seminars aiming at teaching sensitivity toward cultural diversity to police officials and information sessions for candidates from visible minorities, and talked to fellow social scientists in the field of the police and ethnic minorities. Although brief, this experience was instrumental in preparing my research; it trained my eye to issues and concerns, which were to come up—or not—in the German fieldwork. This little expedition made me realize that the "bearers of difference" were not, in Germany, those who had for the most part contributed to the acknowledgement of difference within the forces (Lavoie 2006).

Once in Germany I started interviewing people whose official mandate—according to the literature available—had to do with the treatment of difference within the police forces in the 1990s.[10] This first led me to people in charge of initiatives to recruit and counsel police officers from postmigration backgrounds, an area which has attracted most scholarly attention (see Franzke 1999; Blom 2005; Behr 2006; Hunold 2008). At the same time, I also interviewed experts and took part in police conferences. Talking to them, it also seemed obvious to explore areas where differences were being formally addressed such as seminars for police officers dealing with intercultural education, equal treatment, and gender mainstreaming.[11] For this reason, I participated in such seminars—stretching from one-day to one-week—in Hamburg and Berlin over the course of 2006 and 2007.

Next to recruitment and in-house training, that is the field of activities mentioned in the reviewed literature, I decided to expand the frame of my research. I contacted and met people who, I gathered from other readings and former research experience in Germany, might have contributed

---

10 For works on the treatment of difference outside the police forces and the interactions with citizens, see Schweer (2008), Sterzenbach (forthcoming), and Gauthier's (2012, 2011) work with a Berlin police unit specialized in the control of illegal immigration and prevention in neighborhoods with large immigrant populations.

11 Gender mainstreaming aims to evaluate the effects of policies or programs on women and men.

through their work to the framing of difference and its pragmatic recognition. Other fields of activities were thus included: counseling, teaching, and the commemoration of the past. In particular, political education (*politische Bildung*) was drawn upon as an area where efforts to broaden the ideological spectrum of the police had been made in the past. Investigating the history of the Berlin police forces, Liang (1970: 72) had pointed to attempts to broadening the social basis of the police forces through personal policies, such as the (failed) recruitment of trade unionists and efforts to change the police through political education. These areas helped me construct and understand the multiple aspects the object of inquiry may take on in the German context while being attentive to the past. From my previous work on churches in Germany and the related literature (Thériault 2004), I also knew that the police chaplains, as specialists of ethical issues, might play an important role in dealing with issues related to difference. Extending my reading to police forces in other countries, it soon seemed obvious enough that trade union representatives might also be concerned with such issues (Holdaway and O'Neill 2004; Hunold *et al.* 2010: 127 ff.). My field grew larger yet again as I realized, in the course of researching and taking part in conferences, that human rights specialists might also have played a role in dealing with difference (Schicht 2007).

Having identified the people who had been officially mandated or might have, according to the evidence I gathered, contributed to the acknowledgement of difference, I contacted them for an initial formal interview, which was, when allowed, taped. I asked the first informants about initiatives that were going on in their police department and their federal states and the context of their inception. When broaching recruitment, I inquired about those who were deemed to be the ideal candidates ("Who would be, in your opinion, a good candidate?") and problems encountered. I was also interested to find out about their person, their work, their background and how they had come to occupy their function. While asking my questions, I usually had photos and brochures in front of me (the above mentioned Montreal police advertisement, a photo of policewomen wearing a hijab in the color of the London Metropolitan Police, a brochure of an association of black law enforcers in Canada), which did not fail to spark comments. Through a snowball principle, the first interviews led me to other people and to loose networks between police departments in different federal states or between police forces and partners such as NGOs. Not all the people I met at this stage had left an imprint in the police forces. Trade union representatives, for example, were present at conferences and police meetings; however, I did not come across any concrete initiatives (see also Lautmann 2010). Not all field of activities identified turned out to be actual channels, or vectors (*Weichenstellungen*), for the recognition of difference within the forces.[12]

The interviews and observation that were to follow this first stage narrowed the field and delineated it with more precision: they targeted people as well as fields of activities that promised to instruct me on the relation to difference in the police forces. Who were the people I met in this second phase and where did they work? Most of them were police officers. However, they were neither "street cops" nor "high management cops" (Reuss-Ianni 1983); instead, they were middle management, members of the elevated service, often police inspectors or chief police inspectors (*Polizeikommissar* [PK] or *Polizeihauptkommissar* [PHK]). Because police officers generally change their position within the organization in five-year turns, my informants had occupied other positions before I met them and often changed it at a later stage of their career. They were not trained in public relations or used to answering questions and they were not necessarily the people met at police conferences touching upon issues of difference. Officers holding high mandates and representative functions typically attended—sometimes accompanied by practitioners—these conferences. Police officials usually exhibited enthusiasm toward projects and initiatives that aimed at the opening of the forces. Meeting informants took me to police departments, academies, a museum, meetings organized by NGOS in Hamburg and Berlin as well as to four other federal states. Next to the city-states, two other federal states are important to this study, but—because they involve more difficult and personal cases—are not named so as not to identify my informants.

I chose to meet those I came to identify as carriers of diversity several times for discussion. In the course of researching this book, I adapted and improved my questions, added new ones (such as, for instance, "Who should, or would, be likely to replace you once you move on to another po-

---

12 *Weichenstellungen*, or the switches that change the direction of railroad tracks, is an expression used metaphorically by Weber to refer to, and assess, possible loci of change (Weber 1978b [1921]: 1209; Weber 1972 [1921]: 252).

sition within the forces or when you retire?), and became more attentive to the dilemmas pertaining to my informants' work. Next to formal conversations, I also accompanied them in their daily work and took field notes: participating in the activities they organized, meeting them at police conferences, seminars, in-house trainings, and meetings, observing them teaching and in interaction with colleagues, or in a car or train on their way to work or on special occasions. This was instrumental to carry out informal conversations and observe their colleagues' reactions to them. I conducted most of the interviews and participant observation while on leave in 2006-2007 and in the second half of 2009; with shorter visits in between and again in the first half of 2010. Overall, I conducted 64 interviews as well as several informal conversations.

Meeting my informants in different settings (mostly at work, but also at conferences, ceremonies, seminars, visits to mosques, information session for people of Turkish background, meetings of the historical society, parties) and, most of all, on several occasions, turned out to be pivotal for the present study. I could witness their successes and failures as well as the effects they had on them. Some of my first impressions were contradicted in subsequent meetings, whereas a simple intuition sometimes turned out to be an important lead. This methodological strategy was worthwhile for interpretive sociology: it enabled me to uncover—and later reconstruct—the importance of motives underlying the work of my informants and how they change over time as a response to the consequences of their work and the reaction it provoked within the forces. Furthermore, I could witness the resistance the officers met, the tensions emerging between their work and an organization with homogenizing principles, the ambivalences pertaining to them. This strategy also facilitated me having access to internal police documents and archives material (internal studies, press cuttings, reports, letters), secured my participation in seminars and police events, which might have been difficult to attain access. After some time, the fieldwork became autonomous: I got invited and, being mobile, I could attend events.

2.2 Leaving the Field: Ideal Types

Researching this book was a process. Observing, taking notes and memos, I refined my questions and shaped my object in accordance with the constant comparative method (Glaser and Strauss 2008 [1967]: 101-115) while watching reflexivity at work for my informants and myself (see Martucelli and de Singly 2009: 97). Generating, around the actors' motives, ideal types of carriers of diversity was also an ongoing process between collection and analysis of data, between theorization and observation.

While still in the field, I could roughly delineate three ideal types. In accordance with the criteria of theoretical saturation, I left it when no new data involved the creation of an additional ideal type (Glaser and Strauss 2008 [1967]: 61, 111). Although being attentive, it is possible that I missed some initiatives and that new people entered the field as I was leaving it.[13] However, I have no ground to think that these newcomers would alter the ideal types. Admittedly, some ideal types might become more important, others less. They would nonetheless remain valid for mapping out possible positions one could reasonably expect to find when tracking the relation to difference within German police forces. Comparing the ideal types to observations in the field indicates paths that were actually taken. More than classifying or describing, the aim of the present study is to interpret and understand (*verstehen*) through ideal types—as opposed to merely know (*wissen*) facts properly speaking (Disselkamp 2012: 155).

Gradually leaving the field, I spent more time in my office and went on to refine my three core ideal types. As I move along in this book, I describe how I constructed the ideal types. I will come back to more formal aspects of ideal types in chapter two. For the moment, let it be said that the types at the center of the chapters are contrasting ones (Gerhardt 1986: 61). Combining different cases—present and past—, they are constructed in dialogue with another. In their foreground, are the specific motives of the people I came in contact with. My reflection always starts with and feeds on concrete situations and individuals. This choice, or strategy, helps me to construct ideal types—abstractions of the actual or possible paths or relations toward difference—and ground them in a particular cultural context. Be-

---

13 Due to some technical problems, one federal state was left out where I had conducted some interviews. When Criminal Police Inspector Schmitt, the woman at the center of one of the chapters, showed me a picture portraying the invited guests at a conference she had organized with recruitment officers in the 1990s (chapter four, see section 1.2), I realized that—beyond the time of my fieldwork—I had met the members of the first generation of carriers of diversity, those of the 1990s.

sides the situations depicted through vignettes, I introduce throughout the chapters, four (and a half) portraits are at the core of the chapters constituting the second part of this book. I bring the characters of the portraits in dialogue with the ideal types; indeed, once clearly delineated the types are mirrored back on the actors. This exercise brings individual dilemmas to the fore and, in turn, another dimension to the analysis, a more existential one. Through the portraits, I intend to help the reader easily grasp the ideal types.

Because the choices I made while constructing the field had an impact on the architecture of the book and the relation between the cops and the sociologist, I touch upon these aspects in the final sections of this introduction.

3. Division of the Book

The present book is divided into three parts. The first part is dedicated to the sociology of Max Weber, motivational understanding, and the possibilities it offers for empirical studies. This first part provides a frame for the second, and most substantive, one. Outlining through several portraits the motives of the people interviewed and observed, in the second part I construct three ideal types, or sociological portraits (Nisbet 1976: 72): the empathetic, the type devoted to a principle, and the opportunist. The third part goes beyond the analysis of the individual portraits: it assembles the ideal types together to create a group portrait.

After proposing a reflection in chapter one on how to apprehend the individual in Weberian sociology and laying down the tools for examining the police forces, the chapters of the second part are each dedicated to one ideal type, and one possible way to deal with difference. As the photo inserted at the end of the preface conveys, each chapter combines two levels of analysis: they focus at times on the abstract models (the mannequins, or the ideal types), at times on the flesh-and-blood individuals behind them (the real police officers). While lending the study its structure, each portrait is also linked to a central theme that grounds the outlined motives in a cultural and historical context: a Christian heritage, a particular shade of liberalism, a Kantian resistance to opportunism, and the spirit of the social movements of the 1960s onward. These themes stand in tension, or share affinities, with the ethos of the police officers and the image they cultivate—the "we-ideal" of the forces (Elias 1998 [1989])—as well as with the values of the observer. As such, the ideal types draw attention to value understanding, not least to the values of the sociologist.

Vignettes, interwoven in the chapters, act as miniatures devoted to particular situations and people (a "pastoral"-like meeting between a recruitment officer and his recruits in Hamburg, a meeting where the recruits and officers from post-migration backgrounds poke fun at the attention given to them, efforts in Berlin to commemorate a Weimar high police official of Jewish descent and the naming of a square, a trip to the Netherlands, a much repeated anecdote, an altercation at a conference gathering between a social scientist and high police officials and police researchers). The portrayed situations represent moments when the alchemy of theory and empirical material constitutive of the ideal types, the creative tools of Weberian sociology, set in. They provide the analysis with interpretative keys while giving a voice to those who are otherwise not at the center of the inquiry, the recruits and officers from post-migration backgrounds in particular.

Chapters two and three are dedicated to two inspectors—Dietmar Piontek and Klaus Bobkowski—and their colleagues. Both men are close—though not identical—to the types constructed, the empathetic and the principled ones respectively. In the subsequent chapter, I then go on to construct a third type, the opportunist. The motive underpinning this type was met to various degrees in most people encountered while researching this book. The reaction opportunism created is epitomized in the portrait of a police researcher. To the cases outlined, one is added, that of a group of specialists for whom diversity is a profession and a vocation. Though I expected to find representatives of this group of specialists in the German police forces, they were largely absent during the fieldwork. Why did diversity as a principle remain a mere "logical possibility" (Weber 1949 [1904]: 93)? This question constitutes an enigma that turns out to throw light on all ideal types and on the complex relation between actors, ideas, and interests within the police forces. Far from being useless, this missing group of specialists (and one version of the principled type) serves as a counterpoint, enabling me not only to contrast the other types, but also to point to, beyond all differences, the similarities and specificity of those who contributed in one way or another to the recognition of difference within the German police today.

Whereas the ideal types in part two are treated on equal grounds, I attempt to put them together into a single and three-dimensional picture in the third and last part of the book. Being attentive to the types that were most present in reality, I put them in perspective: some types thus appear on the foreground and others more on the background. Instead of ending the study with different possible positions when tracking the relation to difference within German police forces, this exercise enables me to see what they have in common. In so doing, I can identify and account for the particular imprint of the relation to difference—the specific spirit of diversity—within the police today. While assembling the ideal types, two details catch my eye: the striking similarities of the actors on the foreground and the outdated character of the picture that was emerging. In chapter six, I come back to the first detail, the social characteristics and ideas pertaining to the carriers of diversity. This leads me to a discussion of the activity of representation (*Stellvertretung*) and normative issues inherent to talking and acting on behalf of others. In the seventh and concluding chapter, I reflect on the second detail, the seemingly outdated character of the picture, and the types of connections that tie the actors to the past.

The chapters entailed in this book follow a certain chronological order. I tell the story as I go along, first making my way in the police forces and then shedding light on the history of the initiatives. This enables me to account for change, in the vocabulary used, but also in the types of measures put forward, their acceptance, or resistance to them. The chronology of the initiatives also points to how the motives of the actors involved have changed. Although the chapters do not systematically focus on specific federal states, there are some overlapping between particular ideal types, some initiatives, and federal states. As is often the case, the people who first got involved in the initiatives often laid down tracks for subsequent developments and patterns for the treatment of difference. For this reason, they are subjects of particular attention.

4. THE SOCIOLOGIST AND THE COP

It is often said that it is difficult to investigate the police (Manning 1974; Waddington 1999; Monjardet 2005; Hunold 2008: 16); that suspicion, an often identified trait of cop culture, is a barrier to sociological work on the police. Whereas getting information from the police in Montreal proved difficult, the treatment of difference being judged as a sensitive topic and a matter of organizational priority, contacts with the police officers in different police departments in Germany were unexpectedly easy. Although I could not have access to particular areas and could certainly not reveal all aspects of their work, the contact with officers proved easy because—and this seems to be a decisive factor—the people I met occupied rather marginal positions within the police forces. They were sometimes flattered by the attention given to their work by someone who came from far away for their sake—and would also conveniently go away. Most informants agreed to have our conversations taped; and of course, I changed their names.[14]

Working on the police turned out to be more difficult than I had first expected among the colleagues I share affinities with. At an early stage of the research, the young social scientists who helped me transcribe the taped interviews, reacted to what was being said, pointing to values and their conflict as well as to different relations to difference and, hence, conceptions of diversity. My colleagues often commented I should work on police victims, not cops. The sociologists' value relation to the police and, ultimately, its legitimacy, as a research object is a central issue of the next chapter. Inspired by certain annoyances and dilemmas encountered during fieldwork, the reflection takes the shape of a three-party fictional dialogue with Max Weber, my fellow sociologists, and police officers encountered in the course of my research.

In the next chapter, I stress the Weberian conception of motives underlying the action and at the core of the investigation. I distinguish three pairs of concepts: the fictional and the "flesh-and-blood" individual, motive and intention, the consequences of action and individual destiny. I insist upon

---

14 Some of my informants would not have minded or would have even liked being named by their real surname. Some insisted that they "had nothing to hide" or were "not afraid," attesting to what seems to be an attempt at independence within the forces.

the notion of motive in the Weberian sense in order to advocate an approach—and a technique—that would take social action into account so as to stress the interpretative task that such an approach presupposes, and to question anew the relation between the values of the researcher and the object of his investigation. In so doing, I reflect on what the (Weberian) sociologist and the police officer have in common: the study of motives and inquiring as a professional activity. Accentuating this trait no doubt constitutes a romantic bias: if police officers do cultivate the image of the investigator, they also concede that they spend an important part of their time—as sociologists generally do if they work in a university—writing reports, dealing with recalcitrant colleagues, and attempting—with more or less conviction—to reform the organization they belong to.

Apprehending the Individual

My colleagues raised their eyebrows when they heard about my work on the police. Even if it is considered a legitimate subject, it undoubtedly remains an unpopular one. Sociologists without what one might call a "police background" and who adopt a perspective exterior to the organization generally maintain a negative value-relation (*Wertbeziehung*) toward the police. As P.A.J. Waddington (1999: 298) has rightly stressed, the police tend to offend the liberal values to which sociologists often subscribe. Because police officers exercise a coercive authority over citizens who themselves only grudgingly confer legitimacy on them, the former occupy a necessarily delicate position within liberal democracies. This distinctive tension shows up in the dilemmas of police work, which are most palpable during demonstrations (where police officers must sometimes take action against peaceful citizens), as well as in the constant fear of criticism and the need often felt by the police to reestablish their image as a democratic organization.[1] This tension is also reflected in the work of the observer who wishes to understand—without necessarily endorsing—this sensitive object of study.

In the course of my work with police officers, I have myself felt this tension whenever I was being treated in a manner I considered too courteous. This tension was made all the more acute by my knowledge of the literature touching on the subject of the police, which never fails to mention

---

1 For example during the demonstrations of January 1990 in East Berlin, where a group of police officers was lined-up before the crowd to shout "We too are the people," appropriating the slogan of the popular movement: "We are the people" (*Wir sind das Volk*) (Förderkreis Polizeihistorische Sammlung Berlin e.V. 2003: 14).

the difficult relations between researchers and police officers (see, among others, Waddington 1999; Monjardet 2005; Hunold *et al.* 2010).[2] In my case, this tension expressed itself in a certain conceit that encouraged me to distinguish myself from sociologists specializing in the police in Germany, often ex-police officers whose bearing and insider perspective on the organization was at first little different, to my eyes, from that of the police officers themselves. For my part, I considered my work to be decidedly different from that of the people I was observing. On the other hand, for the police officers I had the chance to accompany—like the one who, at the end of a conversation added amiably: "Good luck with your investigation!" (*Viel Glück bei Ihrer Ermittlung!*)—it seemed entirely natural that my work resembled theirs, both in its methods as in its purpose.

This allusion to the investigation made me stop and consider possible parallels between sociological procedures and those of the police. We both investigate, yes. But what is the object of investigations? In his "Basic Sociological Terms" Weber writes that "[i]t is the task of the sociologist to be aware of this motivational situation and to describe and analyze it" (Weber 1978a [1921]: 9-10). Interpretive sociology (*verstehende Soziologie*), as Weber conceives it, involves motivational understanding, or the reconstruction of the motives underlying action. The translation "to be aware of" stands for the German *ermitteln*, a term referring to a police investigation and used by the amiable police officer who wished me good luck.[3] In reflecting on investigation, my point of view is that of a sociologist outside the police milieu, but one who has accompanied police officers during her fieldwork. My perspective is shaped within a Weberian cosmos, a particular way of organizing empirical material and to handle relation to values. Such an exercise in comparison is not foreign to Weber himself, who was in the habit of comparing the work of the sociologist to that of the journalist, the politician (2004 [1919]) and the jurist (1949 [1906]) in order to underline its object and specificity as well as its finality.[4] As always in Weber, it is

---

2   Specialized literature on the police is presented in chapter 7.
3   "*In diesem Fall steht die Soziologie vor der Aufgabe, diesen [Motiv]Zusammenhang zu ermitteln und deutend festzustellen*" (Weber 1972 [1921]: 4).
4   Comparing the social scientist to the jurist, in particular the judge (Weber 1949 [1906]; Eberle 1999), was quite common before Weber's time (see Saupe 2009).

the practical problems that I have encountered in my research which are the center of these considerations. These problems arose in encounters with police officers and other researchers as well as in the process of portraying the carriers of diversity.

In comparison, this exercise will bring me to define the motives of action, to identify the limits and potential slippages between the work of sociological and police investigators in areas that are particularly sensitive due to the moral and political interests attached to them, and the dilemmas of writing about individuals. Finally, I will suggest—again following Weber—a possible way to avoid or overcome these potential slippages, which, as we shall see, is not completely foreign to the work of police officers. But before I do so, let us first return to the title of this chapter: How to apprehend the individual?

1. THE PLACE OF THE INDIVIDUAL IN WEBER'S SOCIOLOGY

If one may assume that the individual is the point of departure in Weber's analyses, one is compelled to recognize that, in the reception of his writings, this idea has been translated in various manners. It is presented now as a methodological aim, now as what one might call an "existential" aim, following the two most prominent interpretations of the guiding insight of Weber's work. The first interpretation appeals to the development of the theme of rationalization (Rehberg 2004: 452) and to the late project of developing a Weberian *paradigm*—a school that never took form during the lifetime of the author (Schluchter 2006; Albert *et al.* 2003)—while the second appeals to the problem of the fate of the modern individual (Hennis 1987). But besides these opposed readings, it is possible to argue that, in Weber's sociology, the individual manifests himself through three different

---

There is, in this respect, a whole literature on the links between law and the social sciences. Foucault (1994 [1974]) insisted notably on the importance of transformations of the juridical model and its methods of inquiry. On another level, Turner and Factor (1994) see a close connection between Weber's sociology and the legal thought of his time.

facets—polemical, methodological, and existential—which I here summarize and place in relation with each other.

The concept of the individual is firmly rooted in Weber's time. Because it is opposed to the collectivist notions of the late 19th century, it had for him a *polemical* function (Rehberg 2004: 452). In fact, one might take the concept of the individual as a critique of Marxist, romantic, and organic conceptions of society, which Weber was careful to avoid (see Schluchter 1991a: 26; 1991b: 631). Following the Kantian tradition, the individual in his action and passion offered for Weber the possibility of a grasp of the real, while collective notions like the community or the state existed only in the heads of individuals (Hidas 2004: 44). The "objectivized" (*versachlicht*) individual is the basis of Weber's *method*. Besides the methodological consequences Weber draws from this (and which will be the object of the following section), we find in his writings a third dimension: the modern individual confronted with his fate. This *existential* dimension is found in the figure of the modern scientific man and the capitalist entrepreneur as well as in various metaphors such as the "polytheism of values" or the "iron cage," and constitutes the tragic moment of Weber's sociology.[5]

1.1 Individuals, Fictional and Real

If individuals occupy a central place in the foundations of the program of Weber's sociology, one finds them most often in his substantive writings in the guise of the *ideal type*, for example in the figure of the soldier, the monk, the bureaucrat, or the entrepreneur. Sometimes it is a matter of a particular individual presented in a kind of vignette, as in the example of Benjamin Franklin, which contributes to the construction of the ideal type of the "spirit" of capitalism.[6]

---

5   One thinks in particular of the last pages of *The Protestant Ethic and the Spirit of Capitalism* (2007 [1904/1905]) and the lecture *Science as a Vocation* (2004 [1917/1919]).

6   One also finds "historic individuals" in Weber, which he defines as a "complex of elements associated in historical reality which we unite into a conceptual whole from the standpoint of their cultural significance" (Weber 2007 [1904/1905]: 13). These entities (among which is ranked the spirit of capitalism), therefore, do not correspond to historical personalities, but to empirical re-

Let us linger a while on this example incarnating the ideal type of the capitalist entrepreneur. Franklin, an author of sermons and of an autobiography, is not merely a construction of the observer. He is a real person, a case-study of the spirit of modern capitalism. What draws Weber's attention to him was the fact that Franklin's economic activities were guided by moral convictions (Weber 2007 [1904/1905]: 14). It is the kind of motives underlying action exemplified by the figure of Franklin that are at the heart of *The Protestant Ethic and the Spirit of Capitalism*. They allow a glimpse of the causal relations that constitute the book's initial problem as well as its polemical character.[7]

But if motives (*internal* sanctions) are at the heart of *The Protestant Ethic* and the "Basic Sociological Terms" of *Economy and Society* (Weber 1978a [1921]), one cannot fail to recognize *external* (for example, market-related) sanctions. When reading the "Basic Sociological Terms" beyond the definition of social activity, one encounters concepts ranging from the smallest to the greatest scale of analysis. A sociologist following Weber could quite well begin a study at a level other than the individual, for instance at the level of orders.[8] If individuals are forced somewhat in the background when the sociologist examines, to use Weber's language, the empirical validity (*Geltung*) of an order and its maintenance, they invariably reappear in the forefront during struggles, as is found, to take two examples from the "Basic Sociological Terms," in the concepts of legitimacy (Weber 1978a [1921]: 31-38) and conflict (Weber 1978a [1921]: 38-40).

If one considers the *methodological* character given to the individual, the aspect of Weber's writings which has drawn the most attention in their reception, one finds it expressed in three different forms: as a particular case, an average, or as a pure constructed type (Weber 1978a [1921]: 9). As can be seen not only with the example of Franklin but also with the concepts of legitimacy and conflict, there is always one or several flesh-and-

---

alities brought under a stable and systematic perspective by the sociologist (Weber 1949 [1917]: 101). Oakes (1987: 126) defines historic individuals as cultural phenomena that appear important to us from the point of view of our values.

7 On the polemical character of the essay, see Weber's reply to his critics (2001 [1910]).

8 Elsewhere I have suggested a reading of the sociology of institutions that begins with the notion of legitimate order in Weber (Thériault 2005).

blood individuals lurking behind these formal constructs: "Behind the particular 'action,' stands the human being" (Weber 1949 [1917]: 38). In disentangling these phenomena—in distinguishing the objectivized or fictional individual from the real one—we can delineate the moments of the Weberian program. Apart from the fictional and the flesh-and-blood individual, I distinguish two other pairs of concepts: motives and intent, and the consequences of action and individual fate in both the realms of the observer and the actors.

2. THE OBJECT OF TYPICAL SOCIOLOGICAL INVESTIGATION: MOTIVES (AND NOT INTENT)

In order to avoid a frequent misunderstanding, it seems to me essential from the beginning to distinguish "motives" (*Gründe*) from intent or reasons invoked *post facto* (*Begründung*). Motives do not necessarily correspond to what the actors report themselves in order to give an account of their action, for instance in the course of a conversation. In the *Protestant Ethic*, motives constitute, above all, a psychological sanction and social incentives. Weber notably observes them through religious or moral maxims for living (*lebenspraktische Maxime*) that are not explicitly justified from a precise theological viewpoint, but have an influence on practice.[9] To uncover the "motives" of an action, then, corresponds not simply to an account of the arguments given beforehand by the actor, or to what Colin Campbell in a critical commentary on Charles W. Mills calls "motive talk" or reasons invoked to justify an action to oneself or others (2006: 214).[10] As such, ethnological observation is surely a good method for reconstructing

---

9 An exasperated Weber, in the *Protestant Sects*, writes an essay which follows the *Protestant Ethic*: "To repeat, it is not the ethical doctrine of a religion, but that form of ethical conduct upon which premiums are placed that matters. Such premiums operate through the form and the condition of the respective goods of salvation. And such conduct constitutes 'one's' specific 'ethos' in the sociological sense of the word" (2001 [1906]: 146).

10 The reappropriation of the Weberian conception of motive in Mills (1940) shares affinities with instrumental motives ("*um-zu*"-*Motive*) found in Alfred Schütz (1974 [1932]: 115 ff.).

the motives at the heart of action, motives that might have otherwise gone unnoticed in, say, interviews.

The motives identified by the sociological observer may receive the assent of actors under scrutiny (who will eventually take over the sociologist's concept for their own use), but on the contrary they may equally be found irritating. They point first and above all to the observer, to the task of *interpretation*. In other words, if the conscious intention of the actor does not necessarily correspond to the motive, it is because the latter is a *construction* of the sociologist. It is an objective possibility that "appear[s] in full conceptual *integrity* either not at all or only in individual instances" (Weber 1949 [1904]: 94). The motives point to a sociology that proceeds by the reconstruction, and not the constitution, of action, which has, for its end, the understanding and thereby the explanation of a phenomenon we have before our eyes and try to render intelligible. For Weber, the interpretation or study of motives is intimately connected with intelligibility and the act of explanation. No motive, no causal explanation.

It is sometimes argued that it is impossible to identify the *real* motives of an action. In addition to the fact that people "proceed through their lives as one proceeds *in the fog*" (Kundera 2001 [1993]: 238) as they are not always conscious of the motives for their action, the motives themselves may be numerous and interwoven. This is also true for the observer. For us, Weber stresses, "(…) it is not possible to arrive at even an approximate estimate of the relative strength with which diverse significant relations are expressed, and which oppose each other in the 'conflict of motives' even though they are all equally comprehensible."[11] The tensions within life conducts, between different spheres of activity, but also between the researcher, his values and the object of his research is a theme dear to Weber. Due to the entanglement of interests (material and ideal) within the actor, as well as with the values of the observer (Weber 1949 [1904]), the motives that underlie the action can only be of the kind of an ideal type. But this heterogeneity of motives need not keep the sociologist from tearing them

---

11 "*In welcher relativen Stärke aber die verschiedenen im 'Motivenkampf' liegenden, uns untereinander gleich verständlichen Sinnbezogenheiten im Hanldeln sich auszudrücken pflegen, läßt sich, nach aller Erfahrung, in äußerst vielen Fällen nicht einmal annähernd, durchaus regelmäßig aber nicht sicher, abschätzen*" (Weber 1972 [1921]: 4).

out of the fog, "from systemizing his concepts by the classification of possible types of subjective meaning. That is, he may reason *as if* action actually proceeded on the basis of clearly-conscious meaning" (Weber 1978a [1921]: 22, my emphasis). As in a detective novel, the Weberian (or neo-Kantian) sociologist attempts "at organizing chaos" (Gombrowicz 1993: 160).[12]

Like the work of the sociologist, the task of the police investigator is to discover and reconstruct a network of motives underlying the action. William B. Sanders emphasizes that "the concept of 'motive' (…) plays a central role in many [police] investigations.... Without such a guiding concept, there would be no starting point for an investigation and no grounds on which to build a theory or finish an investigation" (1974: 4). The police officers isolate a motive that explains a crime; they talk of "motivated crimes," such as in, say, racially or sexually motivated crimes, or crimes motivated by greed or vengeance. The prosecutor, with the evidence submitted to him by the police officers in the course of a prosecution, also reconstructs the motives of the defendant and proposes a theory of his actions by means of legal categories (Turner and Factor 1994: 169).[13] The more sensitive the problems all three figures will treat, the more they will require a suspension of their own values; a posture that finds expression in the objectivity of the sociologist, the professionalism of the police officer, or the impartiality of the judge.[14] This is what allows them to carry out their work

---

12 An aim and a question are at the heart of Weber's sociology. The aim is greater intelligibility and can be achieved through inventing ideal types and making up "genetic" models such as in the *Protestant Ethic*, an essay which attempts to account for the genesis of a particular order, that of modern capitalism (Turner and Factor 1994: 157). The question could be put like this: How can an order exist in spite of the diverging motives? In *The Protestant Sects*, Weber looks at the empirical validity of an order and points to the different motives sustaining it.

13 Prosecutors are also confronted with diverse motives, which are often unconscious and unarticulated. The pleading of a case will emphasize an ensemble of motives contributing to the elaboration of a judgment on the basis of demonstrations and reasonable grounds (Turner and Factor 1994: 169).

14 In a similar fashion, Kundera (1988 [1986]: 158) speaks of the wisdom of the novelist.

even with individuals for whom they might have particular contempt.[15] If police work aims at an intervention, be it to come to someone's aid or pursue an individual, and that of the prosecutor aims at a decision, a sentence, the Weberian sociologist is marked by an entirely different end (Weber 1949 [1906]: 168-169): he limits himself to rendering intelligible the causes of the cultural phenomena that appear to be important from the point of view of values—his own and those of his contemporaries.

2.1 Possible Slippages

Colin Campbell (2006) observes an interesting paradox: although a great number of sociologists claim Weberian roots, we are forced to admit that motives—understood in Weber's sense as a "complex of subjective meaning which seems to the actor himself or to the observer an adequate ground [*Grund*] for the conduct in question" (Weber 1978a [1921]: 11),[16]—are today practically absent from empirical studies. Contemporary sociologists tend much more to favor the reasons invoked by the actor himself to explain or justify an action ("motive talk"). In fact, we generally study not so much motives (*Gründe*) as discursive strategies employed to ground or justify an action (*Begründung*). Such a conception of motives often—though not always—places the observer in the position of a moral judge insisting on the bad intentions of some, and the naïveté of the others.

---

15 Thus, the literature on the police reveals that officers can hold racist opinions and nonetheless respect a citizen's civil rights (Waddington 1999: 291; see also Cashmore 2001: 653).

16 Martin Albrow translates the Weberian definition of motive as the "meaningful basis for behaviour" (1990: 164), which corresponds better to the original *Grund*, not reason nor *ratio*, but basis, fundament. Milan Kundera, the most "Weberian" of contemporary writers, observes that "[i]n all languages derived from Latin, the word 'reason' (*ratio, raison, ragione*) has a double meaning: first, it designates the ability to think, and only second, the cause. Therefore reason in the sense of a cause is always understood as something rational. A reason the rationality of which is not transparent would seem to be incapable of causing an effect. But in German, a reason in the sense of a cause is called a *Grund*, a word having nothing to do with the Latin *ratio* and originally meaning 'soil' and later 'basis'" (1999 [1990]: 243).

In the case of the social scientists investigating the police, an accusatory attitude becomes all the more likely since the forces, as I have underlined earlier, tend to offend liberal democratic ideals. Such a conception of motives can add an air of deception to arguments brought forth by actors; a deception sometimes unconsciously influences the actors themselves. I often encountered such an attitude in discussions with fellow sociologists or anthropologists driven by a moral incentive to unmask power relations and give a voice to actors in a minority position. For them, the carriers of diversity within the police forces as well as some of their initiatives (meetings with minority groups, information sessions, intercultural training, and the recruitment of officers from post-migration backgrounds) were to be acknowledged as well intentioned. However, my colleagues did not fail to point out to me the naïveté of these "progressive" actors—and in turn my own—in their blindness to the fact that despite their goodwill, police officers remain no less in a position of domination toward minorities. I have also frequently observed a similar type of reaction among police officers during intercultural training. While visiting a mosque, for example, they were listening to the host and politely asking questions. At the exit, however, they showed distrust and suggested lip service, doublespeak, cover-up plans, and hypocrisy.[17]

The distrust found among social scientists outside the police forces as well as that of the police officers do not share the same object: the police for the former, some minority actors for the latter. To be sure, this situation accounts in part for the frequent irritation aroused in sociological studies on the police and police participation in these studies. For all their differences, the results seem in both cases to be known in advance. However comprehensible, this posture also testifies to an entanglement of values that attribute those of the actor with those that animate the observer; a posture that seems to make empirical work redundant. This confusion is relevant to the interests of investigators and, to borrow Mills' terms (1940: 910), to the "accepted vocabulary of motives." The greater the number of people among

---

17 The officers used the term *Scheinheiligkeit* (literally: apparent saintliness). It has been often noted that police officers become distrustful in the course of their career. The professional habitus of police officers institutionalizes this doubt and their techniques encourage them to play this double game (Hess 1997: 51-52; also Manning 2005: 195).

whom this confusion is shared, the less likely it will be noticeable or able to be called into question. Such an entanglement of values constitutes an obstacle to approaching the field of inquiry and, in the end, to the advancement of knowledge. We must be all the more vigilant as the object of our research is controversial and touches on power issues as in the case of research on groups we, as social scientists, feel inclined to agree with or oppose.

In the pursuit of an interpretive sociology, it is the study of motives, and not the truth of the meaning aimed at by the actor, that will be the primary guide of our inquiry.[18] Putting intentions on trial is an uneasy task for the sociologist. On the one hand, we know that the actor's intentions are prone to change. Mills (1940: 904) emphasizes that the mere fact of expressing a "reason" is already part of the action. On the other hand, we know that moral or theoretical dualisms are all too often weak indicators of the empirical reality (Rehberg 1994: 51). One may think at the level of individuals of processes portrayed in such a film as Ingmar Bergman's *The Best Intentions* or, at a more general level, in terms of the history 20th century, which is marked by developments that we consider horrific but are actually the product of good intentions. Conversely, outcomes judged as happy may be the product of physical and mental coercion. The motives underlying actions are multiple; they are subject to transformation, and they are sometimes detached from their consequences (Weber 1949 [1906]: 168), a principle at the heart of Weberian sociology.

2.2 Weber's Desertion

One ought to acknowledge the desertion by sociologists of this study of motives and reflect on its possible causes. It seems that it was in part Weber himself who unwittingly led us into this trap. Albrow states that "[it] is this Kantian emphasis on responsibility which probably accounts for the rather exclusive emphasis on motivation as an element in explaining the course of human action in Weber's comment on the nature of sociology" (1990: 200). In Weber's works, motivation and responsibility are intimately connected

---

18 One must concede a certain sociological sense to the writer of the film *The Brave One*, when his detective says in an interview with a journalist that "people lie all the time, but they don't lie for nothing—they're also saying something."

(Weber 1949 [1906]: 168-169). This alliance makes sociology the inheritor of a long juridical and religious tradition and sets Weber and his contemporaries under the colossal shadow of Kant.[19] It testifies to the historical and normative grounding of our own theories.[20] When we give importance to intentions and to the truth of the actors' subjective meaning over the consequences of the action, we bear the stamp of this grounding.

Besides the emphasis on motivation, one might invoke multiple causes for the disappearance from sociological research of motives as Weber understands them: the reception of his writings (Gerhardt 1986), competing sociological definitions, or a fear of using concepts that might be turned against real individuals and groups with little means of protest. It is true that Weber's abundant usage of inverted commas and italics, just like his rigorous, even pernickety elaboration of concepts, does not perhaps provide a sufficient antidote to abusive interpretations, appropriations of his concepts in social practice, or to their essentialization. Moreover, Martin Albrow (1990: 212) underlines that Weber did not seem worried about the impact that his types might have. It seems to me, however, that the discredit into which the study of motives has gradually fallen, to the profit of discursive aspects and "motive talk" that focuses on reasons invoked by the actors, has had among others the consequence of removing from sociological study what Weber called its "genetic" aspect, that is the challenge not only to understand, but also to put forth explanations that casually account for the course and consequence of social activity (Weber 1978a [1921]: 4).

Dialoguing with Max Weber brings another aspect to the fore: he is not our contemporary. He was a (left) liberal of the cultural bourgeoisie of the beginning of the 20th century whose sensibility toward difference we sociologists no longer share, at least not entirely. As his writings attest, Max Weber, the man, confers the individual with a high degree of responsibility.

---

19 Among other sociologists, Hahn (1982) shows that in the 12th century there is a shift in interest from the external deed toward the intention, which conferred a great importance to confession, and eventually to scrutiny.
20 A point always stressed, and criticized, by Norbert Elias (1978 [1970]: 116-117).

His individual is a stoic, heroic man bestowed with a strong sense of duty.[21] He has to make choices and face up to what often turns out to be a tragic fate.[22] This individual is not our contemporary. Reading contemporary sociological writings on issues related to difference—as well as teaching Weberian sociology—hints at a sensibility, a value relation the researchers and—students—maintain toward a "spirit" of diversity, which might have been foreign to Max Weber. This "new" sensibility tends to favor actors one wishes to give a voice to and "let speak." It is on the one hand argued that interrogating the motives might, unwittingly throw doubt on the sincerity of actors who may already be in a minority position (Beaman 2008: 202); on the other hand, letting the actors speak might counter the constructed character of sociological concepts. Seen in such a light, the question "How can one let the individual speak without abandoning the interpretation and the causal explanation of social activity?" becomes all the more relevant.

By investigating diversity—a particular relation to difference—in Germany and its "carriers," I attempt to cement the three moments of the Weberian program: besides distinguishing motives and intention, I differentiate the consequences of action and individual fate. These distinctions allow me to play with different analytical levels, that of the objectivized or fictional individual and that of the flesh-and-blood individual. Though Weber had stressed the importance of motives, one cannot indeed reduce his approach to this aspect alone. In reality, he had not neglected another important dimension of sociological inquiry, namely the consequences of action and their effect in relation to their intentions (which one is really to become clear about "in the face of critical and absolutely concrete problems" (Weber cited and translated in Manasse 1944: 30). It is there that individuals reintroduce themselves in the sociological narrative; they resurface through

---

21 In his lecture entitled *Politics as Vocation*, Weber promoted an ethics of responsibility or *Sachlichkeit*—the political equivalent of scientific objectivity—and of a "resigned voluntarism" (Despoix 1995).

22 For Weber, the fate of the man is a tragic, even Faustian one. It corresponds to the force "which ever seeks the good but ever creates evil" (Weber 2007 [1904/1905]: 116). Weber inverts here Mephistopheles' sentence from Goethe's *Faust*.

the chasm opened by the force of the tensions between the effects of action and initial intents.

3. THE CONSEQUENCES OF ACTION, FATE, AND THE RETURN OF THE INDIVIDUAL

Here we arrive at another aspect of Weber's sociology. While we often associate Weber with the theory of action, his enterprise could just as easily be characterized as a theory of the paradoxes and consequences of action (Turner 2007: xi), a discovery that ought to be ascribed, before sociology, to literature (Kundera 1988 [1986]: 24). The Benjamin Franklin of *The Protestant Ethic* is part of a process of mediation of which he is not the master and which even runs counter to his will. For this reason he has been described as a "vanishing mediator" (Jameson 1973). The consequences of action considered in relation to intention often point to what is, from the sociologist's vantage point, the paradoxical nature of action, or the relation between will and the effects it often produces. However, for the flesh-and-blood man (including Max Weber the man behind the sociologist) they constitute his fate.

Weber defines fate (*Schicksal*) with an interesting formula. It is "(...) the consequences of one's action, compared to one's intention."[23] This formula, which provides the narrative framework for the *Protestant Ethic* (the Puritans' motives for action, the paradox of their action and the emergence of modern capitalism as well as the fate of modern man), also makes it possible to harmonize the two main interpretations of the guiding thread of Weber's corpus: the historico-sociological interpretation emphasizing rationalization as its central theme (Schluchter 1998 [1979]) and the more "existential" interpretation that places the fate of modern man (*Menschentum*) at the heart of the analysis (Hennis 1987; also Breuer 2006).[24]

---

23 "(...) *die Folge seines Handelns gegenüber seiner Absicht*" (Weber 1988 [1920]: 524).

24 Danilo Martuccelli writes in this respect: "what is vocation becomes destiny. However, within these constraints, just like the return of *charisms* in modernity, Weber never ceases to define social action as a function of the conscious intentions of the agent. There is a strong tension between his subjective-

Needless to say, the suspension of values at the heart of the ideal-typical method is not equivalent to indifference on the part of the sociologist. The importance accorded to fate, a word encountered often in Weber's writings, invokes the existential dimension of the individual, the flesh-and-blood individual standing "behind every action." It constitutes, in a way, the humanistic moment of Weber's sociology. The theme of fate notably appears when Weber evokes the necessity of facing the consequences of rationalization, the polytheism of values and the anguish of solitude. If there is a judgment of value, it consists in an entirely Kantian partiality for a person who feels himself charged with a mission (*Dienst an einer Sache*), however irrational it might be.

The cases I present in this study highlight the three underscored moments of the Weberian program as I see it: the motives, the consequences of action, and individual fate. The real individuals I also wish to give a voice to precede the types, but they also follow from them: they feed in the types and, once constructed, they in turn help me to understand them. The confrontation between the types and police officers gives expression to the dilemmas individuals encounter and a more existential dimension. Casting light on these three moments allows one to apprehend the individuals, the real police officers who are at the center of the study as well as the person of the researcher, and that of Weber lurking not too far behind. Before presenting the ideal types of the carriers of diversity in the police in Germany, which are at the core of the book, let us pause and consider one possible way to discern the motives of action and, thus, delineate the types, which will be instrumental in weaving the individual chapters together. As we will see, this technique is not entirely foreign to police work.

---

comprehensive reasoning and the social reality described in his socio-historical analyses" ["*Ce qui était vocation devient destin. Pourtant, en deçà des contraintes, tout comme du retour des charismes dans la modernité, Weber ne cesse de définir l'action sociale en fonction de l'intentionnalité visée de l'acteur. La tension est forte entre sa démarche subjectivo-compréhensive et la réalité sociale décrite dans ses analyses socio-historiques*"] (1999: 227).

4. Investigating the Motives of Action: A Proposition

In his programmatic text "The Objectivity of Knowledge" (1949 [1904]), Weber enjoined the construction of rigorous concepts in order to manage the tension existing between the values of the researcher and his object of study. Thomas Kemple argues that such an approach:

"helps us to understand how Weber's text mediates between the generalizing, nomothetic, and even universalizing objectives of the sociological writer, on the one hand (who must sustain a principle of 'value-freedom') and the particularizing, ideographic, and even critical judgments that readers may wish to draw, on the other (insofar as their concerns more overtly moral, political, or aesthetic)" (2006: 9).

Comparison, logical reasoning, and counterfactual argumentation are some of the techniques that Weber privileges for the refutation or confirmation of hypotheses. I would like to emphasize a technique sometimes employed by Weber to isolate the motives of action and which had a particular imaginative appeal for him. Though it might well seem ironic to qualify Weber's tortuous writings as literary, he certainly utilizes a literary *method*: the "fictional dialogue." In the course of a fictional debate staged by the researcher, ideal typical characters are led to confront their values; in his comparative studies in the sociology of religion, Weber quite ably composed a dialogue between two opposed types, the Protestant ascetic and the Confucian monk (Weber 1988 [1920]: 512-536; Passeron 1996: 37). In this we have a method that seems to me particularly well suited to the handling of subjects where a polemic can blur the sociological gaze. This procedure allows the comparison of characters from very different horizons, the isolation of their specific characteristics, their values and dilemmas within the spaces constructed according to a questioning that is appropriate to them, and where the values of the researcher are suspended. Moreover, the contrast permits Weber to assess the importance of the religious motive in the conduct of the actor's life and thus to address the thesis at the heart of his *Protestant Ethic*.

It might be worth noting that this technique is not entirely foreign to the work of police officers. It is not unlike the confrontation between arrested suspects in the course of an interrogation (in German, "confrontation,"

Gegenüberstellung, also means "cross-examination"). The purpose of this technique is to make the suspects talk, to observe them and to uncover their motives. In literature, this type of dialogue reaches its climax in Milan Kundera's *Immortality* (1999 [1990]). In this novel, where motives as well as the question of fate occupy a central place in the reflection accompanying the story, the novelist puts his characters on the scene, makes them interact and speak while always talking to them. This would not be surprising at all but for the fact that the novelist, the real man, confronts his characters and becomes himself a character in the novel. To the extent in which the questions we address in our work concern us as sociologists and flesh-and-blood persons, and we maintain a value relation toward them, we too are more or less discreet characters in the sociological investigation. It is precisely this relation of values that is the source of our questioning and causes the social sciences, as Weber insists (Weber 1949 [1904]: 104; Turner and Factor 1994: 164), to remain eternally young sciences.

Throughout the book, I also used imagined comparisons, or invented dialogues between the types. This exercise is inherent to the construction of typologies. Sometimes, I also stage dialogues or conversations. The main character in chapter three, Inspector Bobkowski, is cross-examined by the representatives of other types; this gives expression to different reactions, points of view, and moral dilemmas. In an attempt to distinguish subjectively intended and objectively valid "meanings," toward the end of the book, I assemble the people portrayed in the chapters into a conversation over one central issue, the activity of representation. This also allows a discussion of normative dimensions pertaining to this type of activity.

In this chapter I have insisted on the notion of motive, understood in Weber's sense, in order to advocate an approach and technique that would take account of social action, to underline the task of *interpretation* that such an approach demands. In the context of questions connected to difference, diversity, and tolerance, where the values of the observer are strongly questioned and his sociological vision can easily become blurred, Weber's suggestions seem to offer material for reflection on the analytical and existential levels. For one to interpret the *motives* of action is to take account of its *consequences*, but also, in turn, to concern oneself with the fate of the individual. With this in mind, in the next section of the book, I will portray the police staff I accompanied in their daily work between 2004 and 2009-2010 through four typical characters. The next chapter is dedicated to the empathetic type: it sets the stage for outlining other types for comparison in delineating the acknowledgement and treatment of difference in the German police force. It is set in Hamburg where I met Inspector Dietmar Piontek and his colleagues at the recruitment unit.

These are their stories.

II. Dealing With Difference. Four Portraits and a Half

> "The portrait becomes a starting point (and not an ending point with the illustration): they [the sociologies of the individual] start with the singular for understanding the social" / *Le portrait devient un point de départ (et non plus d'arrivée avec l'illustration): partir du singulier pour comprendre le social* (MARTUCCELLI AND DE SINGLY/2009: 111).

> "Understanding rather refers to something creative than knowing strictly speaking; fragments, that is positive facts of which the life of human beings is made are united in a construct, product of the imagination without being imaginary" / *le comprendre relève davantage du créatif que du savoir à proprement parler; les fragments, c'est-à-dire les faits positifs, dont se compose la vie des êtres humains, sont réunis en un tableau, produit de l'imagination sans être imaginaire* (DISSELKAMP ON SIMMEL/ 2012: 155).

Inspector Piontek, or *Sorge um die Seele*
The Empathetic Type

Investigating diversity in the police, I started with the most obvious, as in the poster that had attracted my attention in Montreal: the initiatives to hire officers from post-migration backgrounds. This is the expression used as I write these lines; the person I first contacted talked about "candidates of non-German origin." This person was Inspector Dietmar Piontek. Because his work turned out to be instructive on one possible way to deal with difference within the police forces, I was to meet him on several occasions.[1] Without him, the project underlying this study may never have seen the light of day.

Slowly building on Dietmar Piontek's work, in this chapter I examine the initiatives to recruit police officers from post-migration backgrounds in Hamburg, the changes incurred, and the resistance they met. At the center of this chapter is a vignette portraying the inspector and his colleagues, the ones to whose recruitment he had contributed. Interpreting the gathering enables me to draw the contours of the motives underlying the work of Inspector Piontek and, thereby, outline the first ideal type of the carriers of diversity, actors who have contributed, as a consequence of their actions, to greater recognition of difference within the police. To be sure, this type neither characterizes in an "ideal" form all the actions nor the motives of the officers met; however, it serves as a reference point for delineating, comparing, and engaging a dialogue between the types (as well as between them and sociologists) in the subsequent chapters, while hinting at its cultural foundation. In the final section entitled "Forth in Berlin, Back in

---

1 I met him four times in 2004 and once more in 2006.

Hamburg," I return to Hamburg and present a second vignette with a different point of view, that of the recruits.

1. INSPECTOR PIONTEK: RECRUITING OFFICERS FROM POST-MIGRATION BACKGROUNDS IN HAMBURG

I met Inspector Dietmar Piontek for the first time in 2004. This was at his office at the Personnel Selection Center within the Hamburg Police Academy in the Carl-Cohn Straße. Stepping into his office, I saw posters of exotic places and, right above his desk, a board with small pieces of paper with names fixed on it. Before I could ask about the board, Piontek offered me some coffee.

Dietmar Piontek was a bearded inspector in the prime of life. He was wearing a green uniform with three stars, which made him a member of the elevated service, a Chief Police Inspector (PHK). An officer of German origin, he was appointed in 1994 as the first advisor for candidates of foreign origins (*Berater für ausländische Bewerber*) within Hamburg Police Academy. The inspector had, until then, worked as first officer in a neighborhood known for its sizeable Turkish community. This experience, combined with other personal experiences (he mentions being married to a woman of South American origin), seemed to predetermine him for holding such an office.

A legal frame was provided in 1993 for the work of Inspector Piontek at the police academy. In the midst of flashes of xenophobic violence, combined with police scandals and tense relations between police officers and foreigners in the early 1990s, the Conference of Ministers and Senators of the Interior then adopted an exception rule to the civil service law (*Beamtengesetz*) that granted permission to hire foreigners living in Germany into the police force—provided there was an "urgent professional necessity" (BBG § 7, Absatz 3). Because the people hired eventually were to be sworn in and become civil servants, sometimes without a German passport, this dispensation turned out to be quite extraordinary: German citizenship was no longer considered a prerequisite for becoming a police officer.[2]

In Hamburg, the Christian Democratic Union (CDU) proposed to the then Social Democratic Party (SPD)-led Senate to follow suit and also resorted to the exception rule. In the case of Hamburg, pragmatic concerns were voiced that echoed those on the federal level: it was contended that foreign police officers would enhance police efficiency and competence; that is, the acceptance of police work in neighborhoods characterized by a high percentage of foreigners and the use of foreign police officers in the struggle against organized crime (Bürgerschaft der freien und Hansestadt Hamburg 1993). Already by the end of the 1980s, attempts were made in another German police department—in Berlin—to recruit foreign police officers with the pragmatic aim of infiltrating certain criminal milieus and increasing the acceptance of police work in neighborhoods characterized by a high percentage of foreigners.[3] Second generation German Turks and Poles, and later Yugoslavs were thus to be trained for the task.

The exception rule, together with the Hamburg Senate's resolution, was worded as a permission and not an injunction. Dietmar Piontek was nevertheless hired to deal with and *promote* nonnational applicants (Bürgerschaft der freien und Hansestadt Hamburg 1993: 1). The committed and dedicated inspector introduced several measures on his own initiative. Breaking new ground, he enjoyed freedom in shaping his work, which eventually included (1) shaping the rules of entry for foreign candidates, (2) leading recruitment activities, as well as (3) representing and accompanying recruits through their integration in the forces. A closer look at Inspector Piontek's multifaceted work enables us to better grasp some of the issues involved in these initiatives.

1.1 Shaping the Rules of Entry

At the beginning, the initiative's stated goals—increasing police efficiency and fighting criminality—influenced the formal conditions of entry for for-

---

[2] The addendum to the civil service law draws on an exception rule, which was introduced in the 1960s for the purpose of hiring foreign academics at German universities.

[3] More details are provided in chapter three.

eigners for complying to the exception clause introduced by the senate. They had to be in possession of a valid residence permit and demonstrate linguistic and cultural skills in another culture acquired through socialization. Besides meeting these criteria, the candidates had to meet all criteria required from German candidates. In the Hamburg Police Department, candidates must be holders of a school diploma, be under the age of 31 and meet the physical standard of being at least 165 cm tall. Candidates who meet these requirements are invited to pass another set of tests (written, oral, intelligence, sport, medical), which are followed by an interview. Subsequently, they are screened to ensure their "police suitability" (*Polizeitauglichkeit*), which includes inquiries about such things as contracted debts, family members' background as well as body piercing and tattoos. As a rule of thumb, recruitment officers in all federal states said that only one in ten candidates are found suitable.

Once selected, candidates go through socialization at the police academy, which comprises a two-year training period and a six- to twelve-month internship. The locus of entry for the incorporation of the foreign candidates in Hamburg is the police academy. There is no fast-track program, which would allow recruits to join the force within a few months, and Inspector Piontek stresses on many occasions the importance that all candidates enjoy the same instruction.[4] The training, as a type of organizational socialization, is considered something worth preserving and a guarantee of successful integration. The incorporation in the police, an organization known for its *esprit de corps*, is ultimately deemed a matter of personal effort and conformity. This type of inclusion requires, Piontek firmly believes, time. Upon completion of their training, the officers-to-be are expected to swear an oath of allegiance.[5] According to the Hamburg civil service law, the wording of the oath is the following: "I swear loyalty to the Basic Law of the Federal Republic of Germany and to the Constitution of the Free and Hanseatic city of Hamburg, obedience of the laws and conscientious fulfillment of my official duty, so help me God." The oath was modified after 1945 to allow formulations omitting the reference to God,

---

4   Interview with DP, 10 May 2004. In Montreal's Police Department, candidates with university degrees can go through such a fast-track program.

5   See the information leaflet, *Informationen zur Einstellung in den Polizeivollzugsdienst*, p. 1.

thus accommodating both members of other religions and atheists. Up until then, the oath's reference to God had been a motive invoked to turn down Jewish candidates to the civil service (Pulzer 1992: 340).[6]

In contrast to the Berlin Police Department, candidates are not required to take up German citizenship until the end of their training. The authorities in Hamburg respect the will of those—mainly Turkish nationals—who waive this option. These sworn-in officers become, in Habermas' words (1998: 233), "Germans with foreign passports." In fact, however, many foreign candidates did take up German citizenship.

Complying to the exception clause introduced by the senate requires higher standards than the ones usually required for obtaining German citizenship. Considering the requirements needed to become a police officer, Dietmar Piontek writes, in 1999, with regard to practices from the Weimar Republic: "People who [then] acquired the status of civil servants were automatically granted citizenship." He then suggests: "in view of the perspective to resort to an exception clause for an indefinite period of time, this type of regulation could represent an idea worth considering for the legislator."[7] Yet changes were introduced in European and German regula-

---

6 "Ich schwöre Treue dem Grundgesetz für die Bundesrepublik Deutschland und der Verfassung der Freien und Hansestadt Hamburg, Gehorsam den Gesetzen und gewissenhafte Erfüllung meiner Amtspflichten, so wahr mir Gott helfe."
"(3) Erklärt ein Beamter, dass er aus Glaubens- oder Gewissensgründen keinen Eid leisten wolle, kann er statt der Worte "Ich schwöre" die Worte "Ich gelobe" oder die nach dem Bekenntnis seiner Religionsgemeinschaft oder nach der Überzeugung seiner Weltanschauungsgemeinschaft an die Stelle des Eides tretende Beteuerungsformel sprechen.
(4) (1) In den Fällen, in denen nach § 6 Absatz 3 eine Ausnahme von § 6 Absatz 1 Nummer 1 zugelassen worden ist, kann von einer Eidesleistung abgesehen werden, wenn der Beamte eine fremde Staatsangehörigkeit besitzt und diese durch die Eidesleistung verlieren würde. (2) Der Beamte hat, sofern nichts anderes bestimmt ist, zu geloben, dass er seine Amtspflichten gewissenhaft erfüllen wird.
1) Geändert 11. 6. 1997 (HmbGVBl. S. 193). http://hh.juris.de/hh/gesamt/BG. URL:_HA_1977.htm#BG_HA_1977_rahmen (accessed 10 September 2006).
7 Internal document, Hamburg (1999 [1997]). Inspector Piontek is right in pointing that, with a nomination as civil servant, individuals were automatically con-

tions during his time as advisor for candidates of foreign origins between 1994 and 2005. The Maastricht Treaty gave, from 1993 onwards, European Union citizens access to civil service careers and revisions of the German foreigners' law (in 1991 and 1999) accelerated the granting of German citizenship. Under the backdrop of this general frame, Inspector Piontek contributed to shaping the rules of entry while leading recruitment activities.

1.2 Leading Recruitment Activities

In accordance with the Hamburg Senate's 1993 resolution, Dietmar Piontek's role was defined as attracting new recruits of foreign background. In a first stage, he primarily sought to reach potential Turkish candidates, the largest group of foreigners in Hamburg. He expended considerable effort, ranging from visiting ethnic shops to learning Turkish and informing second generation Turks about job opportunities at the police department.

Figure 3: Poster made by the Hamburg Police Academy for placement in Turkish shops

Poster reproduced with the permission of the Hamburg Police Department.

---

ferred citizenship. He probably does not have Adolf Hitler in mind who, according to Manfred Overesch (1992), was presumably appointed police inspector, and later professor, to become a German citizen and candidate for political office.

In spite of the initiatives undertaken, results in the recruitment of foreign police candidates were modest at first: the police department of the Hanseatic city hired one Turkish police officer in 1995 (Bürgerschaft der freien und Hansestadt Hamburg 1995: 3). Considerable difficulties were met with formal police requirements, the main obstacle mentioned by Inspector Piontek and his colleagues at the academy being the candidates' deficient knowledge of the German language. Recruitment officers in all federal states generally bemoaned difficulties met by candidates from post-migration backgrounds with the language test. If this claim is indeed confirmed by some studies,[8] it is important to note that the failure rate at this particular test is the highest—all categories of candidates taken into account.

To counter these hurdles, Inspector Piontek supported the introduction of German classes at the academy for promising candidates and, more importantly, argued in favor of a change in the rules: the tests to which recruits were submitted were modified so as to avoid possible cultural bias. Also, a point system was developed to favor candidates who might have deficiencies in German, but otherwise had knowledge of a second language, allowing them to accumulate points for particular competences. Although not described as such by its initiators, the revisions brought about a form of affirmative action in police recruiting activities. To counter possible criticism, this new point system applies to *all* candidates.

As time went by, Inspector Piontek sought applicants from non-German backgrounds (*nicht deutscher Herkunft* as opposed to *ausländischer Herkunft*), an expression he coined together with his colleagues at the academy, to acknowledge the various statuses of candidates and those who should be recruited. According to my informant, being of non-German origin (with or without German citizenship)—*not* the initially stated operational needs of the police (*dringendes Bedürfnis*)—justifies local authorities' granting of the exception rule. Although high police officials still stressed operational needs, there was, by 2004, no consideration as to the origin of the candidates or the language skills they might have in a second language. When I went back to Hamburg in 2006, the counselor in charge

---

8   Internal document (2007), Police Academy of Lower-Saxony. The language test is the criteria on which the most candidates—independently of their backgrounds—fail.

was looking for candidates who had at least one parent from post-migration backgrounds (*mit Migrationshintergrund*).

The measures introduced by Piontek and his colleagues have shown results, as more candidates were indeed recruited. From 1993 to 2004, the Hamburg Police Department hired through these measures 148 police officers of which 25 were not holders of German citizenship. Among the 25 officers, 11 were European Union citizens, 9 Turkish citizens, 2 citizens from the former Yugoslavia, 2 Polish nationals, and one Indonesian. These figures remain modest if measured in relation to the whole police department.[9] Inspector Piontek's efforts also moved to other "targets;" he considered as one of his achievements the hiring of a black man. Although his goal was not initially to change the organization, he contributed to modifying the rules of entry in the recruitment process and increasingly aspired to promote more difference within the police forces, as the hiring of a black officer attests to.

Although the exception rule to the civil service law reaffirmed, through its exceptional character, the necessity of German citizenship (and consequently the idea of the national homogeneity of the police forces), it turned out to be a half-opened door for change. And Inspector Piontek's influence certainly played a role in keeping it open.[10] That said, there were no strong institutional foundations underlying the measures he put in place and his work in general. Did I mention that Piontek was faced with considerable challenge? Within the ranks of the police forces his recruiting measures were perceived as jeopardizing the quality of the police body and were vehemently contested. They were said to go against the principle of equality of treatment (*Gleichbehandlung*), an argument I was to hear constantly throughout my fieldwork. Throughout our conversation, my informant stressed that his "vision" neither reflected that of the police as an organization nor that of the majority of his fellow officers and colleagues. Indeed, he perceived himself as a "free-floating atom" and described himself as a strange species (*Exot*). His efforts remained, he reckoned, to a large extent a personal struggle. I remember thinking to myself that he presents himself

---

9   Internal document, Hamburg (2004).
10 According to the same logic, the law on the career structure (*Laufbahngesetz*, par. 33[3]) was amended in July 1999 to allow non-German candidates to be hired in the higher service of the police forces (Blom 2005: 31).

much like Sisyphus, always confronted by the risk of failing and having to start everything over again. When we first met in 2004, Inspector Piontek was not sure whether his initiatives would be carried on if it were not for him and his commitment. His work, he commented, was still dependent on the vagaries of politics. He reported stoically that whenever a new police president is nominated, "you always have to explain the whole program anew."[11] The idea to recruit police officers of non-German background is, he explained, born in the 1990s in a particular climate, which in spite of the senate's formal resolution, is often forgotten.[12]

1.3 Representing Recruits in the Selection Process

Besides attracting candidates of non-German origin, Inspector Piontek represented recruits in the selection process, which includes, as mentioned, a host of tests and interviews. As such, his position was somewhat analogous to that of an equal treatment representative (*Gleichstellungsbeauftragter*). When appropriate, he accompanied candidates at the local foreigners' registration office. With passing time, he also mediated with superiors in cases ranging from freeing officers to participate in activities he organized or intervening in cases of harassment and conflict. Acting on behalf of his recruits and officers, he also became their unofficial representative (see Blom 2005: 40), a function that certainly was not part of any job description.

Inspector Piontek regarded his mandate as counseling, tracking the recruits through their formation and career as police officers, and also inviting them to group discussions. The board with small pieces, which was hanging above his desk and had caught my eyes when I first stepped in his

---

11 Interview with DP, 27 May 2004.
12 Goffman reflects on special programs introduced in the type of organizations he was interested in, psychiatric hospitals, in a similar manner: "Often a special psychiatric service, such as group psychotherapy, psychodrama, or art therapy, is introduced with great support from higher hospital management; then slowly interest is transferred elsewhere, and the professional in charge finds that gradually his job as been changed into a species of public relations work—his therapy given only token support except when visitors come to the institution and higher management is concerned to show how modern and complete facilities are" (1961: 92).

office, turned out to be a collection of the names of all his new and old recruits, together with the position they occupied in the forces. Piontek kept track of them after their hiring and training. His role, as he saw it, was to support the incorporation of recruits from non-German backgrounds in the police forces and, in turn, society. Individuals—and not groups as in other ethnically-based recruiting initiatives in some European and American countries—are the subjects of his particular attention. Once in the forces, Inspector Piontek observed that police officers of non-German background do not congregate in particular groups. Looking at a photo of the Muslim Women Association of the London Metropolitan Police, which was jutting out of one of my files, and comparing the organization to associations of black law enforcers, he remarked that this type of congregation is exactly the opposite of what is usually intended.[13]

Let us now set aside the account of Piontek's work and the changes incurred and offer a close-up of one activity, a group discussion. Because the episode allows for isolating the motives underlying the inspector's actions while hinting at their cultural foundations, the exercise is useful for specifying a first ideal type of an attitude toward difference within the police forces.

"Sorge um die Seele": Pastoral Care of the Soul (Excursus on the Guide)

The activity took place on 17 June 2004. Inspector Dietmar Piontek had invited "his" recruits and officers; twelve participants had taken up his invitation. Some, like me, were there for the first time; others were attending the meeting for a second or even a third time. On his own initiative and free time, the inspector had been organizing these gatherings, which he designated as exchanges of experiences (*Erfahrungsaustausche*), once a year for the past ten years.

The participants, some wearing their uniform, others not, all sat in a circle around a table set with candles, tea, and snacks after a day at the police academy or during a shift. The inspector in charge started by reading an email written by a German Turkish female police officer who regretted not

---

13 Interview with DP, 27 May 2004.

being able to attend. She described, in a moving way, how she had made her way through the police ranks and her family's reaction to her job. The inspector then invited the participants, all of whom he knew, to present themselves in turn. He asked them to state where they came from, when they started their training at the police academy and, when appropriate, where they worked. He then invited them to share their experiences and difficulties: Had they met with particular problems within the police? With the population they served? Or with their families? The individual presentations were to be followed by an open discussion and, finally, comments on Inspector Piontek's part.

The participants' responses were quite different from one another. Whereas some said they had encountered problems with their parents, with people from their "community," or experienced some kind of discrimination at the academy or in the forces, others mentioned that they had not met any difficulties. The participants showed three, not mutually exclusive, kinds of reaction, which Christophe Bertossi (2007: 201-203, 2013) also observed while working on ethnic minorities in the French army. Some said they made themselves invisible (as in the case of a young man wearing a badge without a name tag so as not to hint at his Turkish name, or at least to leave some ambiguity as to his origin); some insisted that they were not any different from other trainees or officers; and some mentioned feeling useful because they brought special competences in the police.[14]

When the discussion moved on to a less formal part, the inspector asked: "What problems do you encounter?" Participants were prompted to further share their experiences and reflect upon them. Let us be clear: it was difficult for recruits and police officers—and even for Dietmar Piontek himself—to talk about some issues, but they confided in the inspector. Police research points out that issues related to racism or discrimination are taboo in the forces (see Behr 2006: 80; Liebl 2004). The principle of equal treatment, according to which all officers are the same because they all make it through the stiff entry tests and police training, is firmly-believed and seems to be reinforced through the donning of the uniform. Problems

---

14 In his comparison of police officers from post-migration backgrounds in Paris and Berlin, Jérémie Gauthier (2012: 270, 2011: 467) has shown that the problems individuals encountered were similar in the two contexts; however, the institutional responses to them were different.

are not thought to be absent; however, they tend to be attributed to the individuals themselves and their potential deficiencies, or lack of stamina. Officers always stress the necessity to have a "thick skin" (*ein dickes Fell*). This principle is used in a defensive manner and was also echoed in the arguments of some of the participants at the gathering who stressed that one should not hire "just anybody" and look for people with perfect mastery of the German language.

The inspector's obvious care combined with the unique atmosphere (the setting reminded me of a moment of reflection typical of the Advent in Germany),[15] were admittedly more reminiscent of a pastoral meeting than the ones typically described in the literature on police culture or police managerial "diversity" (see Behr 2000: 175-181; Blom 2005: 6-50). The rain outside might have added some feeling of solemnity to the evening; still, the gathering itself called to mind the work of a police chaplain, not the work of a uniformed police officer. And although there was no explicit religious motivation underlying the meeting, the religious atmosphere must have struck the officer in charge himself; he felt the need to state, in an assertive manner, as though getting a manful grip on himself, "We're not doing pastoral care!"[16]

It seems instructive that the inspector—and the sociologist—was reminded of pastoral care of the soul (*Seelsorge*). Two important aspects of the situation call the *Seelsorge* to mind. Because Piontek explicitly addressed the first dimension, the scrutiny of one's conscience, or examination of conscience (Foucault 1978 [1976]), let us look on the second aspect of the *Seelsorge*, the guidance of the conscience of others and the inspector's role. During the whole meeting, Inspector Piontek listened carefully while exerting a certain authority on his officers. In contrast to group therapy, the discussion was not dependent upon the help of a professional stranger for, it seems important to note, the "counselor" was a uniformed officer; he was also a member of the group, yet not the immediate supervisor—as one would expect in the police. In contrast also to similar initiatives abroad as in again Canada or England, the recruits from post-migration backgrounds were not encouraged to congregate in particular groups or gather together as trade unions or associations; this was unthinkable for the

---

15 Miroslav Tížik (2001: 86) aptly compares the circle to a mobile church.
16 *Wir machen hier keine Seelsorge!*

inspector (as he had stressed in an earlier conversation). The individual officers were part of the group, but they were believed to need extra protection.

2. INVESTIGATING MOTIVES

2.1 On Ideal Types

The group discussion points to empathy, a Christian theme, and to the particular context of the police, which have yet to be examined. Before going any further, let us linger a moment on the method expanded in this chapter and the following ones, the ideal typical one.

What are ideal types? Above all, they are instruments. Ideal types are for the sociologist what contours are for the painter. Just as contours do not exist in reality, society always being on the move (see Arasse 2004: 98), ideal types do not, or only partially, correspond to social reality—social reality is heterogeneous and shifting. Borne in the mind of the sociologist, ideal types are his or her constructions, an attempt to "bring order to chaos," to render intelligible a phenomenon s/he considers important from the point of view of culture. By showing us "how the world might be, and by using them as our reference point," the ideal types help in pointing to what life is like "in *reality*" (Albrow 1990: 157).

As the long lasting discussion in painting, Max Weber is neither the first nor the only author to think about this instrument and the problems to which it attempts to respond. However, it is the definition he bequeathed sociology that became famous. In his essay "'Objectivity' in Social Sciences and Social Policy", he writes: An ideal type is formed by the one-sided *accentuation* of one or more points of view by the synthesis of a great many diffuse, discrete, more or less present and occasionally absent *concrete* individual phenomena, which are arranged according to those one-sidedly emphasized viewpoints into a unified *analytical* construct (*Gedankenbild*)" (1949 [1904]: 90).[17] Once constructed, ideal the types help the sociologist to throw light back on the very concrete individual phenomena

---

17 For a detailed reconstruction of Weber's (and Simmel's) position on the ideal type, see Gerhardt (2001).

that were instrumental in creating them as well as other phenomena. In sociological accounts the former are always more abstract, more coherent, and succinct than the description of the latter.

In this study I draw contours by discovering and reconstructing possible subjective meanings, the motives "which seems to the actor himself or to the observer an adequate ground for the conduct" (Weber 1978a [1921]: 11). I try to grasp and describe the individuals' "motivational code."[18] In the present chapter, I started from the fieldwork, with a portrait of Inspector Piontek and a reconstruction of his work. The vignette that followed helped me uncover a motive, empathy. In accordance with the new sociologies of the individual described by Martuccelli and de Singly, I use the case of Inspector Piontek as "a starting point, not an ending point with an illustration" (2009: 111). As I will show below, the inspector is neither identical with the type nor an illustration thereof: rather, it is instrumental in outlining one ideal type. In other words, I start with the singular for understanding the social.[19]

With an eye to the question underlying the investigation, the cases at hand, and the literature on the police, I outline in the next section my first type, the *empathetic* one. Once constructed, the type will be mirrored back on Inspector Piontek and extended to other people met during fieldwork such as Tamara Schwarz. It points to their motivations and the dilemmas they confront. Of course not all individuals encountered in the course of my fieldwork and in the police literature in Germany can be accounted by this type, but empathy is important as a contrast to other emerging types.

2.2 The Empathetic Type...

Let us depart from Inspector Piontek and his colleagues and create an abstract model: the empathetic type. Its "motivational code" can be described by two core ideas: care for the welfare of others and guidance.

---

18 I paraphrase Milan Kundera. Looking for "the non-psychological means to apprehend the self," the novelist explains in the *Art of the Novel*: "to apprehend the self in my novels means to grasp the essence of its existential problem. To grasp its *existential code*" (1988 [1986]: 29).

19 Although also written in combination with individual portraits, I start in other chapters with several cases or with a logical possibility.

The empathetic cares for the welfare of others. The others are neither abstract fellow citizens nor groups: they are concrete individuals. It provides guidance to others along their socialization in one organization. More than the material welfare of individuals found in trade unions, this type cares about the welfare—the soul—of the individuals. As such, its work resembles that of the classical *travail sur autrui* (Dubet 2002: 9), the smooth transformation and incorporation of the stranger within an organization characterized by strong socialization.

Instead of the professional "diversity" managers such as those I had met in Canada while doing preliminary fieldwork and that I expected to find from the literature on *diversity* (see, for example, Hannerz 1999), some of the inspectors I was observing could be referred to as sympathetic *Seelsorger*, understood in its literal translation as "caretakers of the soul" of the recruits they represented. If I'm correct in stating that one can talk of the pastoral care of the soul within the police, it does not take place within the frame of church activities.[20] Nor is this practice necessarily religiously motivated. I do not know for certain about Dietmar Piontek's religious commitment (I did not ask him directly) and others officers who emulated him (such as Brigitte Winter, one Berlin Inspector who organizes such gatherings for officers from post-migration backgrounds in her beat, and Gert Müller, one trade union representative in North Rhine-Westphalia).[21] As a *type*, the empathetic shares affinities with a secularized element of a religious and liberal tradition, which bears resemblance to a cultural Protestant cure of the soul. Historically, the expression Culture-Protestantism was coined to refer in an offensive manner to those, mainly an educated liberal bourgeoisie (*Bildungsbürgertum*) at the beginning of the 20th century, who actively sought to develop a modern, liberal cultural synthesis, which would mediate between Protestant reform and the modern world (Graf 1984: 217).

---

20 Indeed, the opposite might be the case. Pointedly said, this guidance is likely to constitute a kind of secular competition to the police chaplaincy.

21 Interviews with BW (6 June 2007; 18 August 2007) as well as with GM and TP (12 June 2007). For Berlin, see Gauthier (2011: 469).

2.3 ... And the Flesh-and-Blood Officers

Inspector Dietmar Piontek obviously cared for his recruits: he took extra time, listened to them, and counseled them while getting feedback on his work. This is how he came to define and exercise his job—and it did not necessarily have to be this way, as we can see when we compare him and his work to most of his colleagues in similar positions, whether in his police department or in other ones. His recruits could rely on him, but he also expected strength on their part (a "thick skin"). Closely connected to the care for the welfare of others and guidance, Piontek also exhibited a strong sense of responsibility and duty one finds in other types. He guided and accompanied, but also acted as a representative of his recruits. In his case, we can identify three, not two, core ideas at the heart of his action: care for the welfare of others, guidance, and responsibility.

If I write my account of Inspector Piontek in the past form, it is because he is no longer a counselor for foreign candidates. **Tamara Schwarz**, a young police officer with two silver stars on her shoulders, took over the job in 2005. Under the supervision of a high-ranking official, she is now in charge, part-time, of recruiting and counseling candidates from post-migration backgrounds. A former training instructor recommended by Inspector Piontek, she advises potential candidates and insures a follow up with the candidates who make it through the entry tests. She also organizes gatherings as her predecessor used to. She lays importance on keeping with, in her own words, the good work of her predecessor for whose approaches she has a great affinity (*auf einer Welle sein*) and is indebted to. While In-Dietmar Piontek stands closer—without being identical—to the ideal type outlined, Tamara Schwarz could also aptly be described as empathetic. Listening to her, I can see that she follows the path already laid by Piontek; however, a different quality and some changes are noticeable. Tamara Schwarz stresses that her goal is that the recruits and officers from post-migration backgrounds "feel taken care of" and are "well counseled."[22] Perhaps her work can be less characterized as guidance or a care of the soul (*Seelsorge*) and more as a care for others. Her work echoes a trend toward management and human relations, which was absent in Piontek's; it is also animated by a strong sense of responsibility. Incidentally, she uses the word

---

22 "(...) *dass sie sich gut beraten fühlen*" (interview with TS, 12 September 2006).

Fürsorgepflicht, the obligation, or duty, to care for the recruits and officers from post-migration backgrounds.

Inspector Schwarz insists, on several occasions, on the necessity to protect the recruits and officers from post-migration backgrounds. I had encountered this sentiment when talking with police officers I met throughout Germany and reading some police researchers (Blom 2005: 49). Evoking the need to protect attests to the responsibility felt by some carriers of diversity within the context of the police forces. Although my informants seldom mentioned the words discrimination or racism to me—except to negate them—,[23] the individual who could be described as empathetic stressed that they were there for others, in case something happens.[24] They feared a lack of internal acceptance for the people they cared for. This attitude is matched in studies on officers of migration backgrounds, which, while not detecting racism toward recruits, evoke anticipated racism (Blom 2005; Franzke 1999). If discrimination prevails within the force, it is in part checkmated by the belief in the principle of equality of treatment, which makes its acknowledgement and denouncement unlikely, and in part by the fact that the practice of the job requires in practice officers to cooperate and rely on each other (Cashmore 2001: 653).

3. Consequences of Action, Tensions and Dilemmas

The relationship between intentions and their consequences, Max Weber points out, always takes us back to the existential and individual dimension of typological sociology. For Inspector Piontek, the changes he has contributed to bringing about—in laying a path for dealing with officers from post-migration backgrounds and the recognition of difference—sprung forth from tensions and dilemmas. In other words, we could consider that empa-

---

23 Visibly compelled by my presence, Tamara Schwarz feels the need to point out that there was no problem in the Hamburg police forces. She stresses that not many recruits from post-migration backgrounds quit and those who take part in the discussions tell positive experiences (interview TS, 12 September 2006).
24 As I know from reading police interrogation books, such a denial might potentially point to a problem.

thy can here be seen both as a motive underlying the action and a consequence of the context of the police, an organization hostile to differences, which leads to those particular tensions and dilemmas.

Inspector Piontek's measures and views were often criticized within the police forces ranks, and the new rules of entry were challenged. Even Tamara Schwarz, who emphatically insists on following her predecessor's footsteps, stresses that she is not specifically looking for "exotic candidates such as Turks or Africans" and insists that the same rules should apply to all candidates. The phrase she uses is one I was to hear often in the course of my fieldwork, "there should be no special treatment."[25] By that derogatory phrase (in German: *kein Extra-Würstchen*), the police officers I met stressed the need to avoid preferential treatment. In the eyes of colleagues, Inspector Piontek had become particularly bold. He was said to have taken risks others would not have dared to take, say in allegedly taking measures to give a second chance to people who had not quite passed the entry tests.

The inspectors I met come to terms—more or less freely, depending on each case—with the tensions inherent to their mandate (and the consequences of their work, that is the greater recognition of difference) and the principles of an organization characterized by strong socialization and great cohesion. Those who can be described as empathetic were and still are confronted with this tension, as Inspector Schwarz' attitude attests to. Inspectors interviewed often feared that people who are in charge of recruiting and hiring candidates from post-migration backgrounds might change their behavior. Some felt that they would show too much sympathy for the recruits and officers from post-migration backgrounds; in other words, one was afraid they would "go ethnic." Through his work, one officer in Berlin reported having gone through a change in the eyes of his colleagues, as though he had converted, in his words, from "Saul to Paul." But commenting himself on Dietmar Piontek, the same inspector also said, distancing himself from him: "With his beard he does not look like a real police officer anymore."[26]

Empathy is one of the many possible paths one can take to acknowledge difference and deal with it; a path, which can be linked, I argued, to the carriers of a religious tradition. In the particular context of the police forces,

---

25 Interview with TS, 12 September 2006.
26 "*Vom Saulus zum Paulus*" (interview with LET, 3 November 2006).

this empathetic way of dealing with difference can paradoxically both hinder and enable the recognition it seeks.

This path hinders the process because of the image the caring police officers may reflect, an image that is at odds with the "we-image" or "we-ideal" of the police forces (Elias 1994 [1990]: 125). The empathetic type is somewhat striking in the context of the police forces. Furthermore, it is marred by a feeling of clumsiness expressed by Inspector Piontek himself when he declares: "We're not doing pastoral care!" Indeed, the group discussion described above would have no doubt irritated officers in charge of similar initiatives in other police departments—as well as some sociological observers. Because it does not bode well with the image of a police inspector and modern secularity, this observation confers upon the situation a somewhat comic character and forces him to constantly reassert, like the recruits and officers from post-migration backgrounds, their identity as police officers, such as in the donning of the uniform, even when this is not required.

At the same time, the empathetic path enables a particular treatment of difference in an organization hostile to difference and lacking strong institutional foundations to underlie the initiatives to recruits candidates from post-migration backgrounds. For the police officers who recognize discrimination, the *esprit de corps* that defines the forces, and feels a responsibility toward recruits and officers from post-migration backgrounds, there seems to be little alternatives to empathy, or caring and protecting. However, the situation is not easy for the inspectors committed to individuals like Dietmar Piontek. They are confronted with resistance within police forces. As a result, a certain capacity to absorb tensions seems to characterize to a high degree the work of the inspectors—and their recruits even more—whom I interviewed in the course of the study: all of them stressed the necessity to have a thick skin.

While researching, I noticed that criticism also emanated from some of my colleagues, avowedly progressive academics. While acknowledging their sympathetic character, they bemoaned that officers like Piontek do not *really* contribute to the autonomy and agency of recruits from post-migration backgrounds; they pointed toward the paternalist way in which they deal with them, and insisted that they are dilettantes. How might have Inspector Piontek responded to them? I write "might have" because he did not see the problem, he did not share my colleagues' sensibility. Given the question, he might have objected that his intention was not to be paternalistic to anybody. On the contrary, as he actually argued, he wanted to encourage and contribute to the full citizenship of foreigners in the forces—that is to say, their full incorporation in the organization. Inspector Piontek did his best in the police to act and speak on behalf of "his" recruits and officers as well as to accompany them at a time and in a context in which he saw no other available alternative. Piontek and those like him are closely related to those Johannes Weiß (2001) refers to as mediators (*Vermittler*) and their dilemmas and ambivalences. The inspectors came to assume a bridging function (Certeau 1998 [1980]: 128): they both potentially unite and separate; they can incorporate young officers from post-migration backgrounds in the forces while threatening their autonomy.

This reaction to the empathetic type points to issues of agency and advocacy we will encounter throughout the study and has several normative and moral implications. Before turning our attention to these concerns, it might be interesting to follow up with the situation in Hamburg and to take a glimpse at those most concerned, the "object of care."

Forth in Berlin, Back in Hamburg (Excursus on the Recruits)

While in Berlin some time later doing fieldwork, I went back to Hamburg to participate in another exchange-of-experiences with recruits and officers from post-migration backgrounds.[27] Inspector Tamara Schwarz had this time convened the meeting. There were more participants than two years before and two high-ranking officials were also attending the event, conferring upon it an official seal.

As at the former meeting, the participants were invited to present themselves and to share their experience in turns; however, the serene but earnest atmosphere had given way to a different, pastiche-like, situation. Indeed, there was a flair of rehearsal about the gathering. The same questions were being asked and the evening dragged on as police officials were taking considerable time to present their view on people from post-migration backgrounds; I could feel that participants were getting nervous. One of them pointed out that there was, as far as he was concerned, no problem.

---

27 Participant observation, Hamburg Police Academy, 23 November 2006.

He then started talking cheekily about "police officers from an East German or Berliner background" [*Polizisten mit einem ostdeutschen oder Berliner Hintergrund*]. As it happened, some 500 Berliners had gone to Hamburg between 2003 and 2006. Because of budget cuts, the Berlin Police Department could not hire the recruits it had selected and trained and who had been promised a job. The unemployed trainees could be hired in the Hamburg police forces. The label "police officers from an East German or Berliner background" was an allusion to these officers whom, for the most part, came from the new federal states, that is the territory of the former German Democratic Republic.[28] Those officers, he argued, were the ones said to form a special group and have a problem, and not him and his colleagues present at the gathering. With a malicious grin he pointed to the incongruity of the situation, thus distancing himself from the category he was assigned to. More than criticizing the "officers from an East German background," the "identity joking" (Goffman 1961: 112) was a reaction to the labeling and restoring his identity as a full-fledged police officer and a Hamburger by creating another category for a silenced or invisible minority.[29] Half-mockingly and half-defiantly, he suggested inviting the colleagues from an East German background to join them at a future gathering.[30]

---

28 In the 1990s sociologist Andreas Glaeser (2000) studied the unification of the East and West Berlin police from an ethnographic angle. The case of the 500 young officers would represent an interesting fieldwork to write a follow up to his book *Divided in Unity*, a similar experiment, ten years on. When I told him about the label, an officer at the Berlin Police Department commented, both in a resigned and sarcastic tone: "I knew that the reunification would mean the easternification of Berlin" ["*ick hab ja jewusst, dat die Wiedervereinigung die Ostfizierung Berlins bedeuten würde*"] (interview with KB, 24 November 2006).

29 "We find identity joking, when a member of one group briefly acts like a member of the other, or briefly treats a co-member as someone of the other category, for the avowed purpose of amusement. I assume these identity concerns point to the difficulty of sustaining a drama of difference between persons who could in many cases reverse roles and play on the other side" (Goffman 1961: 112).

30 Murat Topal, a Berlin police officer turned stand-up comedian hailing from a German-Turkish family, also plays in his sketches with the frontiers of ethnicity. In *Kreuzberger Schule* (Topal 2005), to take just one example, he imitates

From their reactions, it was not quite clear whether Inspector Schwarz and the police officials grasped the irony and played along themselves or if they were giving the remark some serious thought. Inspector Schwarz took a reassuring stand, saying that the participants were of course not a problem; but by then nobody was listening to her for the other participants had all started talking and joking about "police officers from an East German or Berlin background." Two years prior, Inspector Piontek was put a similar question as to whether such gatherings were necessary. He had come to the tentative conclusion that the next meeting should perhaps be open to all, something that was not to happen. Attending my second meeting, I could not resist the impression that such events had become quite funnily normal.

Together with other officers met while working on this study, the case of the inspector depicted in the vignette can help us delineate one type, an empathetic one. This type is closely connected to what François Dubet (2002: 306) calls the "work on the other" (*travail sur autrui*), professionals activities, which aim at explicitly transforming the "strangers," and, we might add, incorporating them in the police forces. Its representatives act out of empathy for (future) fellow officers. The inspectors I met often became committed to individual police recruits and their incorporation. But empathy is not the only possible path, as we will see in the next chapter. Perhaps not so surprisingly, political education (*politische Bildung*) at police academies, a subject where a lot of energy is devoted to addressing issues of basic and human rights and where people devoted to the democratization of the police can be found, turned out to be a field of activities—besides recruitment initiatives—for issues related to difference during my fieldwork.

---

young people interrogated by police officers. Because of the way they speak, we are led to believe that the youth are of Turkish origin until we learn their names, Florian Hufschmidt and Nadine Rüggers, two German names.

Inspector Bobkowski, or Liberalism
The Principled Type

Investigating the people in charge of initiatives to recruit and counsel police officers from post-migration backgrounds took me from Hamburg to other police departments, notably, to Berlin. There, I explored another area where ethnic, cultural, and religious difference was being formally addressed: teaching. Because my informants had mentioned it and because it promised to be an important channel, I turned to political education and its teachers.

Politische Bildung

Political education is a political or democratic science, a unique form of "nonpartisan propaganda" (Hébert 2006: 171; Mannheim 1929: 158). This intellectual groundwork was laid in Germany in the context of the discussion on opposing political forces and on the role of intellectuals in the interwar period. Born out of the tension between *Wertfreiheit*—"value-freedom" or non-imposition of values—and propaganda in the context of education (Kalinowski 2005: 198-199), it aimed at presenting different positions without imposing them. During the Weimar Republic it was embodied in institutions such as the *Deutsche Hochschule für Politik* (DHfP), an institution meant to be democratic, independent, and open to all (Drews 1921).

After the Nazi era, and in the shadow of the Holocaust, political education was institutionalized as a means to inculcate the broad population with the embrace of democracy and to promote liberal attitudes (*demokratische Gesinnung*) and institutions in the newly founded Federal Republic (Buse 2008; Widmaier 1987). Independent of particular

> political parties, political education today is coordinated at the federal and state levels by agencies (*Bundeszentrale* and *Landeszentralen für politische Bildung*) that support teachers, publications as well as press information, and organize conferences and public events.
>
> Political education is also a subject taught in schools, including police academies.

At the Berlin Police Academy and Training Center, Inspector Klaus Bobkowski is Director of the Political Education Unit. We first met in his office filled with files of newspaper clippings and books on the police and German history and later at the Berlin Police Museum (*Polizeihistorische Sammlung*), an institution that he played a key role in creating. Because talking to him and accompanying him and his colleagues throughout their work day turned out to be instructive about the treatment of difference in the police forces, we met several times between 2006 and 2010. Besides being a police officer and a teacher, Inspector Bobkowski is also a hobby historian. His efforts to portray the police's past are of sociological relevance for grasping the treatment of difference and how officers who were confronted with a great deal of resistance have contributed, sometimes against their initial intentions, to its greater recognition within the police forces.

After introducing Klaus Bobkowski and describing his work in the field of political education, in this chapter I present a story within a story—or what literary scholars refer to as a *mise en abyme*—that documents the attempts undertaken by the inspector and his colleagues to commemorate Bernhard Weiß, an observant Jew who became deputy president of the Berlin police force in the 1920s. The conflation of the inspector's work and that of the people he helped commemorate represents a key moment for constructing a second ideal type of carriers of diversity, the *principled* one. Comparing and contrasting today's officers and the measures they have taken with Weiß' supporters allows me to isolate common motives underlying their action and ground them in a liberal tradition. Once the type is outlined, I will focus back on Inspector Bobkowski, the dilemmas he is confronted with and the normative issues he raises. If the arguments propounded by the main protagonist of this chapter do not fail to raise reaction among other carriers of diversity and social scientists, we will see that they are convincing for a lot of police officers. Indeed, they resonate with a way to grasp the individual in the forces.

1. THE POLITICAL EDUCATION TEACHER

1.1 Inspector Bobkowski

Like most of the teaching staff at the police academy, Klaus Bobkowski is a police officer.[1] As it turned out, he is also a keen hobby historian: "Well, during the evening, the weekend, others... while others watch soap operas or pick their nose, I usually read some books [laugh]."[2] Upon finishing high school, he joined the Berlin police force in 1968, the year of the massive student demonstrations. In a tongue-in-cheek manner, he refers to himself as "an old 68er" and a full-fledged police officer.[3] When we met for the first time in 2006, Inspector Bobkowski had been teaching political education to police trainees and officers for thirty-two years.

Political education takes a lot of time in German police academies and particularly in the capital. This used to be a very sensitive subject in the geographical and ideological enclave that was West Berlin in the Cold War era, a city often described as an "island in the red sea." Even now, during the police officers' two-and-a-half years of training, four hours per week are dedicated to political education, a considerable number of hours equivalent to the time allocated to what is considered the core of police teaching: intervention law (*Eingriffsrecht*). Trainees are taught the mechanisms of the German parliamentary system as well as state and constitutional law, with a particular emphasis on basic rights. At the Berlin Police Academy, the subject can be described as a combination of political science and history. Next to the history of the Third Reich, Inspector Bobkowski particularly stresses in his teaching the history of the Weimar Republic (1919-1933) and the ex-

---

1   There are also academics teaching at police universities. These institutions are attended by students intending to join the higher service (*höherer Dienst*).
2   "*Also, ich hab dann abends, am Wochenende wie sich andere... Andere gucken sich eine Soap an oder bohren sich in der Nase, dann les ick meistens irgendwelche Bücher* [laugh]" (interview with KB, 23 August 2006).
3   Interview with KB, 23 August 2006.

tremist threats it faced from the Right and the Left of the political spectrum, which embodies, he says, "all the good and the bad" in German history.

After an incident involving the harassment of a recruit of Jewish descent at the beginning of the 1980s, political education was thoroughly reformed. What was a theoretical course on state and constitutional law became geared more toward practice and current events. Klaus Bobkowski explains that "fieldwork" was added to the theoretical part of the teaching so that trainees would gain concrete experience of what political education was about:

"I mean, with the basic rights and the rule of law it is always so, you can't say: 'I've done it and now we've got it for good,' or something like that. Or: 'We're a democracy and we'll always stay one.' This is like in a marriage, well, love will not always stay, one has to do something for it. It is just the same thing with some topics in the police. They can't say, because they had during their training basic rights, the rule of law, racism, anti-Semitism, xenophobia, that'll [the spirit of the basic rights] last till their 63rd birthday, well till the officer retires."[4]

Stressing the need not to "stew in one's own sauce" (*nicht im eigenen Saft schmoren*) leaders of non-governmental organizations and local ethnic communities were invited to give talks and share their experiences with recruits and officers, podium discussions were organized, excursions were planned (such as visits to the Bundestag or to the Memorial to the Murdered Jews of Europe), and participation in activities such as the *Reichspogromnacht* commemorative ceremony became part of political education courses. Through the changes they introduced, Inspector Bobkowski and his colleagues became acquainted with associations as well as with city of-

---

4 "*Und ich sach mal, mit den Grundrechten und der Rechtsstaatlichkeit is es eben immer so, sie können nicht sagen, 'Ick hab dit mal jemacht und jetz haben wa se imma,' oder so. Oder: 'Wir sind eine Demokratie und wir werden sie immer bleiben.' Es ist so wie mit einer Ehe, also die Liebe wird nich immerwährend sein, sondern man muss wat dafür tun. Und jenauso is es mit bestimmten Themen in der Polizei. Sie können nicht sagen, wenn wir in der Ausbildung das Thema Grundrechte, Rechtsstaatlichkeit, Rassismus, Antisemitismus, Fremdenfeindlichkeit hatten, dann reicht dit bis zum 63. Lebensjahr, bis der Beamte also in nen Ruhestand jeht*" (interview with KB, 23 August 2006).

ficials such as the foreigners' commissioner.[5] Because of their existing contacts, the officers of the Berlin Police Academy and Training Center were entrusted with the coordination of a two-year European Union-financed project, NAPAP (Non-Governmental Organisations and Police against Prejudice).[6] "Well, we actually started with it [BT: contacting associations and city officials] around the mid '90s [BT: during the wave of European Union-founded initiatives and conferences on discrimination]. Yes, the mid '90s. That was, well, forced upon us, well also by the foreigners' commissioner at that time."[7] The project was, at the inspectors' initiative, institutionalized as a one-week intercultural skills seminar, compulsory for all new police recruits at the end of their training.[8]

In the 1990s Klaus Bobkowski and his colleagues took part in numerous conferences and met with city officials. Thanks to their contacts and the experience they gained, they became active networkers and self-taught experts regarding intercultural matters. Under their impetus and with the passage of time, political education drew into its orbit—besides education and in-house training—an array of other activities, and established a key position, a *Schlüsselstellung* (Mannheim 1958 [1935]) or *Weichenstellung* (Weber 1972 [1921]: 252, 1978b [1921]: 1209) for the pragmatic recognition of difference in the police.

---

5   When I first met Bobkowski, eight officers were teaching political education. The team had peaked at twenty-four teachers at the beginning of the 1990s when the East Berlin section of the People's Police was incorporated into the West Berlin Police Department. For an account of this process, see Glaeser (2000) and Jobard (2003).

6   NAPAP was launched in 1997 and followed by a second project, Pavement (see Leiprecht 2002: 79-81).

7   "*Na, wir ham so Mitte der 90ier ham wa eigentlich damit anjefangen. Ja, Mitte der 90ier. Dit wurde also och forciert, also och durch die damalije Ausländerbeauftragte*" (interview with KB, 23 August 2006).

8   The seminar was led by workers of the Office Against Ethnic Discrimination in Berlin and Brandenburg (Büro gegen ethnische Diskriminierung in Berlin und Brandenburg) who were trained for this purpose in the context of the NAPAP project.

1.2 In the Orbit of Political Education

Although not directly falling under the rubric of political education, a so-called *Clearingstelle*, a mediation office for conflicts between the police and "foreigners" (*Ausländer*), was set up under the aegis of Inspector Bobkowski in 1993. The *Clearingstelle* is led by an ethnic German police officer who also teaches, using real cases, at the police training center.[9] Other examples of activities included recruitment initiatives. Through the crystallization of contacts between the Berlin Police Academy staff, the Turkish Union in Berlin-Brandenburg (a Kemalist organization lobbying for German Turkish interests), the senator of the interior, and the city's labor office, a ten-week-course for Turkish unemployed youth was created. This course was set up to help candidates prepare for the rigorous police entry exams.[10]

---

9 A similar position, that of a foreigners' counselor (*Ausländerbeauftragter*) was set up in Frankfurt (Main) in 1993; it was—and still is—led by a civil employee with a migration background and training in social sciences (interview, 23 March 2005).

10 Participants get courses in topics such as German, general knowledge, mathematics, information on the police career (*Berufskunde*), sports, and—to bolster, Inspector Bobkowski stresses quoting representatives of the Turkish association, their self-confidence—Turkish language as well as exercise interview situations. In 2002, all the participants could take part in the entry exams, but none were, at least in Berlin, hired (see section three of the last chapter for more details). Due to financial cuts there was between 2003 and 2006 no new hiring in the Berlin Police Department and the program was temporarily interrupted. In 2007, the program resumed with another Turkish organization as its partner.

Figure 4: Für türkische Berliner stehen die Sterne besonders gut

Poster from an advertising campaign of the Berlin Police Department targeting young people of Turkish background (November 1999), reproduced with the permission of the Berlin Police Museum.

Next to education and recruitment initiatives, the commemoration of the past became an object of concern for the Political Education Unit. In the late 1980s, the Berlin Police Museum and archives were set up at the police headquarters at Tempelhof. The members of the Police Historical Society and the staff of the Political Education Unit played a key role in creating them. As deputy president of the Police Historical Society, Klaus Bobkowski conceived an exhibition on the history of the Berlin police force (from the foundation of a Prussian police in the mid 19th century to the clashes with the city's squatters in the 1980s and the unification of the East and West Berlin police forces in the early 1990s). He has also been receiving visitors at the museum, publishing articles in police internal organs, and getting involved in commemoration activities, all of which were incorporated into the political education of recruits and officers.

Amongst these commemoration initiatives, one in particular struck my attention because of the similarities it bore to the object of my own research and the kind of *mise en abyme* it brought to light: the case of Berlin police official Bernhard Weiß.

Excursus: A Story Within a Story.
The Planned Bernhard Weiß Square

Michel de Certeau wrote: "Every power is toponymical and initiates its order of places by naming them" (1998 [1980]: 130). In the wake of German unification, Berlin has witnessed numerous attempts at renaming streets and public spaces. The police were no exception. Being known as a keen lay historian, Inspector Bobkowski was mandated by the chief of police in 2002 to survey police history and make recommendations as to who deserved particular recognition. While being wary to stress that the history of the police was far from immaculate, he stressed two figures from the Weimar era deserving particular recognition: Ernst Gennat, one of the founders of modern criminology and forensics, and Bernhard Weiß, a deputy chief of police. Of these two popular figures, which are also the stuff of numerous historiographical accounts, novels, and films,[11] Weiß was at the center of the majority of efforts.[12]

A Prussian lawyer by training, Bernhard Weiß (1880-1951) was a decorated officer who became a high-ranking police official in Berlin during the Weimar Republic. An observant Jew, Weiß embodied the archetype of the "established outsider," the expression of a relationship embodied by German Jews under the Empire and the Weimar Republic who belonged on the cultural and linguistic level firmly within the majority while not being fully recognized as such (Elias 1994 [1990]: 121 ff., 1996 [1990]: 158 ff.). Needless to say that Berhard Weiß was a rare exception in the civil service of the Prussian state (Angress 1998). The rules of entry in the police and the civil service in general included, next to the stiff entrance examinations, the pledging of an oath to the constitution. For Jews who generally lacked career opportunities in the civil service, meeting the criteria of entry often

---

11 See for instance Philipp Kerr's crime novel *March Violets* (1993 [1989]) and Jason Lutes' comic *Berlin. City of Stones* (2008 [2001]); for a monograph, see Todd Herzog's 2009 *Crime Stories. Criminalistic Fantasy and the Culture of Crisis in Weimar Germany*.

12 Already in 1989 a former chief of police wrote to the *Jüdische Gemeinde* to expose a plan to honor Weiß in an exhibit at the newly created police museum and to inquire about available material (Schertz's letter to Galinski, 9 May 1989).

meant baptism, sometimes combined with the changing of names (Pulzer 1992: 63).

Bill Drews, the last Prussian ministry of the interior under the monarchy, nominated Weiß in June 1918 as a civil servant, as *politischer Beamter* (Bering 1992 [1987]: 132; Hamburger 1968: 102). He was the first unbaptized Jew in the Prussian ministry of the interior. From 1918 to 1924 he was chief of the Berlin political police and, from 1925 to 1927, chief of the Berlin criminal police. Weiß became deputy chief of police in 1927 until he was removed by the Nazis in 1932 and forced to emigrate.

With the aim of acknowledging Weiß as a prominent police figure during the Weimar Republic and, as Inspector Bobkowski emphasizes, "the main opponent to Goebbels [the Nazi propaganda man],"[13] an initiative was set up to name the square in front of Berlin's famous Friedrichstraße train station "Bernhard Weiß Square."[14] In January 2004, the Police Historical Society's recommendation was brought in by the Berlin section of the FDP (*Freie Demokratische Partei*, or Free Democratic Party), to the Berlin parliament (Antrag der Fraktion der FDP 2004). The party was approached, Inspector Bobkowski stresses, because "it imposed itself as an obvious choice as successor of the DDP and Weiß' party."[15]

The German Democratic Party (DDP) was between 1918 and 1932 a predominantly protestant Left-liberal party whose electorate encompassed, in the Weimar era, a large segment of the educated liberal middle class, among whom were many Jews (Hamburger and Pulzer 1985: 8-14; Pulzer 1992: 217-225; Langewiesche 2000 [1988]: 304-305). This liberal party is

---

13 Bernhard Weiß was one of Goebbels' favorite targets. Articles and caricatures in the propaganda magazine *Angriff* portray him as a conspirator and a wirepuller who had successfully infiltrated the police. For a detailed account of Goebbels' attacks on Weiß and the latter's counter-attacks, see Bering's book, *Kampf um Namen. Bernhard Weiß gegen Joseph Goebbels* (1991).

14 "But Weiß was *the* main opponent to Goebbels here [*"Aber der Weiß, dat war der Gegenspieler von Goebbels hier"*]. He carried on: "We have to name a street after him. And not in Lichtenrade or in Frohnau [BT: districts at the outskirts of Berlin] but were he worked" [*"Nach dem muss man doch eine Straße benennen. Und nich in Lichtenrade oder in Frohnau, sondern da, wo er jearbeitet hat"*] (interview with KB, 23 August 2006).

15 Interview with KB, 3 November 2006.

also remembered for its efforts to defend the new republic against its opponents on the Left and the Right. After 1945, Dieter Langewiesche argues, the liberal program of the Weimar Republic is best found in parties such as the Christian Democratic Union and the Social Democratic Party (SPD) and in the social institutions of the Federal Republic, rather than in the FDP (2000 [1988]: 306 ff.). Notwithstanding the questions as to whether the FDP, a party generally characterized by its liberal economic orientation, can be seen as more than the DDP's nominal successor and to whether Bernhard Weiß would today hold a membership card, it is worth noting that the support of this particular party was sought by Klaus Bobkowski and his colleagues in their efforts to commemorate Weiß.

Having ensured local political backup, the members of the Police Historical Society were confident that their initiative would be realized. It thus came as a surprise when the recommendation was rejected on the grounds of a new district policy. One week prior to the petition brought in by the FDP, the district's leading coalition of the SPD and the Party of Democratic Socialism (PDS, since 2007: *Die Linke*, or The Left]) had agreed to name (or rename) the city's streets and public places only with women's names, as long as women remained underrepresented.[16] Contesting what could be referred to as a form of "positive discrimination backwards," and what was described as intransigence by the petitioners, the president of the Police Historical Society, as well as a former chief of police, wrote several letters to local politicians before turning to the press.[17]

The letters written to lobby city officials emphasize Weiß' quality as a representative of the police, a proud Prussian democrat, and Goebbels' unflagging opponent.[18] They underscored the exceptional character of the former police deputy president—as an outstanding personality with "no

---

16 The district's policy takes into consideration women who died at least five years prior to petitions to rename public spaces. Interestingly, its wording is identical to the one used in the federal and federal states' legislation on antidiscrimination laws (*Gleichberechtigungsgesetze*).

17 Some articles were also published on the issue in *Der Tagesspiegel*, see Bemmer, Ariane, "Frauen-Quote für den Stadtplan" (28 June 2004) and Oloew, Matthias, "Männer hinten anstellen" (18 April 2006).

18 Letter of the president of the Police Historical Society to the city councilor responsible for construction, 27 September 2004.

comparable example" (*kein vergleichbares Vorbild*)—and the urgent necessity (*dringendes Gebot*) to honor him. Despite finding a new possible location and ensuring the support of Berlin's mayor, the initiative failed again in 2005, to its supporters' dismay. Although visibly disappointed, Inspector Bobkowski felt compelled to point out that at no moment did the Police Historical Society either raise the argument or seek the help of the Berlin Jewish community, not wanting "any preferential group treatment."[19] One of the feared assumptions was that Weiß would have been commemorated "only because he was a Jew"—to the detriment of the recognition of his merit as a Prussian police official.

These arguments would most probably also have met with agreement on the part of Weiß himself who yearned to be recognized as a Prussian civil servant (Liang 1970: 158-160) and fought through legal means against individual discriminations. During the monarchy and the Weimar Republic, as Pulzer noted, middle class Jews, among whom were incidentally many jurists, became important figures in the fight against discriminations (1992: 327), generally valuing individual effort and merit in contrast to more corporatist tendencies typically championed by Catholics (Pulzer 1992: 53). They "wanted a society in which the individual was judged by his merits and in which all groups had equal access to the decision-making of a neutral, impartial state (…). Such a state the Weimar Republic promised to be, and the DDP the nearest embodiment of its principles" (Hamburger and Pulzer 1985: 11).

When I met with him in August 2008, Inspector Bobkowski had not lost all hope to find a suitable place to honor the former deputy president.[20] In February 2008 he had contributed to organizing the launch of a small biography of Weiß,[21] which contains a foreword by the chief of police and was bought in great numbers by the police department and given out to trainees.

---

19 Interview with KB, 5 October 2006.
20 Attempts were made to find a suitable place near a new shopping mall, in vicinity of the police headquarters' original location at Alexanderplatz in the center of the capital.
21 Rott, Joachim. 2008. *Bernhard Weiss. 1880 Berlin-1951 London. Polizeivizepräsident in Berlin — Preussischer Jude — Kämpferischer Demokrat*. Berlin, Hentrich & Hentrich.

Figure 5: Photo of Bernhard Weiß with Daisy Grzesinski, Charlie Chaplin, Albert Grzesinski and Lotte Weiß in Berlin

This is one of the photos of the deputy chief of police, which Klaus Bobkowski likes to use in his publications and at the police museum. Bernhard Weiß, standing, with (from left to right) Daisy Grzesinski, Charlie Chaplin, Albert Grzesinski and Lotte Weiß in 1931 (reproduced with permission of the media service of the Berlin Police Department).

2. ENTANGLED HISTORY

These efforts at commemoration constitute one example of recognition of difference within the police forces. Interestingly, the argument invoked in favor of the Weiß initiative echo those that have been proffered since the 1990s in favor of the recruitment of candidates from post-migration backgrounds in the police forces—a domain where, as we have seen in the previous chapter, organizational change has been most explicitly sought. Both types of initiatives typically refer to a logic of exception that seeks recognition while striving to confirm the principle of equality deemed so constitutive of the police forces. Furthermore, they both appeal to an "urgent necessity" (*dringendes Bedürfnis*). The dispensation clause to the civil service law that was adopted in several federal states in the early 1990s to recruit nonnational candidates was grounded in an urgent necessity of police work in certain milieus. Seen in this light, the effort at commemorating the past seems relevant in grasping a model of inclusion, or "we-ideal" (Elias 1998 [1989])[22] and a way to talk about difference within the police force.

There is perhaps no surprise in encountering—in Berlin as well as in other police departments—those I have referred to as carriers of diversity among the political education teaching staff.[23] After all, this represents a well-worn track for talking about and dealing with difference that is specific to post-war Germany. However, the similarities between arguments and principles invoked to appoint Bernhard Weiß and other outsiders in the 1920s and those to commemorate him in the first decade of the 2000s were more striking. Today's officers stress in particular—as Weiß and his patrons have done—the efforts and merits of the individuals and the formal principle of equality in a neutral organization. They also explicitly refer themselves to institutions of the Weimar Republic. The DDP mentioned by Bobkowski and his colleagues from the Police Historical Society—and with it the liberal agenda of civic equality it stood for—is such an example.

Moving beyond the arguments, principles, and institutions called upon in the context of the commemoration initiative, in this section I approach the linkages between such figures as Inspector Bobkowski, his colleagues, and Weiß' patrons at the beginning of the 20th century. In order to do so I borrow from *histoire croisée*, or entangled history (Werner and Zimmermann 2006). Building on comparisons and cultural transfers, *histoire croisée* opens up the comparative method beyond the usual logic of national framework and synchronicity and allows one to consider objects of research "in relation to one another but also through one another, in terms of relationships, interactions, and circulation" (Werner and Zimmermann 2006: 38). Entangling the case of Weiß and his defenders with that of today's inspectors and their teaching, recruiting, and commemorating activities enables me to isolate common motives so as to delineate the contours

---

22 In the sense of an ideal deemed to be reached by the actors, not of an ideal type.
23 Such could notably be found in Mecklenburg-Western Pomerania, Hamburg, and Bremen.

of a particular ideal type of carriers of diversity, to which real individuals can be compared and measured against.[24]

What is to be entangled here? In both cases, I examine individuals and the motives—again: a "complex of subjective meaning which seems to the actor himself or to the observer an adequate ground for the conduct in question" (Weber 1978a [1921]: 11)—underlying action taken toward organizational change. Next to the motives grounding action, I pay particular attention to the measures taken to change mentalities and the organizational context, as well as the consequences and dilemmas pertaining to these measures. Just as Inspector Bobkowski—who admittedly felt uneasy presenting the FDP as the natural successor of the DDP in the context of the Weiß commemoration initiative—,[25] I neither assume continuity nor causality between the cases. Similarly, I am aware that the image of police officers, who are mostly of lower middle-class origin, sits uneasily with figures who belonged to the educated liberal middle class (*Bildungsbürgertum*).[26] I use the comparison as a heuristic method for constructing an ideal type.[27]

---

24 Siegfried Kracauer attributes a similar process to Georg Simmel: "Often Simmel must first completely pick to pieces the familiar, commonplace image of whatever object he is examining, so that the aspect it shares with other objects can come to the fore. What it always at stake for the thinker in this process is the liberation of the thing from its isolation. He turns it this way and that way, until we recognize in it the fulfillment of a lawfulness that is simultaneously embodied in many other places, and we can thereby weave it into an extensive net of relations" (1995 [1920]: 235).

25 For this reason, he tried to evade my questions on this issue (Interview with KB, 3 November 2006).

26 The *Bildungsbürgertum* can be described in Weber's term as a status group—as opposed to a class proper—whose members were more aptly characterized by high education and refined cultural lifestyle than by capital ownership (1978a [1921]: 305-307). They made out the bulk of liberalism under Weimar and were concentrated in professional occupations such as professors, teachers, pastors, and lawyers.

27 For more details on this comparison, see chapters six ("A Second Detail: The Weimar Connection") and seven.

2.1 Investigating Motives

Who were Weiß' contemporary supporters? And what were their motives in supporting him? They were non-Jews with a liberal outlook. These men were for the most part, like Weiß, members of the Defense Association against anti-Semitism (*Abwehr-Verein gegen Antisemitismus*), an association composed mainly of Protestants and Jews who fought against anti-Semitism. They adhered to the abstract principle of equality before the law (Pulzer 1992: 106; Suchy 1983),[28] which characterizes all of the various shades of liberalism. They did not abandon assimilation as a goal; rather, they held on to the idea of a German, yet heterogeneous culture.[29] This German culture, or spirit (*Geist*), was deemed an achievement accessible to all through education (see Drews 1921: 7-17).

Among them, the aforementioned Bill Drews (1870-1938), the liberal conservative jurist who first appointed Bernhard Weiß to a post in his ministry, should be especially considered. The jurist made what could be described as a classical career in the Prussian civil service: he became administrative head of Oschersleben in 1903, chief administrator in Köslin in 1911, then state undersecretary in 1914 before being nominated minister of the interior in 1917. He is remembered for his administrative reforms of the Empire toward a republican federal state, including that of the police law. A liberal conservative and a proud German nationalist, he was a member of the DDP and taught at the *Deutsche Hochschule für Politik* in the 1920s.[30] Another was Albert Grzesinski (1879-1947), an SPD Prussian minister of the interior under Weimar who hired Weiß as his deputy police chief.

---

28 For a long time women were largely excluded from this agenda of civic equality (Langewiesche 2000 [1988]: 12).

29 Let us here note that the word "German" is not only an ethnic category for Inspector Bobkowski; it is a more encompassing category, which may include people whom representatives of the other ideal types would not recognize as German. Klaus Bobkowski and his colleagues do not abandon assimilation as a goal; rather, they also hold on to the idea of a German, yet heterogeneous culture. Culture is for them somewhat elastic.

30 After 1933, he remained in office but did not become a party member (see Otto 2003: 20-26).

Because he wrote his memoirs (1974 [1939]), we know more about Grzesinski than Drews.[31] He is remembered for the democratization of the civil service—including the police, which was under the auspice of the ministry of the interior—under the newly founded republican order. A dispensation clause to the Prussian civil service law had been introduced, which made possible the hiring of "outsiders" (candidates who were not trained for a civil servant career, among them socialists, Catholics, Jews, democrats and liberals) in small numbers as *politische Beamte*, civil servants without guaranteed job security (Pikart 1958: 126-127). This clause constituted a half-open door for making change in the civil service possible. Albert Grzesinski mainly proceeded to such changes and what was called the "democratization of the civil service" through personnel politics (Albrecht 1999: 210 ff.; Glees 1974). In his memoirs, he notably recalls appointing reliable "outsiders" (1974 [1939]: 112),[32] such as Bernhard Weiß whom he describes as a "convinced republican and democrat" (2001 [1934]: 227). As it turned out Grzesinski acted more in the name of the new democratic order than out of particular sympathy for the "outsiders." And he was faced with considerable resistance. As the supporters of Jews and other outsiders in the Weimar higher administration, he encountered a lot of opposition within his own ranks.

Similarly, Inspector Bobkowski's motivation in pursuing his activities (education, training, commemoration of the past, and recruitment) are not grounded in empathy for individual officers and their welfare.[33] Rather, he acts according to a principle, the democratization of the police forces. Making the organization more democratic involves here, at the individual level, education in the basic rights of the democratic order and the respect of civic

---

31 Born in Prussia from a poor family, he became a metal worker. He joined a trade union, then the SPD. He made a career through trade unions, notably in Offenbach and Kassel before becoming holding offices in the high administration of Hesse and Prussia. In 1926 he became Prussia's minister of the interior.
32 In the German edition: *nichtzünftig* (Grzesinski 2001 [1934]: 204).
33 Incidentally, Inspector Bobkowski mentions that Bernhard Weiß was not a particularly likable figure and that he only reached such a high position thanks to orders (*Befehl*) and achievements (*Leistung*). The police deputy president must have been, the inspector says, "a grouch [*Stinkstiefel*]" and a "very pernickety man" ["*ganz akkurater Mann*"] (interview with KB, 23 August 2006).

equality within an organization that is bound to occupy a marginal position in liberal democracies. On an organizational level, it notably involves collaborating with NGOs and the recruitment of officers from post-migration backgrounds. Throughout our conversations, it became clear that Klaus Bobkowski's leitmotif in pursuing all these activities was to enlighten trainees and officers. Through instilling basic rights and their spirit (understood in light of the quote cited above as a never ending project—"as in a marriage, well, love will not always stay, one as to do something for it"), the inspector sees his mandate as making the police a more civil or democratic organization. Democratizing the police has also long meant departing from the military tradition (Liang 1970: 37, 57 and 72), which Bobkowski says was still very much "Prussian" when he started his training in the 1960s. He mentions the ranks, salutes, uniforms and the training in general and adds: "Well, I mean, the training here in the police forces was nothing for sensitive souls at the end of the 60s, one has got to say. In the meantime it's been totally changed, totally changed round to civil activities."[34]

Admittedly, Weiß' patrons under Weimar were faced with illiberal policies and a situation that cannot be equated with the context of contemporary Germany, in which liberal values are accepted and institutions are committed to liberal standards.[35] If police officials are today generally in favor of the initiatives—developed in the orbit of political education (education, training, commemoration of the past, and recruitment—the latter being considered both in Weimar (Liang 1970) and now (Leiprecht 2002)—the main means to transform the forces,[36] a majority of police offi-

---

34 *"Also, ich sach mal, für zarte Gemüter war die Ausbildung nichts hier bei der Polizei, Ende der 60iger Jahre muss man sagen. Völlig umjestellt worden [ist] inzwischen alles, völlig also auf zivile Tätigkeiten umjestellt worden also"* (interview with KB, 23 August 2006).

35 Furthermore, the background of today's police candidates from post-migration backgrounds is admittedly very different from the "outsiders" wishing to gain access to public service under the Weimar Republic.

36 Hsi-Huey Liang mentions suggestions made by some high police officials in the early days of the Weimar Republic to recruit "organized workers from the labor movement" to strengthen social-democratic elements within the forces (1970: 58). That said, it proved difficult to attract them and Liang concludes that the forces were not a "people's police."

cers show skepticism toward them (Dudek 2009: 164 ff. and 201 ff.). This unreceptive attitude is even to be found amongst recruiting officers, teachers, and trade union officials who are mandated to train, recruit, or counsel candidates from post-migration backgrounds, and whose efforts sometimes seem at best half-hearted.[37] It is no surprise, then, that most commentators have described the initiatives to recruit candidates from post-migration backgrounds as a dismal failure (see Jaschke cited in Behr 2006: 124), a failure that can be attributed to internal resistance but also to bureaucratic inertia.[38]

2.2 Measures Taken in a Hostile Context...

As in the case of patrons of Jews and "other outsiders" and the higher Weimar administration, the officers I met in Berlin and in other police departments I have encountered—admittedly to varying degrees—demonstrated resistance within their own ranks. In fact, the inspector's attitude and that of his colleagues within the police force bring to mind historical accounts of the Weimar Republic, which usually distinguish among the carriers of the new democratic and republican order, a small group of republicans "by conviction" or *Gesinnungsrepublikaner*, from a larger group of republicans "by reason" or *Vernunftrepublikaner* (Langewiesche 1993: 29). Given this context, it is no surprise that the first police recruits from post-migration backgrounds were—just as the "outsiders" into the Prussian administration—sometimes more "smuggled" from above into the police by their patrons than welcomed by a majority of fellow colleagues. Furthermore, these hiring practices, have been, in both cases, condemned either

---

[37] Alluding to the initiatives striving to recruit candidates from post-migration backgrounds he was responsible for, an interview partner told me, referring to a widespread image of the civil servant, in a candid manner: "You know, I'm rather the bureaucrat type" [*"Wissn Se, ick bin eher der Beamtentyp"*] (interview with CC, 6 September 2006).

[38] Bobkowski stresses the bureaucratic character of the police forces and sometimes refers to some police members as "energy-saving lamps" (*Energiesparlampen*).

within the rank and file or in the press for what was seen as an infringement to the established procedure and tradition.[39]

Faced with resistance, Klaus Bobkowski does not shy away from a top-down model—which can be seen as a compromise of democratic and liberal principles. Some things, he believes, just have to be imposed on officers and the police organization. He mentions the preparatory courses for German Turkish youth in Berlin and the initiatives to recruit officers from post-migration backgrounds. Although criticized,[40] the latter measure is considered necessary in order to avoid what the inspector sees as an upcoming legitimacy problem facing the police as the city's post-migrant population continues to grow. He also stresses the necessity to confront the population: "Also the lawyer in Zehlendorf [BT: a well-to-do district in Berlin] has got to get used to being talked to in German by a police officer of Turkish origin. He also has got to come to grips with it."[41] Both now and in the past, the authoritarian manner by which the objectives were formulated did not always square with the democratic ambitions, though it could be argued that—at least in view of the context of the Weimar Republic (Glees 1974: 824)—there was, in fact, no alternative to this line.

2.3 ... and Pertaining Dilemmas

Like the patrons of Jews who were accused of being "half Jewish" (for Grzesinski, see Glees 1974: 814; also Grzesinski 1974 [1939]: 18), the officers described as carriers of diversity are, as a consequence of their activi-

---

39 Interview with MS, 12 September 2006. For Weimar Prussia, see Grzesinski (1974 [1939]: 112) and Pikart (1958: 122).
40 See "Streit um Polizei-Einstellung: Erste Klagen angekündigt. Abgelehnte deutsche Bewerber wollen gleiche Chancen wie ausländische Jobanwärter," *Berliner Morgenpost*, 14 February 2006; "Einstellungspraxis für Bewerber/-Innen mit Migrationshintergrund. Rechtswidrig und diskriminierend," Press report by Junge Gruppe Berlin, Gewerkschaft der Polizei. URL: http://www.gdp.de/gdp/gdpber.nsf/id/jg_presse_1 (accessed 24 June 2006).
41 "*Och der Rechtsanwalt in Zehlendorf, der muss sich och jefallen lassen, auf Deutsch von einem Polizisten türk'scher Herkunft auf Deutsch anjesprochen zu werden. Damit muss er och fertig werden*" (interview with KB, 23 August 2006; also interview with KB, 28 June 2007).

ties, often identified with those they have helped incorporate into the forces. They are perceived as a strange species (*Exote*), a reality to which they have to measure up inwardly. This situation often forces them to reassert, not unlike the recruits and officers from post-migration backgrounds, their identity as police officers, such as the donning of uniforms even when this is not required.[42]

Assessing his own image, Inspector Bobkowski says he cannot be considered a strange species within the police, though he admits to being perceived as a "bit theoretical."[43] In the eyes of the trainees and young officers, Bobkowski and his colleagues are conveyed as having a somewhat antiquated, but nonetheless respectable appearance. Because his arguments fare well with members of the police force itself, an organization characterized by strong socialization and homogenizing principles, and because they are often much in line with the attitudes of the resistant officers toward the recognition of difference, it could be argued that he has good grounds not to feel as if he were, as he puts it, "swimming against the current." As a matter of fact, Bobkowski and recruitment officers, or teachers I described as "half-hearted," often argue in a similar fashion: they usually talk about equality and stressed the need to avoid preferential treatment (and the latter typically express the view, when talking, for instance, about recruitment, that "it would be nice to hire more foreigners, but it's difficult. We just don't have enough good candidates"). The sociologist is well aware that there may be a different basis for behavior behind apparently similar arguments. Indeed, people may talk and act in the same way for different motives. As Weber writes: "(…) processes of action which seem to an observer to be the same or similar may fit into exceedingly various complexes of motive in the case of the actual actor" (Weber 1978a [1921]: 10).[44] It is

---

42 Interview with DP, 27 May 2004; interview with LET, 3 November 2006.
43 Interview with KB, 3 November 2006. This self-assessment echoes Bobkowski's scholarly knowledge as well as the image of the street cop who embodies—as opposed to the one working in an office—the "real" police officer (Waddington 2005 [1999]: 377).
44 As Kundera points out when commenting on the act of interpreting: "Whether a man loves a woman or not, whether he is lying or sincere, he would say the same thing […] with no regard to their individual psychology" (2001 [1993]: 125).

the sociologist's job to discover, interpret, and reconstruct the motives of action. Taking up this task, I argue that in contrast to some police officers who may be against the initiatives I have here associated with the treatment of difference, others—as Inspector Bobkowski—might not be motivated by such a negative reaction, but may well act according to a liberal principle and agenda of civic equality.

Because it sits well with the police forces, this principle does not confront Klaus Bobkowski with the dilemmas encountered by some of his colleagues. The tensions otherwise felt by the latter between their work and the police organization are largely passed on to individual trainees and officers—as in the case of Jewish civil servants under Weimar. A telling example is illustrated by a report, which followed the work of an *ad hoc* commission made up of a police doctor, high-ranking officers, school staff, and Inspector Brigitte Winter (the woman who organizes gatherings with police officers from post-migration backgrounds in her beat) on the eventual need of special support for employees from post-migration backgrounds. The report, which happens to have been authored by Bobkowski, stresses that potential problems, such as discrimination, are to be prevented by the vigilant monitoring of teachers and immediate police superiors (*Dienstweg*). While explicitly arguing against special measures, the report nonetheless recommends the training of teachers and instructors who would act as guides (*Bärenführer*) to police trainees. Problems, which would not be solved by such monitoring, are imputed to insufficient individual autonomy and ability to face up to police work and realities.[45]

---

45 Further commenting on the mentioned report, the inspector points out that problems that were encountered and initially raised by police doctors should not be imputed, as one might expect, to discrimination, but rather to cultural problems encountered by officers coming from a particular background ("an Eastern European or Muslim-oriental cultural background" / "*osteuropäischen oder islamisch-orientalisch geprägten Kulturkreis*") which undermines the individual autonomy required by police work (interview with KB, 28 June 2007).

3. A Principled Type

Investigating the motives of those who contributed to the recognition of difference within the police forces and drawing on Weber's method in the previous chapter, I constructed a first ideal type: an empathetic one, whose motivation is grounded in the welfare of individual fellow officers and their guidance. With an eye to the question underlying this investigation, observations made during my fieldwork, and the *histoire croisée*, that of Weiß and its supporters and of Inspector Bobkowski and his colleagues in Berlin, I suggest constructing a second option, the principled type.

The principled type is not characterized, at least in its pure form, by empathy for others nor self-serving interest. Its central motive is grounded in a commitment to a principle or, in Weberian terms, "an inner devotion to a cause" (*Dienst an der Sache*)—not concrete persons. The cause, or task, to which the representatives of this type feel devoted to can have different contents. As a pure type, the content of a task is not important, duty is.[46] In the particular case of the police and organizational change,[47] the principled type shares affinities with a classical liberal tradition, a particular way to apprehending the individual and, in turn, difference. It places a lot of responsibility on the individual, who is framed as a strong, even heroic, citizen. The type's core can be summed up as follows: basic rights, individual autonomy, and the becoming of a citizen by means of educational work.

3.1 Bobkowski Cross-Examined

Returning to the case of Inspector Bobkowski, he frames his work in the language of basic rights, civic equality, or the democratization of the police—that is to make it a more civil organization through the instilling of the basic rights and their spirits, which sometimes have to be forced upon the officers and organizations. His original motive was not to contribute to the recognition or promotion of difference within the police forces. Rather,

---

46 Notably because duty is for Max Weber of prime importance, he would most likely have been sympathetic to his type. Martin Albrow points out that Weber was in thrall throughout his life to duty, "that sublime concept in the Kantian world-view" [1990: 166]).

47 I will come back to the police as a particular type organization in chapter 7.

this was much more a *consequence* of his work, but an effect he is admittedly proud of today. When we met in February 2010 at his retirement party, Inspector Bobkowski mentioned the arrival of nine new political education teachers and stressed that two of them were from post-migration backgrounds, something of which he had made sure. Even if he embraces the initiatives mentioned in this chapter, however, he is not a fervent promoter of difference as such and is more inclined toward assimilation. His "motivational code" could be described by a few words: democratization, basic rights, and assimilation.

Klaus Bobkowski's attitude might cause some indignation in the real men and women. They might be tempted to submit him to cross-examination. Because he is sometimes cynical about gays and lesbians as well as feminist activists whom he occasionally refers to with tongue in cheek as "suffragettes" (*Suffragetten*), he is likely to raise criticism. While we generally confer nobility and value to principles such as the basic rights, Bobkowski's attitude also offends some of today's sensibilities; indeed, the people who are most likely to be sensitive to difference and entertain a positive value relation toward it are the most likely to be indignant at the language sometimes used by Inspector Bobkowski.

The empathetic officers, whose motivation is grounded in the welfare of individuals, might, for example, criticize Klaus Bobkowski for not being sensitive enough to "possible problems" (the word discrimination might not be used). They might suggest special measures for those who might be victims of discrimination. As we have seen, difficulties that potentially might be encountered by police trainees or officers from post-migration backgrounds should, according to Bobkowski, be prevented by immediate police superiors and faced with manly strength. Keeping the stress on the needs of recruits and officers from post-migration backgrounds for extra protection—the officers I interviewed use the word *Fürsorge* (welfare),[48]— the empathetic officers would be prone to criticize Inspector Bobkowski for not doing enough and, by merely stressing an abstract, bloodless, individual, not caring for real people.

---

48 Interview with MS, 12 September 2006.

4. Epilogue

In March 2007 accusations of anti-Semitism were leveled against police trainees at the Berlin Police Academy. The press addressed an incident that occurred during a political education class when a Holocaust survivor who had regularly visited the police academy gave a talk. Police trainees are reported to have said that all Jews were rich and that they did not want to hear about the Holocaust anymore.[49] Following the incident and its disclosure to the press, the chief of police mandated a team of educational scientists from one of the city's universities to look into it and submit a report. The report did not detect noticeable signs of anti-Semitism, but a second team of social scientists was commissioned to evaluate the work of the Political Education Unit. They criticized the teaching methods used in political education; they were deemed not interactive enough and the language used was not entirely free of a nationalistic pathos. They then suggested different measures for talking about and dealing with difference in police education and training.

What happened after the stir around political education? Klaus Bobkowski was distressed. When we met much later, at the beginning of the 2010, he confided that he still had to struggle with the reports and the accusations. When the Political Education Unit along with his teaching and the initiatives he had set forth came under criticism, he revealed something he had not wanted to talk about before, namely that he was of Jewish descent. This was a knockout argument that silenced his critics.[50] He felt compelled to add that until then, he had not wanted to use this argument because he did not want to be treated any differently—an argument he had used in the context of the initiative to honor Bernhard Weiß. Only when faced with criticism did he talk about the issue. Only then did he feel somewhat rehabilitated.

---

49 "Polizeischüler brüskieren Holocaust-Überlebenden," *Franfurter Rundschau online*. URL: http://www.fr-online.de/in_und_ausland/politik/aktuell/?em_cnt =1099256 (accessed 21 March 2007).
50 Interview with KB, 27 August 2009.

Attempting to investigate diversity within the police forces in Germany, political education turned out to be of sociological relevance in Berlin as in other federal states since it represents one channel for acting and talking about ethnic, cultural and religious difference, and contributes to its pragmatic recognition within the police. This is admittedly not surprising, though rarely seen as such in the literature.[51] Emphasizing the spirit of the constitutional rights in modern police work, some officers promoted a liberal agenda of civic equality compatible with the recognition of some differences By combining present and historical perspectives, in this chapter, I outlined a principled type of carriers of diversity in the police forces whose central motive could be characterized by a commitment to a principle or "an inner devotion to a task." Concretely, the content of such a task could be found in different guises, be it basic or human rights, police professionalism, or the promotion of difference *per se*. In the case of Inspector Bobkowski depicted in this chapter, his actions were motivated by the democratization of the police forces and were linked with a liberal agenda of civic equality. In the next chapter, the principled type and its empathetic counterpart will be contrasted with another possible way of acknowledging and promoting difference, that of the opportunist type.

---

51 Interestingly, the book entitled *Diversity Studies* (Krell *et al.* 2007), which has the goal of grounding a new field of studies; one of the fourteen chapters is dedicated to anti-Semitism, a typical theme of political education.

Criminal Inspector Schmitt and the Police Researcher

(The Opportunist Type and Its Mirror Image)

> "Act so that you treat humanity, whether in your own person or that of any other, always as an end [*Zweck*] and never as a means [*Mittel*] only" (KANT/1990 [1785]: 429).

> "You've read too much Kant" (LATOUR/ 2009).

Leaving Berlin, I headed off to another federal state where much publicized initiatives to recruit police officers from post-migration backgrounds had been underway in the 1990s. They were responding to calls for changing the police forces' culture and image. Their instigators, I was told, worked in human resources.

In this federal state, I met officers who are at the source of a third ideal type, the *opportunist*. It illustrates one way, or path, to deal with difference, which is encountered and largely talked about in the forces. While I was working on this type, something unexpected happened: a response to the *opportunist*, its mirror image emerged. It is born out of a vague yet persistent irritation I was confronted with all along my research, both in conducting fieldwork and reading police research. It was not concretized in initiatives, if only negatively—as a critique of the people I describe as opportunist and the motives underlying their work. Once outlined, this response turned out to be key in grasping the ambivalence, uneasiness, and partial reservation toward the initiatives police officers were putting in practice and researchers were observing; more generally, it hints at elements characteristic of the attitude within the forces toward difference.

As in the previous two chapters, my reflections in the following two parts, which constitute the present chapter, feed on concrete situations and individuals. The portraits gained help me to construct a type, an abstraction, and ground it in a particular cultural context. In the first part, I examine the case of Criminal Inspector Schmitt and her mandate to put into practice a strategic plan to increase the number of police officers from post-migration backgrounds in the forces. In the second part, I then turn to a research team and the efforts of one of its leaders to come to grips with "diversity" within the police force.[1] Because his writings and our conversations turned out to be instructive on the ambivalences toward the initiatives one encounters in the police forces, I use his example in a similar way to Criminal Inspector Schmitt's to further delineate the types and clarify their theoretical status.

Part One: Opportunism as Motive

1. Working in Human Resources: Criminal Inspector Schmitt

When I started to establish contacts with people in human resources and to meet them for interviews in 2005, my informants in one particular federal state kept referring to a woman, Criminal Inspector Elke Schmitt. She was said to be putting her heart and soul (*mit Leib and Seele*) into her job and was considered a pioneer for all matters related to minorities within the police forces.[2] I tried to meet her, but it proved difficult. She was at that time

---

1   Bar in the expression "diversity management" and as noted in the introduction of this book, I put diversity in quotation marks to refer to efforts in human resources to make greater use of personal competences and in italics to indicate the use of the word in English by my informants or in the German literature.
2   Interview with KW, 24 March 2005.

working somewhere else, in another field of police activities. In the spring of 2007, I finally managed to meet her at her new workplace, in the countryside.

In contrast to many of my interview partners and in particular those portrayed in this book, I met Criminal Inspector Schmitt only once, for a long interview.[3] Though cordial, she did not take me very seriously, at least not until I mentioned I might write something about her. In spite of its limitations and its retrospective character, our conversation conveyed, in a condensed form, many of the things I had heard before when talking to the police rank-and-files. Criminal Inspector Schmitt echoed certain widely expressed views reflecting mistrust toward the initiatives aiming at the recognition of difference in the police forces, and therefore a type of mistrust not wholly absent from the discourse of officers in charge of these initiatives themselves. Although I felt the importance of our conversation, I was reluctant to write about it; something irritated me about her. Because I was to encounter the same kind of irritation in the academic literature on *diversity* in the police forces, I finally decided to go back to her case.

As we sat down, Criminal Inspector Schmitt gave me—not without a touch of coquetry—her account of initiatives to recruit police officers from post-migration backgrounds in the 1990s. She was working in recruitment, when she joined a working group set up by the minister of the interior in 1996 to increase the presence of officers from post-migration backgrounds within the police forces. Back then, this topic was an urgent one: some time before, in 1995, a study commissioned by the Conference of Ministers and Senators of the Interior was made public. This study (in fact, there were two studies) was carried out by a group of researchers at the Police Federal Academy (Bornewasser and Eckert as well as Ahlheim and Heger) and commonly known as the Bornewasser-Studie or PFA-Studie (1996). It followed a series of incidents involving police officers' interaction with members of visible ethnic minorities. Without concluding to a systematic trend, the final report nevertheless hinted at racism within the police forces; and it

---

3 Next to the interview carried out on 3 April 2007, in this chapter I also rely on interviews with other officers in the same federal state and other ones, on police internal documents, and on a book section dedicated to her in the police literature.

received considerable media attention.[4] The federal state's minister of the interior was compelled to take measures: in 1996, he mandated the director of the Recruitment and Selection Unit of the police forces, along with five other people working under him, to draft a strategic paper, an action plan. Criminal Inspector Schmitt was among them.

Like the inspectors introduced in the previous chapters, Criminal Inspector Schmitt was a newcomer to the field. Schmitt had followed an unusual career path; a determined young woman, she had gone straight to the criminal police after her training and had worked 15 years in the investigation service. She said she had made people talk in her time: she had not gone through all levels of the organization as most of her colleagues had to, and she neither had to go on patrol nor to wear a uniform. She did not need to don a uniform to hold herself up straight; she was proud and gave the impression of being very confident in her abilities. Prior to working on the action plan, she was working in human resources.

1.1 The Action Plan

A year after its call into being, Criminal Inspector Schmitt's team presented an action plan to the minister of the interior. It included a statistical overview of police officers from post-migration backgrounds, a review of what had been done so far to recruit officers from post-migration backgrounds in the federal state and elsewhere as well as a catalog of measures to reach more young people and promote their acceptance within the forces.

Criminal Inspector Schmitt mentions that a lot of time went at first into choosing the right concepts to be used, should we talk about "foreigners? Ethnic minorities? What are Ethnic minorities? Migrants? People from post-migration backgrounds? And so forth, and so forth."[5] The goal set was to hire more recruits from ethnic minorities—the term decided upon—

---

4   The authors concluded that "police violations were neither the results of isolated cases nor of a systematic pattern of behavior within the forces" / *"bei Polizeilichen Übergriffen [handele es sich] 'weder um bloße Einzelfälle noch um ein systematisches Verhaltensmuster der Polizei'"* (Murck 1996: 6).

5   *"Ausländer? ethnische Minderheiten? Was sind eigentlich Minderheiten? Migranten? Menschen mit Migrationshintergrund (...) und und und."*

without infringing upon the police's principle of formal equality.[6] Indeed, the authors are wary to stress equal treatment and the exceptional character of the rule to the civil service law, which underlies the plan. Seen in this light, Inspector Piontek's achievements (the changes in the entry tests, the point system, the extra language courses, the counseling) can be considered bold. Upon closer inspection, one notices that while denying special treatment, Schmitt and her colleagues foresee several exceptions. For example, they suggest that the criteria of entry should be left untouched; however, their application should be flexible; the same goes for the principle of selection (*Bestenauslese*), which should remain; however, they recommend that two lists be produced, one for the German candidates and one for the candidates from post-migration backgrounds, thus avoiding what is seen as unduly competition (N.N. 1997: 39-40).

The minister accepted the action plan and a job was created to translate it into action. Criminal Inspector Schmitt was appointed to this position. The new job was an exciting one; Criminal Inspector Schmitt's speech tempo accelerated as she remembered the time. She got down to business: she gathered the recruitment officers of the federal state (some 82 people at the time), organized various meetings, and taught seminars to people who would spread the message ("*Multiplikatoren [, die] dann auch im ganzen Land Folgeveranstaltungen machten*"), getting in contact with ethnic associations and mosques. She also enthusiastically told me about traveling across the federal state, interacting with the media, and going through all levels of the police forces to promote the action plan, talking to police officials and, as she underscored on several occasions, not shunning to discuss with the old and conservative colleagues where resistance was mostly felt and acceptance most needed.

Criminal Inspector Schmitt said remarkably little about the contents of the plan: she stressed talking to colleagues and carrying out in-house training, on her own or with the help of consultants. She mentioned seminars touching upon "Islam, etc." She spontaneously talked about the forces' role in integrating foreigners and, yet again, about Islam. Listening to her and

---

6 The authors entitled their plan Conception to Increase the Proportion of Foreign Fellow Citizens (*Konzeption zur Erhöhung des Anteils ausländischer Mitbürgerinnen / Mitbürger im Polizeidienst*) in the Police Forces, but used the term "ethnic minorities" (*ethnische Minderheiten*) in the text.

glancing at the empty chair of her office companion—one of the newly nominated liaison officers for Muslim institutions (*Kontaktbeamte muslimischer Institutionen*)—I remember thinking to myself that our conversation was probably more instructive on the themes that were most talked about in the media at the time we met in 2007 than on those that were deemed important at the time the action plan was originally put into practice.[7]

Trying once again to steer the conversation back to the action plan, I asked Criminal Inspector Schmitt about its inception. What was it like? She then mentioned a trip the minister of the interior had taken to the Netherlands. Both in the police research literature and during the course of my fieldwork between 2004 and 2009/10, the country was often mentioned and referred to as the multicultural country of Europe. A brief look at Elke Schmitt's and her colleagues' account of the Netherlands casts light on their conception of the initiative.

A Glance at the Netherlands

Measures to improve the level of recruitment among members of ethnic minorities had already been set forth in the Netherlands in the 1980s and a lot of new officers, Criminal Inspector Schmitt told me, had been hired. Along with her colleagues, she wanted to get acquainted with these endeavors.

"And then we first said: (...) 'let's look at ... [BT: name of her federal state], but there is also of course 15 other federal states in Germany. What does it look like there?' And we have also looked around in other countries like the Netherlands, also other European countries, because we knew—through contacts with the Nether-

---

7 In the context of the post 9/11 measures against terrorism and as a means to "build confidence" with the Muslim population, liaison officers for Muslim institutions have been nominated since 2004 (interview LC, 31 August 2010). See "Brücke für Polizei und Muslime." *Islamische Zeitung*, 26 February (3 March 2008).

lands—that they were already well ahead of us in that department and because we did not want to repeat all their mistakes once more (...)."[8]

Drawing on instruments stemming from human resource management and organization development, the Dutch police put an ambitious program into place. Herman Blom, a police researcher with expertise on initiatives both in the Netherlands and Germany highlights the *difference principle* characteristic of the Dutch police forces, that is the recognition and promotion of cultural differences as a means, even a condition, to more efficient police work in a pluralistic context. Such a principle stresses the employees' potential and resources for the organization; this is contrasted by the German *principle of equal treatment* and its trend toward assimilation (Blom 2005: 41-42).

German police officers often depict the Netherlands as a counter-example.[9] They generally do so by underscoring management-fixed quotas

---

[8] "*Und dann haben wir erst mal gesagt (...): 'gucken wir sind* [BT: name of her federal state]*, aber da gibt's ja noch 15 andere Bundesländer in Deutschland. Wie sieht's denn da aus?' Und wir haben uns da auch mal umgeschaut in anderen Ländern wie die Niederlanden also das europäische Ausland, weil wir wussten—durch Kontakte mit den Niederländern—, dass die auch schon auf dem Gebiet viel weiter sind als wir und weil wir deren Fehler nicht alle noch mal machen wollten (...).*" According to Anne van Ewijk, 5,6% of the police officers in the Netherlands were from post-migration backgrounds in 2008 (2012: 81).

[9] Next to the Netherlands, Canada was also sometimes mentioned as a counter-example. I was sometimes given to think, when presenting myself to interview partners: "Germany is not Canada" and was warned not to project my experiences onto Germany. A prominent British scholar who had strongly criticized German police officers at a conference held at the Police Federal Academy was not countered with acrimony as I had expected, but was simply ignored. For the police officers, the scholar needed not be taken seriously; for he did not, so I was told, know the German context. I was reminded of Marx reporting on the English situation to a German audience in the German preface of *Capital*: "In this work I have to examine the capitalist mode of production, and the conditions of production and exchange corresponding to that mode. Up to the present time, their classic ground is England. That is the reason why England is used as

and high dropout rates. Criminal Inspector Schmitt shared this negative view:

"(...) they were in the Netherlands a lot more stringent or a lot more—how should I put it—they opened up more massively and also a lot of massive exceptions were authorized (...) and in doing so they made mistakes (...) such as, they [BT: the candidates] could apply with an interpreter; they did not speak any Dutch and they were hired (...) and that was a total catastrophe! They had to fire half of them."[10]

Criminal Inspector Schmitt made clear that her federal state should not champion the Dutch experience, but rather favor a "cautious implementation" (*behutsame Umsetzung*) of the plan. That was, she said, "her philosophy." As far as recruiting was concerned, there were, Criminal Inspector Schmitt said, no fixed goals. The team members had hoped the hiring of officers from post-migration backgrounds would improve: "Well, we simply said, one should keep an eye on the numbers, if they increase, then our goal is reached, we didn't say anything more."[11] Given the resistance she encountered when promoting the action plan and the importance she conferred onto its acceptance in the police forces, she stressed her federal state should take things slowly. While sometimes underscoring Germany's more tranquil yet steady approach (*der ruhige, aber stetige Gang*), Blom encour-

---

the chief illustration in the development of my theoretical ideas. If, however, the German reader shrugs his shoulders at the condition of the English industrial and agricultural labourers, or in optimist fashion comforts himself with the thought that in Germany things are not nearly so bad; I must plainly tell him—*De te fabula narratur* [BT: it is of you that the story is told (Horace)]!" (Marx 1965 [1867]: 8).

10 "*... weil die in den Niederlanden viel stringenter oder auch viel – wie soll ich mich ausdrücken – die haben (...) viel massiver sich geöffnet und auch viel massiver Ausnahmen zugelassen (...) und dabei so Fehler gemacht wie, sie* [BT: the candidates] *konnten sich mit nem Dolmetscher bewerben, sie sprachen gar kein Niederländisch und wurden eingestellt (...) und das war eine einzige Katastrophe! Die haben die Hälfte alle wieder entlassen müssen.*"

11 "*also wir haben einfach nur gesagt, man soll beobachten, ob sich die Zahlen verändern und wenn sie steigen, ist das Ziel erreicht, mehr haben wir dazu nicht gesagt.*"

ages the forces to take more risks and use more modern techniques (see Blom 2004: 23, 2005: 44-45, 49).[12]

1.2 Consequences, Dilemmas, Motives

Consequences

Returning again to her own personal experience, Criminal Inspector Schmitt mentioned that the new job was promising in terms of career advancement and it indeed turned out to be a good career move. Showing me a photo of the participants of a seminar she had organized—many of whom I had already encountered while researching this study—she reminisced about the past:

"(...) for me, all on my own, it [BT: the job] was hard. But it brought me a lot for my career, to be honest, because I was after some time known all over town [*bekannt wie ein bunter Hund*]. I flew all around and everybody knew me. And because one becomes even more known through television and because I did it all pretty well, the chief was also very enthusiastic about it and it was of course for my career a [BT: leap forward] (...) and then I said: 'OK, I do it' and, besides, I also enjoyed being engaged so intensively in such a theme."[13]

Criminal Inspector Schmitt was in charge of the action plan for the next three years, from 1997 to 2000. As her boss retired, she succeeded him as head of the Recruitment and Selection Unit (*Werbung und Auswahl*) of her

---

12 In his writings, Blom's attention goes to the recruits. His motto could be summed up as, "it's not what police from post-migration backgrounds can offer to the police, but what the police can offer them."

13 "(...) *für mich ganz alleine war's heftig. Aber es hat also auch für meine Karriere ne Menge gebracht, das muss ich auch ehrlich sagen, weil ich also ja bekannt war wie ein bunter Hund nach ner bestimmten Zeit, überall flog ich so rum und alle kannten mich und weil vom Fernsehen wird man noch bekannter und das weil ich das alles ganz gut gemacht habe, war also der oberste Chef auch sehr begeistert davon und es war für meine Karriere natürlich schon ein* [BT: leap forward] *[...] und da hab ich auch gesagt: 'ok, ich mach's und es hat mir ja ganz nebenbei auch Spaß gemacht so intensiv mich mit so nem Thema zu beschäftigen.*"

federal state, thus moving to a higher position in management and to other activities. At the time she started this new job, the unit was confronted with a challenge, which absorbed much of her energy: the hiring of high school graduates (*Abiturienten*) to the detriment of junior high graduates (*Realschüler*). Unprompted, she assured me that the measures her team had introduced had taken their course and that candidates from post-migration backgrounds were applying in greater numbers.

As I knew from other interviews and my own research, there were signs of institutionalization: between 1999 and 2004, some 7 percent of all officers hired in that federal state were from post-migration backgrounds, figures comparable to those of Hamburg and Berlin (Hunold 2010: 138). This is no doubt a considerable achievement, but it remains rather modest if we look at the whole of the forces in this federal state: about 1 percent of all officers in 2004 and 1.5 to 2 percent in 2009.[14] Intercultural seminars had also become part of the police formation; and individual initiatives were organized for recruits from post-migration backgrounds at the police central head quarters.[15] Things had set in, but still remained fragile. When Criminal Inspector Schmitt became head of recruitment and selection, another officer took over her work. However, as he himself confided, the action plan was not a priority for him.[16] A new petition on the recruitment of officers from post-migration background was brought in the Parliament in 2006 and a new government commissioned, a year later, a new plan to the Police Training and Continuing Education Institute,[17] attesting both to a renewed urgency and a fragile institutionalization. In 2009, a research project on intercultural qualification and promotion of cultural diversity was commissioned to a group of researchers on intercultural matters.

After her work in recruitment and selection, Criminal Inspector Schmitt started working in 2005 in a completely different field and in a new location, managing to work closer to her home. I do not know the exact circum-

---

14 Police internal document, 3 August 2004.
15 Such as the seminars organized by GM, a trade union delegate (interview, 12 June 2007).
16 Interview with KW, 24 March 2005.
17 Lautmann (2010: 113) remarks that these demands emerge from all political parties, from left to right ones.

stances of this change. When we met, she had moved on and knew little about new developments or literature on the subject.

Dilemmas?
There is a tension underlying the actions of Criminal Inspector Schmitt and her colleagues, which is also expressed in the action plan: its authors are committed to the principle of equality of treatment while stressing the need to change toward more difference. This tension characterizes the initiatives presented in this study and the resistance their instigators encountered, especially those who were committed to them. As such, Criminal Inspector Schmitt reflects a general trend in the police forces: she tries to legitimize the initiatives to hire more officers from post-migration backgrounds while, at the same time, not openly and fully endorsing such changes. Contradictory principles or maxims can orient action within a same individual (Weber 1978b [1921]: 32); the resulting tensions can lead to uneasiness, ambivalence, and dilemmas. What about Elke Schmitt? Was she confronted with such dilemmas? She did not seem to be plagued by dilemmas; in fact, she did not seem to care that much at all.

Chitchatting about her work, I asked Elke Schmitt once more what her job was about back in the days of the action plan. Since our conversation seemed to systematically shift back to her personal trajectory, I could not easily make out her mandate in the specific context of the initiative: was it about increasing the presence of members of ethnic minorities within the forces? Was it about integrating ethnic minorities? Or about promoting the action plan within the forces and thus favor greater acceptance toward minorities? The goal the group she was a part of had set itself, she had insisted several times during the course of our conversation, was integration. Yet, it was not her direct job: unlike Inspector Piontek, Criminal Inspector Schmitt neither recruited police officers herself nor counseled them; she held a high management position in a large federal state. During our conversation, she remained vague and evasive about her goals and the plan. True, the plan had been a long time ago, but she seemed reluctant to even think about it. Or was it too painful to think about? It cannot be ruled out that the job had been a difficult one, and that Elke Schmitt was more hard-skinned than half-hearted or unmoved. In any case, she eventually put an end to my questioning by telling me she would send me some written materials.

Motive: Career Advancement

What might have been Criminal Inspector Schmitt's motives to get involved in the plan? In trying to reconstruct her account and its underlying motives, I will first look at the consequences of her action and the dilemmas she might have faced. The confrontation with the consequences of one's action, Weber writes (1988 [1920]: 524), brings us—the individual and the observer—back to the intentions.[18] In delineating her motives, I also compared her case to that of the other officers I met with.

Compared to the Hamburg Inspectors we encountered in chapter two, Elke Schmitt did not seem much concerned about recruits and officers from post-migration backgrounds and their welfare. When talking about the resistance encountered while promoting the action plan, she neither mentioned the importance of protecting recruits nor the need to prevent discrimination—as some informants who were described as empathetic did. It was not her job either:[19] Criminal Inspector Schmitt was in charge of all police departments in her federal state; the recruitment officers were the ones on the field. Nor was she explicitly motivated by a principle, or a cause—such as the promotion of difference or the democratization of the police forces. Whenever I pressed her to be more specific about her role and the action plan, she preferred talking about the good times and the friendships that characterized the beginning of the job. If there was a cause underlying her work, its substance was difficult to pinpoint. She worked with energy and determination, but it was hard to identify what she was actually working for; her cause seemed *devoid of substance*.

Elke Schmitt might have believed in the action plan she wrote as a contributor and had been mandated to set forth; however, she seemed indiffer-

---

18 We find a similar idea in Weber's *Gesammelte Politische Schriften*: "Convinced by long experiences and also by systematic reflection, I hold the view that the individual becomes clear about his real intentions only by testing his supposedly 'ultimate' position (*Stellungnahme*) in the face of critical and absolutely concrete problems" (cited and translated in Manasse 1944: 30).

19 Following the tradition of the gatherings with recruits and police officers from post-migration backgrounds, Dietmar Piontek told me, when talking about Tamara Schwarz, his successor, and her efforts to walk in his footsteps that it was not part of her job, that it was all extra time (interview with DP, 23 November 2006).

ent to the content of her work. It could probably have been something else, which she might have carried out with the same energy. Like many other individuals, her career and its advancement—her job was one with an undeniably glamorous side—seemed to be at the heart of her considerations.[20] Self-interest, it seemed, had primarily guided her work.

Theoretical Excursus I (The Opportunist Type)

In this study, when I investigate the spirit of diversity in the police forces, I start by examining what Weber calls an order, or patterned action. Following the example set by the sociologist in his *Protestant Ethic*, I first consider the tangible manifestations of this attitude to difference (in recruitment initiatives, teaching, in-house training, counseling, commemoration of the past) with an eye at the resistance they encounter. I then trace back to the actors responsible for these manifestations and their motives. This loop between motives and order helps in turn to understand and, thereby, explain the spirit of diversity and its genesis while underlining the insight that an order "arise[s] out of various and conflicting individual motivations" (Albrow 1990: 164). As in Weber's study, my efforts are geared at understanding and explaining the presence of one particular spirit in the face of several motives or ideal types of carriers of diversity.

In his writings, Max Weber argues that many motives may uphold an order: they may range from a purely customary basis, the belief in its binding character, to pure expediency. An order based on self-interest, though, is likely to be less stable (less legitimate) than one founded on usage, customs and—especially—the belief in its binding character; such an order will, Weber suggests, be more prone to change (1978a [1921]: 31). What can be deduced from those considerations for the case of the police forces? Following Weber's insights, two hypotheses can be put forth. First, people like Criminal Inspector Schmitt, whose prime motivation lies in self-interest, can lead to the emergence of a new order or the stabilization of an already existing one. Second, the representatives of the opportunist type are likely to disappear when the hype about *diversity*—as a theme in the police forces, media, and politics—fades away; they are likely to move on to

---

20 Job advancement is a motivation for a lot of recruits joining the forces; in all advertisement campaigns, the forces do not fail to insist on the career advancement possibilities they offer to their members.

something else, whatever is fashionable, urgent, or promising for the achievement of personal interests. Following Weber, such an order, is likely to be less stable, less legitimate, than one based on commitment to values.

Let us now think about the opportunist type. Seen in contrast to the other ideal types outlined in the previous chapters, the opportunist's action is neither governed by the welfare of others, such as in the case of the empathetic type, nor by duty to a cause, as in the case of the principled one. Self-interest motivates the opportunist's action. What can be expected from an opportunist person? In reality, s/he will employ different means to attain the goal s/he sets himself or herself to, whatever serves best his or her interest. More than any other type, s/he will be likely to be wary of possible consequences, calculating and watching out for his or her interests. S/he may invoke different arguments—practical, moral—to account for his or her action. S/he may believe in the cause, or not; or come to believe in it for motives can change.

As a pure form, opportunism is also a tool sociologists often use to understanding action and its subjective intended meaning as well as to anticipating action. There is another dimension to opportunism: indeed, it is also related to arguments explicitly invoked to justify an action or an organizational goal, what I referred to as motive talk or vocabularies of motives in chapter one (*Begründungen*). While these dimensions often lead to confusion, one thing remains clear: either as a motive or as motive talk, opportunism can provoke a reaction, hinting at yet another dimension, a value relation. Moving to this aspect, in the second part of this chapter, I leave the realms of tangible initiatives to acknowledge or promote difference within police forces and turn to the reaction, to the critique, of the people who can be described as opportunists and the motives underlying their work. Because the critiques talk and write about it, I also turn to opportunism as motive talk and the often mentioned trend toward diversity management.

PART TWO: REACTION TO OPPORTUNISM

While pondering about Criminal Inspector Schmitt, the initiatives aiming to acknowledge or promote difference and the reactions they got, I could not help but remember a German police researcher and his irritation—and own resistances—toward these initiatives. Drawing on conversations we had and on his writings, I examine his conception of culture and diversity. In so doing, I make a brief foray into the police literature in Germany.

1. STUDYING POLICE CULTURE: THE RESEARCHER

The researcher's name is Rafael Behr. A former police officer, he is a prolific author: he has written and commented on, and also criticized police forces in Germany. His main focus is on police culture.[21] In general, research on the police puts a particular emphasis on police, or cop, culture; it has a strong qualitative and empirical component (Bigo 2000; Bittner 1990; Chan 1997; Loftus 2010a; Reiner 2010 [2000]; Skolnick and Bayley 1988; Waddington 1999; Manning 1974). Next to the study of culture, these traits are often combined—particularly in the German context—with a concern for police reforms (Lautmann 2010: 119-122).

With colleagues, Behr took up a new research theme in 2005: migrants in the police forces. This was a timely topic. With a project entitled Migrants in Law Enforcement (*Migranten in Organisationen von Recht und Sicherheit*, MORS), the group secured financing. Not unlike the authors of the other studies on *diversity* in the police (see Blom 2005), the team set out to study initiatives to recruit and hire candidates from post-migration backgrounds and the situation of those officers within the forces with the goal of making recommendations.[22] And because a trend toward diversity management had, in the meantime, gained popularity at the political level as a means of modernizing public administrations through new management methods, it seemed obvious enough to include it in the new project. While

---

21 *His Cop Culture — Der Alltag des Gewaltmonopols — Männlichkeit, Handlungsmuster und Kultur in der Polizei* was published in 2002 and reedited in 2008.
22 The MORS-project was carried out between 2005 and 2008. Its members notably organized conferences and workshops with academics and practitioners from different European countries. The results of the studies undertaken within the project are gathered in a book, *Fremde als Ordnungshüter* (edited by Daniela Hunold, Daniela Klimke, Rafael Behr, and Rüdiger Lautmann. Wiesbaden: VS Verlag für Sozialwissenschaften).

most of those I refer to as carriers of diversity did not talk much about managerial approaches to differences at the beginning of the fieldwork—except for the case of the Netherlands, which I observed in passing, along with a few cynical remarks—, diversity management was now being discussed: it was the annual theme of the Berlin police force in 2008 and the object of a federal campaign for firms and public administrations.

Diversity Management

Diversity management corresponds to strategic concepts at work places, both in firms and public administrations, which represent one set of institutionalized relations toward difference within human resources (recruitment and career management). They typically target specific categories such as ethnicity, gender, religion, disabilities, age, and sexual identity. Diversity management is a relatively new field with its own instruments, idiom, body of authors, and iconography.[23]

Because accounts of its origin diverge (some authors claim it was born in the American Civil Rights Movement) and because it is translated in various policies and programs in work contexts, diversity management can be best described by a tension between the use of economic and cultural resources (for innovation and productivity) and antidiscrimination (for equal employment and chances). The criticism expressed toward diversity management—and the responses provided by its advocates—reflect this tension.

In Germany, three categories have been at the center of attention: gender, ethnicity, and disabilities (Krell 2007). Management efforts related to the last two categories could build on ideas and expand on institutions, which have been put in place since the 1980s around the representation of women. Following equal treatment legislation for women and men in individual federal states, the German federal government adopted an antidiscrimination law (*allgemeines Gleichbehandlungsgesetz*) in 2006. A year later, big firms launched a "Charter of Diversity;" it

---

23 For example, promotion posters or book covers often portray smiling people from visible minorities or, alternatively, a handful of candies or tokens from different colors.

was supported by the federal government and voluntarily ratified by branches of the private and public sectors. At the same time, the federal government instigated the campaign "Diversity as Chance" (*Vielfalt als Chance*).[24] These initiatives followed up directives of the European Union, which has championed—particularly since the 1997 Amsterdam treaty (Doytcheva and Helly 2011: 394)—such policies and measures.

The police researcher entertains an ambivalent value relation toward his new research object: the initiatives undertaken to broaden the social basis of the forces and diversity management. Talking to the researcher, I gained the enduring impression that he considered the object of his study disheartening and frustrating, hard to pin down, and somehow hollow. Behr is critical of people like Schmitt and her counterparts in other federal states. He bemoans what he sees as a lack of consistency and enthusiasm among the police forces. He tells me that they "say they want diversity, but they do not want to change."[25] Besides the lack of enthusiasm, he criticizes arguments invoked within the forces to justify the recruitment initiatives. One example should suffice to make this point manifest.

A Much Repeated Anecdote

When we met, Criminal Inspector Schmitt told me a story. I had heard it in differing versions many times before when listening to people who were officially in charge of promoting greater cultural difference in the police forces.

During a Kurdistan Workers' Party (PKK) demonstration, men were under police observation. Some of the demonstrators were eventually apprehended, and started mumbling something in Kurdish. As it turned out, a dispatched cop from post-migration backgrounds could understand their language and surreptitiously followed their conversation; he could thus gather important information, which led to the demonstrators' arrest. The

---

24 *Diversity als Chance — Die Charta der Vielfalt der Unternehmen in Deutschland.* URL: http://www.vielfalt-als-chance.de/index.php?id=318 (accessed 31 May 2011).
25 Conversation with RB, 14 March 2007.

effectiveness—not to mention the surprise provoked by an officer who, after gathering sufficient information, had suddenly started talking in Kurdish to the demonstrators and, Schmitt added, did not look foreign, "was super!" (*war ganz toll!*).

The arguments involving linguistic skills and tactical considerations seemed to be particularly convincing for Schmitt, but also for police officials and the rank-and-file who might otherwise be against particular endeavors to hire officers from post-migration backgrounds.[26] Incidentally, they are also conspicuous in the dispensation clause, which stresses the "urgent professional necessity" to hire nonnational applicants.[27] However, these arguments are a cause of irritation for police researchers. Indeed, Behr and his colleagues tend to be critical of the utilitarian arguments underlying the anecdote.

Two things bother them: first, tactical considerations are not enough for justifying changes and, second, the idea of "using people" is abhorrent to their sensibility. They are critical of the use of special knowledge for the sole benefice of the forces, regardless of individual persons who are seen as "culture scouts" (Behr 2006: 125; Klimke 2010: 35-40). Police recruits from post-migration backgrounds and officers who could be described as empathetic such as Inspector Piontek also raised—though not always—similar issues.[28] They sometimes argued that one ought to protect the officers from post-migration backgrounds already in the forces against being used for particular purposes such as translation or acting as an interpreter. In so doing, they work against the dominant interpretation of the principle of formal equality generally invoked to *avoid* particular individual treatment; they proffer another one, one underscoring the dignity of the person.[29]

Back from Schmitt's federal state, I take one of Rafael Behr's books from a bookshelf, *Polizeikultur. Routine — Rituale — Reflexionen. Bausteine zu*

---

26 Another argument invoke is to assure a pool of possible candidates (interview with XQ, 4 December 2006).
27 See chapter two, section one.
28 This was for instance the case of Gert Müller, though not of Brigitte Winter.
29 Criminal Inspector Schmitt talks more often of "avoiding unequal treatment" (*Ungleichbehandlung vermeiden*) than "equal treatment" (*Gleichbehandlung*).

einer Theorie der Praxis der Polizei (*Police Culture. Routines — Rituals — Reflections. Elements for a Theory and Practice of the Police* [2006]). It presents the author's first reflections on the treatment of cultural difference within the police forces in Germany. Let me review the sections relevant to my topic to understand the author's reaction, his uneasiness at the initiatives and the arguments generally invoked to legitimate them as well as his own recommendations.

1.1 The Book

In *Polizeikultur. Routine — Rituale — Reflexionen*, Rafael Behr follows three goals: he goes back to, and further develops, his earlier concerns with cop culture and police culture, describes recent trends in German police forces, and brings them together in a "theory of practice of the police"—as the second part of the book title goes (*Theorie der Praxis der Polizei*). The book is a mash-up of textbook and manifesto for police researchers and "reflexive practitioners" within the forces. Two sections concern us particularly: one dealing with the initiatives to recruit officers from post-migration backgrounds (p. 121-143) and one on diversity management (p. 175-191). As most police researchers, Rafael Behr sees the initiatives that aimed at recognizing and promoting difference as a failure—one measured against the statements of politicians or assumed goals.[30] He then quickly moves on to his second topic, one I wish to tackle because Behr equates the treatment of difference with diversity management.

In his book, diversity management is almost invariably presented as a straw man: it was imported from the United States and grafted onto the German context in the late 1990s; springing from management studies, its main goal lies in increasing productivity through the maximized use of the

---

30 Berlin's senator of the interior, as well as his Hamburg counterpart, once suggested that about 10 percent of all civil servants should have a migration or a post-migration background. One of the police officials at the second meeting in Hamburg even talked about a goal of 20 percent (participant observation, 23 November 2006). Similar claims had been made in the press: "Ausbildungs-Aktion: Multikulti im Staatsdienst," *Hamburger Abendblatt*, 7 November 2006. However, as we know from the example of Criminal Inspector Schmitt's federal state, there were often no specific goals stated.

employees' potential in firms (Behr 2006: 175). The police researcher sets out to criticize diversity management harshly. He writes about fixation on competition and the degree of utility; the language he uses points to the artificial character of what he sees as a mere label and the superficiality of the ideas behind it. Whereas the definitions put forward by the advocates of diversity management insist on "the 'positive' effects of cultural plurality and competence for private companies and public service" (Blom 2005: 41; Faist 2009: 177),[31] the police researcher criticizes these attempts for being poorly grounded, both empirically and theoretically. Diversity management pertains, he points out, more to wishful thinking than to realistic goals (Behr 2006: 175-178).

Reading Rafael Behr's book, I see three components that constitute the police researcher's approach, albeit in a negative form: the use of people for instrumental purpose (as noticed with regard to the utilitarian arguments invoked in the anecdote above and in diversity management); the lack of conviction, or belief, he perceives both in the initiatives and in diversity management and, unsurprisingly, the inconsistencies in their application.

As an alternative, Behr suggests a position he calls "institutional patriotism" (*Institutionenpatriotismus*). Some principles, he stresses, ought to ground *diversity* in police culture while also being in tunes with the culture of the organization (2006: 186). With such maxims as "To the outside, we behave like one; inside, we are diverse" (*Nach außen verhalten wir uns einheitlich, nach innen vielfältig*" (2006: 134, footnote 113) or "Cultural unity — personal diversity" (*Kulturelle Einheit — persönliche Vielfalt* [2006: 134]), Behr pleas for a more heterogeneous police organization, which does not give up assimilation as its goal. Self-interest or calculation, either as a personal motive or as an organizational incentive, is for him clearly not enough; instead, he calls for a genuine belief in a principle. He urges the members of the police forces to search for the ethics of the profession; in contrast to diversity management, he stresses the importance of inner convictions and devotion to the initiatives being set forth. Such a plea may call to mind—to draw on religious language—the idea of discerning

---

31 For a positive view—though not related to the police—on diversity management in Germany, see Krell *et al.* (2007) and von Dippel. URL: http://www.migration-boell.de/web/diversity/48_2150.asp (accessed 14 September 2012).

one's charisma or—if we rather borrow from the language of early 20th-century sociology—personality. Behr actually uses a word with strong connotations, which refers both to religious and sexual spheres: *Hingabe* (translated as devotion or passion).

1.2 The Motives, Not the Consequences

For Behr, *diversity*—as a measure for changing the police—has to be embedded both in the cop culture and the principles of the organization (Behr 2006: 185); plus, they ought to be filled with passion. What he sees in the police and in the management literature is "too thin." They are not anchored in police culture; in other words, they are not authentic. This management trend is, Behr stresses, ill suited for the police forces in particular, and to the German context in general (2006: 175).

Let us pause a moment and linger on the relation between culture and diversity. While the concept of culture Behr uses in the first part of his book is theoretically grounded, it gets another meaning when dealing with "migrants in the forces."[32] Indeed, the concept of culture underlying "institutional patriotism" is not unlike the liberal model advocated by Inspector Bobkowski and his colleagues and attempts to create a "German, but heterogeneous culture." Upon closer inspection, diversity management fires his sensibilities; the trend has the significance of an emotive symbol—incidentally, its advocates are neither clearly identified nor much present in the fieldwork but are through discourse. Although theoretically underpinned, the researchers' writings entertain a strong negative value relation to the opportunistic arguments used by people like Elke Schmitt and those he sees at work in diversity management.

Behr is irritated by the motives invoked by the proponents of diversity management due to their content; yet, the effects they seek are not as different from what he himself proposes. A look at a later publication illustrates this point. Four years after *Polizeikultur. Routine — Rituale — Reflexionen*, Behr (2010) revisits his position on "diversity." He calls for greater cultural variation (*größere kulturelle Varianz*) within the police forces as a source of flexibility and organizational change. "For this pur-

---

32 Norbert Elias makes a similar critique of Alfred Weber's concept of culture (see Elias 1994 [1990]: 104).

pose," he writes, "One does not need any *diversity* politics."[33] Considering the researcher's reaction to the endeavors in the police and to diversity management, I come to the following conclusion: *More than the consequences pertaining to action, it is the motives invoked that are contentious.*[34]

Theoretical Excursus II (The Opportunist's Mirror Image)

There is a Kantian twist, or sensibility, palpable in the German police researchers' writings on "diversity." According to Kantian ethics, the motives matter more than the consequences of action. For Kant, as Sullivan points

---

33 "*Dafür muss man aber keine Diversity-Politik betreiben.*" He continues: "For this, one needs not be afraid of conflicts. For it will be the first thing to happen: a growing number of migrants will draw more attention on themselves. One will need to discuss, not as individuals, but as representatives of a group. This can contribute to the positive development of an organization's conflict culture and capacity to act." / "*Dafür muss man den Mut zum Konflikt haben. Denn das wird das erste sein, was eintreten wird: eine zunehmende Zahl von Migranten wird stärker auf sich aufmerksam machen. Man wird mit ihnen Diskussionen führen müssen, nicht als Individuen, sondern als Vertreter einer Gruppe. Dies kann die Konfliktkultur und Handlungskompetenz einer Organisation durchaus positiv entwickeln*" (Behr 2010: 154).

34 The importance of motives and the adherence to them, out of conviction and not out of pure expediency, is a recurrent concern for students of German history and its many radical political changes. German history itself is often framed in this way. We find one variation of this trend in the attempts to come to grip with the failure of the Weimar Republic, an order supported more by people who were republicans "by reason" (*Vernunftrepublikaner*) than by conviction (*Gesinnungsrepublikaner*), a republic without republicans. We also encounter another variation in the account of the early Federal Republic, a democracy without democrats, whose success appears—with this concern in mind—as an enigma. However, things need not be that way. Working on the German Democratic Republic, however, one realizes that some of the ideas that were imposed became valued as something worth keeping; they became binding (Thériault 2004: 141).

out, "the motivation behind an action determines its 'moral worth' or 'moral content'" (1997 [1994]: 27, footnote 8).

While studying opportunism as a motive and motive talk, a response emerged, an image structurally identical to the opportunist one, but an inverted one: while the opportunist acts on self-interest, its mirror image is disinterested. In contrast to the opportunist type, this Kantian response requires a lot of real individuals: for them to show exemplary strengths and to take upon themselves the tensions that may arise from their work. The people who could be described by the former do not need to believe in what they do; for their critique, the motives and the adherence to them is important; one should believe in what one does. By way of example, think of such figures as Max Weber's scrupulous Puritan or Thomas Mann's "achievement-oriented moralist" (Lepenies 1988: 298), Johann and Thomas Buddenbrook, who are primarily acting out of a sense of duty, not self-interest. An action based on self-interest is abhorrent to the sense of duty of these two figures.

The opportunist's mirror image finds its abstract perfection in Kant's ethics and moral law, which is traditionally opposed to the utilitarian ethics we may summon in defense of the opportunistic type. Kant's ethics and moral law is a frame of reference. They are epitomized in the categorical imperative, which—in one of its declensions—enjoins one to "Act so that you treat humanity, whether in your own person or that of any other, always as an end [*Zweck*] and never as a means only [*Mittel*]" (Kant 1990 [1785]: 429).[35] As a pure form, this counter principle is difficult to conform

---

35 One should not be deterred by the terms used: the word "end" [*Zweck*] is here confusing for it often relates to instrumentality (Sullivan 1997 [1994]: 68-69). Georg Simmel opposes the moral of the categorical imperative to prostitution: "Prostitution represents behavior that is the exact opposite of this, indeed, for both parties involved. Of all human relationships, it is perhaps the most significant case of the mutual reduction of the two persons to the status of the mere means. This may be the most salient and profound factor underlying the very close historic tie between prostitution and money economy—the economy of 'means'" (1971 [1907]: 122).

to; and it must remain a model. As such, it is at once an ideal type, a heuristic tool for descriptive purposes and a normative standard for action.[36]

In the context of this study, the Kantian-like reaction was triggered by opportunism (as a motive and motive talk); it is likely to be found at the level of discourse. Emerged while outlining the opportunist type, it enables us to better outline the principled type in adding one more layer to it. As the principled type, their representatives are committed to a cause—whatever it is. What is more, the principle they act upon is impersonal. Indeed, the criticism against the use of people, or instrumentalization, needs not to extend to the concrete individuals, the representatives of the empathetic are likely to care about. The representatives of the former are likely to be against "using people" as a principle while the individuals described by the latter are likely to care for concrete individuals. As Simmel writes when talking of conceptions of individuality: "However unholy man may be, Kant says, humanity in him is holy. And Schiller: 'The idealist thinks so highly of mankind that he runs the risk of despising single men'" (1950a [1908]: 70).

1.3 Back to the Individuals

These considerations help me to better understand Behr's position and return to the police officers described so far. Behr's position displays a belief in duty and echoes the attitude of the representatives of the liberal type—both in today's Berlin and at Weimar. The police researcher exhibits a liberal conception of culture ("a German, yet heterogeneous culture") akin to the same actors and a particular "spirit" of diversity one finds within the forces. That being said, Inspector Bobkowski and his colleagues from the Political Education Unit are not as annoyed about representatives of the opportunist type as Behr and some of the people who could be described as empathetic are.

The problem with the opportunist type is, from the researcher's standpoint, that it is not grounded. In other words, its cause seems devoid of sub-

---

36 Although Weber was wary to point out the heuristic value of the ideal types, value rationality can also be seen as a normative standard for action (Schluchter 1998: 324 ff.; Manasse 1944: 42; Colliot-Thélène 1990: 78-83; Beschorner 2002: 178-183).

stance. Behr calls for a genuine belief in principles and high standards; however, the content of these principles remain vague (there are neither references to history as in the case of Inspector Bobkowski nor to particular social movements or diversity *per se* as we will see in the forthcoming chapter). The principle remains to be discerned. One could say that more than a *cause devoid of substance*; the researcher has a *cause in search of substance*.[37] Behr's motivational code is ambivalent, hard to pin down. His search of substance confers the object of his study with a disheartening and frustrating character while bestowing him with a sad outlook. As we will see when focusing on those who strive for diversity as a fact and a value in the next chapter, the content of the cause one is committed to is not irrelevant in the context of German police forces.

Behr displays the categorical-imperative-like reaction to opportunism, as his general criticism toward his research object bears witness to; yet, he is not merely critical of diversity management and the attempts undertaken in the police forces to acknowledge difference. On the one hand, he is irritated; on the other hand, strictly from the point of view of consequences, the goals he advocates are not so different from the ones claimed by proponents of diversity management. And, in the face of concrete problems, Behr (2010) backs out a little from his original positions.

Behr's positive core ideas, his own categorical imperative, could be summed up as follows: authenticity (to be embodied in the cop culture), objectivity (or: *Sachlichkeit*, to be consistent with culture of the organization), and belief (the importance of motives and the adherence to them, or: sincerity).

PART THREE: CONCLUSION

Because the sociologist, like the police officer, "is looking for the unusual" (Chan 1996: 120), I was drawn to those individuals who were committed to change in an organization hostile to it—and sometimes outright resistant (Criminal Inspector Schmitt estimates at 80 to 90 percent the proportion of colleagues who show resistance to the action plan). Those people who can be described as opportunists occupy a middle position: they are often am-

---

37 At one point, he talks about supervision (2006: 160-163).

bivalent, or indifferent to the acknowledgement of difference, let alone its promotion. I was reluctant to write this chapter, always pushing it back to the next day. I did not particularly like the people who can be referred to as opportunist. Quite frankly, our lack of interest was mutual. Overall, they were difficult to meet: they cared less, they had moved on. This was a vicious circle.

Overcoming my aversion as best I could, I could delineate the opportunist type. It was an important step. In spite of what Behr assumes, opportunism represents one way to contribute to the recognition or promotion of difference one encounters in the police forces as well as in the research on the police; and there were many officers who took this path. The exercise was also instructive because it pointed to the different meanings of opportunism, and to the relation the officers and the researchers (myself included) entertain to it. Next to motive, and motive talk, there is indeed a third dimension to opportunism: value relation. "Egoism," as a German sociologist pointed out at the beginning of the 20th century, "is an immanent counter-principle" (Simmel 1984 [1921/22]: 153). Still today, opportunism does not seem to have the loftiness and value conferred either to the "inner devotion to a cause" or to a commitment to individuals belonging to minorities. For this reason, opportunism was often met by an ambivalent, or negative value-relation while researching this study: very present in Rafael Behr, somewhat less on my part, but nevertheless more than on the part of officers like Criminal Inspector Schmitt.

In the form of a second variant of the principled type, I will present in the next chapter a group of specialists for whom diversity is both a profession and a vocation. This group corresponds to the professional carriers of diversity I knew from Canada and was eager to meet in Germany. Once I bring the second part of this book to a close, I will assess the empirical weight of the individual ideal types in the police forces and thus attempt to provide a three-dimensional picture. While assembling the types, I will return in more detail to a specific—but contested—trait of the relation toward difference in the police forces as well as cultural sources, which have manifested themselves throughout the types: a Christian heritage and a particular shade of liberalism to which a Kantian shadow was added in this chapter. In so doing, I will point to a way to interpret the picture, which will cast light on a particular spirit of diversity one encounters in German police forces.

Ms. Berger, or Social Change
(Diversity as Profession and Vocation)

As I was sipping coffee waiting for a police teacher in his office, one of my police interview partners stood up by his bookshelves and pointed to a small section he sarcastically called his "gender-mainstreaming section." He pulled out a book. Its author, a social scientist, he told me, was to come to work for the police, but it did not work out in the end: "She wrote a letter to the chief of police in which she outlined all that she wanted to change and do better." He paused, "That was not so clever."

In the course of my encounters with police officers, I was to often hear similar stories. This was a surprise. Reflecting on the relation to difference in the police in Germany, I initially assumed that there were those who wanted the recognition of difference and change. I had further assumed that those who would have contributed to it would be people like the social scientists my interview partner was referring to. I had presumed they would have experience in equal opportunity treatment programs, intercultural communication, diversity management and knowledge of the specialized literature on diversity. Had anthropologist Ulf Hannerz not described an industry of interculturalists as, "a new profession of people [...] trying to teach sensitivity toward cultural diversity to various audiences through lectures, simulation games, videos, practical handbooks and some variety of other means" (1999: 396; see also Wetterer 2002; Thomas 2006)? I had met such people in the Montreal Police Department,[1] as well as in other public

---

1   At the time of the investigation, a man of Vietnamese descent with a Masters Business Administration, was in charge of equity access programs in the Montreal Police Department.

and private organizations in Canada where similar initiatives have been undertaken and had expected to encounter people with similar backgrounds in the German police forces.[2]

Although not yet systematically, I found myself constructing one variant of a principled type. At its core, there was a group of specialists who would explicitly seek more diversity. For them, diversity was understood as a fact and a value within the forces; these were people for whom diversity would be both a profession and a vocation. The inspectors in charge of the different initiatives had different motivations to go about doing their work (a sense of duty, professionalism, care for fellow officers, a wish to educate or raise awareness, to contribute to the democratizing of the police, or to advance their careers). Not all officers originally sought to promote diversity within the police or change the organization. In contrast to the other types and their representatives, I expected diversity to be a motive, not a mere consequence of action.

I had yet to realize that these specialists were either largely absent or had failed to find their place *within police forces*, but then my curiosity was aroused. So instead of abandoning the group at this stage, I decided to further investigate. Would the conspicuous absence of specialists turn out to be of sociological relevance? Could it be a key for grasping the specificities of dealing with difference within the context of the German police? Because diversity as a profession and a vocation imposed itself first and foremost from a logical point of view and a theoretical perspective, this chapter begins differently than the previous ones: it first sketches the contours of this variant of a principled type, a construction which may show us "how the world might be, and by using them as our reference point we could show what life was [is] like in reality" (Albrow 1990: 157).

Diversity as a profession and a vocation is here an "objective possibility" (Weber 1949 [1904]: 93), which was not much—but may have been—encountered during the fieldwork.[3] The type was carved out of the literature on diversity (see, for instance, Krell and her colleagues [2007, 2006]; Faist

---

2   This is a trend one could also expect from reading job descriptions for academics in universities and some public institutions in Germany.

3   As Weber stressed, it is part of the ideal typical method that types "(...) appear in full conceptual *integrity* either not at all or only in individual instances" (Weber 1949 [1904]: 94).

[2009]; Hannerz [1999]; Wetterer [2002]), of an implicit comparison with Canada, which underlies this study, and also in contrast to the types already outlined. Having laid out my take on how diversity as a profession and a vocation might be theoretically grasped, I will then introduce a real case from the fieldwork: that of the rise—and fall—of Claudia Berger, the head of recruitment at a police academy where attempts to hire officers from post-migration backgrounds have been undertaken. Comparing Ms. Berger with the other types and the real people behind them, I examine the complex relation between ideas and a group of specialists—with their interests and their ethos—, and ground it in its cultural and historical context. While doing so, I attempt to solve the enigma, the specialists' absence, or failure: are the social characteristics of this group, the ideas they carry, or both, to be imputed for their rejection by police forces? Answering this question leads me to delineating one spirit of diversity, one that was not found in German police forces.

1. DIVERSITY AS A PROFESSION AND A VOCATION

Max Weber's concept of *Beruf* is translated as a profession and vocation, or calling. The concept is a key one to understand the Puritan of the *Protestant Ethic* (Weber 2007 [1904/1905]), but also the politician and the scientist of his two famous lectures (Weber 2004 [1917/1919]). It alludes to an occupation, specialized qualifications as well as high ethical standards—to which Max Weber, the man, was noticeably sympathetic. Drawing on the sociologist's wording, I claim that diversity is, for a group of specialists, both a profession and a vocation.

The types previously outlined emerged though the gaze of the sociologist who observes and interprets the actors' motives and the consequences of action to outline a construct that does not necessarily match the latter's account of their motives. This time, things are different: "carrying" diversity is not for specialists an unanticipated consequence of action: it is a vocation, it is a goal in itself, a value worth defending and promoting. For specialists, diversity corresponds to what is believed to make a difference and what should make a difference. Accordingly, being migrant, female, gay—culturally embedded categories that are constantly changing—is expected to have a positive impact on the actions and perceptions of the individuals.[4] The specialists make their calling a profession: the specific job must be to bring it to bear within organizations and, in turn, within society. It is a full time profession for which one is to be qualified and demonstrate experience in. These qualifications can either be in management and psychology, industrial relations, social sciences, law, or communication; the expertise can be in intercultural, antidiscrimination, or diversity management approaches. Drawing on the terminology previously used in this study, we could sum up the specialists as the only group whose members explicitly seek diversity and—according to the underlying hypothesis—succeed in bringing it about. Put differently, the motives felicitously match the consequences of his actions.

One can think of many contexts in which specialists might be encountered in the police forces: they might be commissioned to take care of officer recruitment from post-migration backgrounds, to carry out equal-opportunity treatment programs, or to conduct intercultural seminars.[5] Accordingly, their official mandate might be the inclusion of groups defined as ethnic or visible minorities, the fight against discrimination, the accommodation of religious and cultural practices, or the attainment of the organization's greater efficiency. The personal motives of specialists might be manifold: besides diversity as a goal in itself, we might assume their will to protect members of minorities or, alternatively, to give them a voice. Furthermore, specialists might draw a particular feeling of self-fulfillment in answering such a calling.

My previous experiences with initiatives dealing with the recognition of difference had led me to believe that specialists were usually key parts in such attempts. I had therefore long expected, in vain, to encounter flesh and blood specialists—until I one day ran into Claudia Berger, a woman who seemed to incorporate diversity as profession and vocation. Let me turn to her case and portray her motives, the initiatives she set up and the context in which they took place. The case is interesting as it allows me to depict a typical unfolding of a second wave of initiatives related to the recognition

---

4 For a compelling account of the constructed character of differences, see Juteau-Lee (1983).

5 Building on initiatives in human resources in the 1980s, the first such seminars were offered to prepare police officers for deployment abroad.

and promotion of difference in the police in the first decade of the 2000 while further developing the idea of diversity as vocation and profession in the German context.

2. ONE CASE: CLAUDIA BERGER

I first met Claudia Berger in 2007 at a conference dealing with police interactions with populations from post-migration backgrounds within and outside their ranks. A group of high-ranking police officers and police researchers attended the event. This was Claudia Berger's first police conference. Full of energy and teeming with ideas, she took an active part in the discussions. She stood out: it was clear to the observer that she was neither a police officer nor a police researcher. Although police researchers typically tend to stress their distance from the forces, their habitus is sometimes difficult to distinguish from those who often employ them and were often their former colleagues. What's more, Claudia Berger's indignation at some of the papers also made it obvious that she had a different stake on the issues that were being discussed.

Ms. Berger's first police conference was quite a typical one; its aim was, as far as the subject matter of this book is concerned, to compare the stated goals of police reforms to recruit police officers from post-migration backgrounds to the results achieved by the measures undertaken in their wake. As the results tended to show that the measures did not meet the objectives originally set, most speakers then went on to criticize the measures or make new recommendations. I could see that Claudia Berger was fulminating and did not agree with what was being discussed. When one of the speakers questioned the necessity of the initiatives that have been put forth since the 1990s, arguing that the acceptance of the police among the population from post-migration backgrounds had yet failed to be realized, she literally burst out with her response. Standing up, she emphatically underscored that the recruitment initiatives went well beyond their initially stated goals, that they were something good in themselves. Her reaction struck me as instructive. Sure, reforms do indeed seldom have immediate results (they have unanticipated effects, their goals evolve); but Ms. Berger's presence and reaction also attested to the transformation of these goals from pragmatic incentives to diversity as a value worth defending and promoting.

After her altercation with the police researcher, we walked down the alley to have a seat and chat. Along the way we came across a female police officer she knew and who, having heard about the theme of the conference, said it was "difficult [*es ist halt schwierig*] to hire these people [from post-migration backgrounds]." After she had gone Claudia Berger shook her head and commented that the remark was typical. "They don't want to change," she added matter-of-factly. This attitude however did not seem to deter her like the police researcher. On the contrary, she seemed to thrive on it. Who was this determined woman with bright colored hair?

Claudia Berger did not don a uniform: she was a civil employee in human resources and was also younger than the people we have so far encountered in this study. We met several times to talk about her work. Her account could be summed up as follows: after a ministerial decision, she had been assigned in 2006 by the ministry of the interior of her federal state as head of recruitment at the police academy. As the officers portrayed in the foregoing chapters, she had first enjoyed freedom in shaping her work.[6] After studying social sciences and traveling throughout Europe, the Middle East, and South America in the 1980s, Claudia Berger had been involved for several years in women's politics, either as a project worker for supportive measures programs for girls and women in industrial and technical professions, or as women's representative in a public service (*Frauenbeauftragte*). She had also been appointed to one of the regional offices of the political education agency and at the European department of a ministry of her federal state and had completed a life coach training along the way.

Although it is not clear whether Claudia Berger wanted to work within the police human resources of her federal state, this position offered her a new field to experiment with, a challenge she proudly took to heart. Let us note that Claudia Berger enters the scene later than, say, Dietmar Piontek, the Hamburg inspector at the center of chapter two. Her entry coincides with a second wave of initiatives related to what was officially referred to as the "intercultural opening" (*interkulturelle Öffnung*) of the civil service

---

6   As I knew from earlier inquiries in her federal state, her predecessors had undertaken little efforts toward special recruitment measures (interview with IX and his team, 21 May 2004).

in general, and of the police forces in particular.[7] Things had changed since Inspector Piontek's arrival: the official discourse on *diversity*, which was not present when the first candidates without a German passport were recruited in the Hamburg or Berlin police forces, was emphasizing cultural diversity (*kulturelle Diversität*)—an expression, which had become usual—for organizational efficiency purposes as well as the integration of migrants through employment in the civil service. The pragmatic incentives legitimating the first initiatives, such as the improvement of police efficiency in securing certain neighborhoods or in dealing with organized crime, have not yet disappeared. As Claudia Berger mentions dispassionately, security issues and the increasing surveillance of Muslim networks, are powerful arguments toward the acceptance of her work within the forces.[8]

Upon getting her job as head of recruitment, Claudia Berger gathered a group of colleagues around her, which included women from Turkish and Russian backgrounds. For her, it was the natural thing to do and it was not an issue that the background of her colleagues would make a difference, bringing fresh ideas. In 2007 her team undertook reforming formal recruitment practices and tests. This implied compiling statistics and getting a glimpse at what had been done in other federal states while taking part in conferences. Her mandate was to reach and attract more candidates from post-migration backgrounds and improve the forces' record in this respect. Not unlike what Inspector Piontek had done in Hamburg and Criminal Inspector Schmitt in her federal state, with the help of her colleagues, Claudia Berger launched a promotion campaign. This included publicity on the police website and in German, Turkish, and Russian-language newspapers, press meetings, and information sessions. Follow-up activities were also encouraged, notably phone calls to promising candidates, inciting them to go ahead with the tests and counseling them. Next to these measures, the formal recruitment practices and tests were modified. Whereas all my interview partners in other federal states had dismissed the idea of reforming the recruitment tests as the latter were deemed "culturally fair," Ms. Berger showed skepticism. Instead of ascribing the low recruitment levels to the

---

7 The minister of the interior of Ms. Berger's federal state had decided to take up the matter and to sign the "Charter of diversity" (*Charta der Vielfalt*).
8 Interview with CB, 18 December 2009. On the subject of the surveillance of Muslims, see Schiffauer (2006).

candidates and their lack of mastery of the German language as most of my interview partners did, she laid particular stress on the aspects that might be detrimental to candidates from post-migration backgrounds (she liked to mention some archaic words used in the tests like *veredeln* [to refine] or *Span* [shaving]). When we met later in 2007, she explained that the next step was to offer intercultural training to the recruitment officers and teach them sensitivity toward cultural diversity.[9] Claudia Berger and her team were then also using computer-standardized tests to determine which candidates were less successful on the basis of different variables.

2.1 Change as Leitmotif

Listening to Ms. Berger, with my ideal types in mind, enabled me to better grasp her while refining, interpreting, and grounding diversity as profession and vocation in a cultural and historical context.

Claudia Berger combines different motives encountered in previous types. Like the empathetic type, she cares for recruits and police students, but does not want to protect them; rather, she is at pains to strengthen their autonomy. In publications by her federal state's political education agency on the local women's movement, she writes about autonomy; she alludes to the issue on numerous occasions during our conversations. For example, she says that upon finishing her university degree, she contemplated working as a humanitarian aid but had grown increasingly critical of the colonial dimension underlying it:

"(...) I went there earlier playing with the idea, 'You now have a look and then decide whether you're going into development aid.' And then I thought, but that's not the right thing (...) the outcome for me was actually, 'they have got to go their own way.' Well, they don't actually need the support of some Europeans."[10]

---

9 This measure ("training the trainers") is similar to the ones found in police forces in many federal states where job promotions are made dependent on participation from in-house training on diversity.

10 "(...) *also ich war früher so mit der Idee dahin gefahren, 'Das guckst du dir jetzt an und entscheidest dann, ob du mal so in diese Entwicklungspolitik gehst.' Und dann danach dachte ich, aber dass so doch nicht das richtige ist (...). Nee, beziehungsweise die Erkenntnis für mich war dann eigentlich, 'Die müssen*

Not unlike the opportunist type, Ms. Berger sees her involvement in the police forces as a career challenge. However, more than being opportunistic, it is a way to realize herself.[11] Planning seminars, talks, conferences and publishing reports and brochures, she describes how she took up initiatives related to the themes she felt to be important and that she found exciting and fun (*spannend* is the word she uses). Retrospectively, she says: "Well, I've always looked for what I really enjoy, what I find really interesting and I had the opportunity to do it."[12] Like representatives of other variants of the principled type, Ms. Berger surely acts according to a cause—but hers seems to be a more *wandering one*. We can trace it back, as Claudia Berger does so herself in her biographical account, from the women's movement to the antiracist one and to what she calls her "baby," interculturalism.[13]

In contrast to the people encountered up to this point and with an eye at the question underlying this study, Claudia Berger's most striking trait is the way in which she believes in diversity and sees it as something in which she wants to serve as a contributor. Drawing on the terminology used in the previous chapters, Claudia Berger's "motivational code" could be summed up by three words: self-fulfillment, progress, and social change. More than a particular principle and beyond the frame of the police forces, her main motive is change, change toward "progressive" values. In her particular case, such values are closely connected to an emancipatory project of group autonomy (*Selbstbestimmung*) and personal self-realization (*Entfaltung*).

---

ihren Weg selber gehen.' Also sie brauchen eigentlich nicht die Unterstützung von irgendwelchen Europäern" (interview with CB, 31 July 2008).

11 Self-realization, in Simmel's language, corresponds to the perfection of personality; it needs not be opportunistic: "[...] the individual's urge toward self-perfection is not necessarily an expression of egoism. It may also be an objective ideal whose goal is by no means success in terms of happiness and narrowly [sic] personal interests but a super-personal value realized in the personality" (Simmel 1950 [1908]: 59).

12 "*Also, ich habe immer geguckt, was macht mir wirklich Spaß, was finde ich wirklich interessant und hatte auch die Gelegenheit, das auch zu tun*" (interview with CB, 18 December 2009).

13 "For Claudia Berger, "cultural diversity," is interesting, exciting, and fun. Conversely, being "German" is plain boring or bad.

Upon closer inspection, we notice that the themes Claudia Berger has dealt with, as well as her diction, echo the institutionalization of the social movements from the late 1960s onwards. Indeed, her trajectory is entangled with their themes and point to the shape they took in the German context. Our protagonist's work was notably framed within European Union-sponsored programs and political education. While working at the political education agency, Claudia Berger took up two themes: intercultural education and right-wing extremism—the latter being a typical topic of political education in Germany, which had gained renewed currency in the midst of flashes of xenophobic violence in the country at the beginning of the 1990s. Europe and political education, as we have seen in the two previous chapters have turned out to be two key positions, *Schlüsselstellungen* (Mannheim 1958 [1935]) or *Weichenstellungen* (Weber 1972 [1921]: 252; 1978b [1921]: 1209), for the pragmatic recognition and promotion of difference in Germany in general and in the police in particular.

What about new trends on cultural diversity? Although she does not make much use of the arguments in which cultural diversity is of potential utility for the organization, Ms. Berger has easily incorporated "diversity" in her vocabulary and is open to intercultural management. The few books I see in her office—books penned by authors like Friedemann Schulz von Thun Kumbier (2006) and Geert Hofstede (2006 [1980])—attest to it.

2.2 An Early Exit

Ms. Berger comes close to the "carriers of diversity" I had first expected to find when I set out to investigate diversity in German police forces: as a woman with a background in social sciences, with experience in equality treatment programs, and whose job it is to promote difference. Indeed, Claudia Berger seemed to have everything going for her. She also shared this expectation: she radiated confidence, felt qualified and competent for the task. She was determined and knew what she wanted; there was no sign of the search of substance, which conferred the police researcher we encountered in the last chapter with a sad outlook, or of the vocabulary borrowed to a liberal register, which sometimes made its holders look old-fashioned. In fact, it may well be that because I had someone as Ms. Berger in mind when I started this project that some police officers appeared somewhat "half-baked" to me.

When we met for a long-planned interview in June 2008, something unexpected happened. Claudia Berger's energy had given way to bitterness. Visibly shaken, she told me that she had been dismissed from her functions as head of recruitment at the police academy. A police officer was now again officially in charge of recruitment. Claudia Berger was demoted and now teaching social sciences at the police academy. Although she was no more in charge of recruitment, she had nonetheless agreed to meet me. She had then notified the new head of recruitment who was, I was informed, unable to attend the meeting. She had also invited another colleague who was new to this task to join us ("He is alright. He does as he is told.").

I was perplexed and did not know how to interpret the situation. Thanks to Ms. Berger's efforts and those of the team she had gathered around her, things had changed. For instance, more recruits from post-migration backgrounds had been hired. In 2009, 9.1% of successful police candidates in her federal state were from post-migration backgrounds. The aforementioned reforms of the recruitment tests had been carried out and, after the high school diploma (*Abitur*), became a general rule for taking police entry exams; an exception measure to allow candidates with a general education development diploma (*Realschulabschluß*) to take the recruitment tests was introduced.[14] Because they often hold such a diploma, Ms. Berger stressed this was also a means to reach candidates from post-migration backgrounds, while keeping the police diversified in terms of social backgrounds. New questions were also added to the standard interview to assess the intercultural competences and outlook of *all* police candidates. Thanks to Claudia Berger, the idea of cultural diversity had gradually been institutionalized in the selection process.

The measures Ms. Berger had initiated were maintained, even extended. Their effects are palpable and, as such, cannot be considered a failure; however, one is wary—in the wording used—not to infringe upon the police's principles.[15] As they were maintained, we can assume that the meas-

---

14 The successful candidates go through a preparatory year. Upon completion they get a high school diploma (*Fachabitur*) and a job within the police forces.
15 Adopting a situational approach, a research group working on intercultural competencies and inclusion in the police's personnel selection (*Interkulturelle Kompetenz und Inklusion in der Personalauswahl der Polizei*) stresses the need not to infringe upon the principle of formal equality (Leenen *et al.* 2011; see also

ures were not the source of her dismissal. What had happened? Before the police officer who was to attend our meeting arrived, I managed to ask Claudia Berger what was the reason for her transfer. She responded that she had not always sufficiently served the hierarchy. She used the word *gedient*, a verb, which resonates with the military, and continued: "You don't see it at first sight, but the police forces are military."[16] I could not find out more, as Ms. Berger's new colleague was entering the room. We talked for a while, all three of us trying to give an impression of composure.

Is Claudia Berger's demotion imputable, as she herself stresses, to the police force's rigid structure? Or, was the rapid tempo at which the modifications were carried out to blame for the surprising turn of events? When talking about change in the police, Inspector Bobkowski uses a mantra-like expression: change in the police forces, he says, "can only be achieved through homeopathic doses." From his standpoint things are clear: "Those who want radical change are bound to fail."[17] Had Claudia Berger made a mistake? I do not know what happened between our last two meetings. I did not have the occasion to ask anymore, and I might not have dared to do so anyway. That said, it came to my knowledge her case was not isolated: there were people dismissed from the forces and others who could not even cross its threshold. The woman I mentioned in the opening of this chapter who had sent a letter to the police president and whom my interview partner had talked about is such an example as well as other women I met at police conferences and within universities and state administration.

Leenen and Groß 2007). It is not clear whether the researchers share the idea or are trying, as sociologists with an ethnological angle might suggest (see Jacobsen 2009), to find a common language.

16 "*Ich habe der Hierarchie nicht immer ausreichend gedient*" (interview with CB, 27 June 2008).

17 "*Die, die radikale Änderungen wollen ... Sie müssen scheitern*" (interview with KB, 24 November 2006). Inspector Bobkowski, who incidentally does not know Ms. Berger, understands the police as a hierarchical organization. For his part, he promotes its democratization from within, through small ("homeopathic") changes. This, he stresses, is a long-term undertaking in a bureaucracy with its fair share of "energy-saving lamps" (*Energiesparlampe*) such as the police.

In the next section, I will look into the fate of the specialists and their enigma: why did they fail to establish themselves and their ideas in the police forces?

3. THE ENIGMA: THE SPECIALIST'S ABSENCE

3.1 The Specialists as Carrier Group

Specialists like Claudia Berger are likely to be women and social scientists with an expertise in antidiscrimination, intercultural matters, or diversity management. This contrasts with the male police officers with a German background who were behind most of the types previously outlined. Could this outsider status hinder the specialists in their efforts to make their place in the police forces? As interesting as this observation might be, it cannot alone solve the enigma. Inspector Dietmar Piontek, the man at the center of chapter two, had been in charge of recruiting police officers from post-migration backgrounds in Hamburg for eleven years when he was unexpectedly sent back to a patrol car. Although, according to the rotation principle, police officers theoretically change positions within the organization every five years, neither his counterparts in other federal states nor his colleagues in Hamburg or he himself had anticipated that he might do so before his retirement. When we met at the end of 2006, Inspector Piontek was still keeping touch with some of his former recruits and collected newspaper clippings on recruitment of candidates from post-migration backgrounds in the police, an issue that had become, as police officials stated, a priority (*Chefssache*) at the management level.[18]

There is, I argue, no direct correlation between the characteristics of those who can be qualified as specialists and their absence or failure within the forces; however, Claudia Berger and female social scientists are more likely than most older male police officers we have encountered so far, to be the bearers of a particular spirit of diversity and to master its specialized

---

18 Interview with DP, 23 November 2006. See the article "Ausbildungs-Aktion: Multikulti im Staatsdienst," *Hamburger Abendblatt*, 7 November 2006.

vocabulary with an assurance and ease police officers generally lack.[19] Is it this spirit—and its related idiom—that we do not find within the police forces?

3.2 The Specialists' Ideas, or Spirit of Diversity

What is this spirit? Max Weber, from whom I borrow the expression, frames the spirit of capitalism as a historical concept, or individual, that is "a complex of elements associated in historical reality which we unite into a conceptual whole from the standpoint of their cultural significance" (Weber 2007 [1904/1905]: 13). For the purpose of the present analysis, the specialists' spirit of diversity could be described as follows: it promotes the recognition of difference as a goal in itself. Such a spirit—grounded differently and subject to controversy in reality—is accompanied by an underlying claim: *one represents best one's own group interests* (see Alcoff Martin 1995). According to this claim, the best possible carriers of diversity would thus be the bearers of difference themselves, members of ethnic minorities, women—or both.

If there were a monument to be erected or a square or a street to be named to commemorate this idea, a majority woman, say a local politician from one of the federal states would have good prospects. Indeed, majority women have successfully claimed the idea according to which the interests of women are best represented by women themselves (see for example Wetterer [2002] and Krell [2007] for Germany and Andrew [2010] for Canada). They have put forth a project of emancipation and autonomy, of self-determination and self-realization, which was sometimes extended to other groups and areas. In the German case, women representatives are seen as self-evident; this claim is even enshrined in a federal law according to which only women can be women's representatives (*Frauenvertreterinnen, Frauenbeauftragten* or *Gleichstellungsbeauftragten*) at workplaces.[20]

---

19 Observing "diversity" seminars, one cannot help but think that police officers feel out-of-place. Coming from their mouths, the specialized language of gender mainstreaming and antidiscrimination is rendered in a satirical-helpless manner or with an impetus to call a spade a spade.

20 Such as in all federal and state administrations and courts (see, for instance, *Gesetz zur Gleichstellung von Frauen und Männern in der Bundesverwaltung und*

As Wetterer (2002: 131) points out, the first women's representatives constituted a carrier group that was—together with their function—instrumental for further development. Indeed, the availability of a group is of sociological relevance as it implies an array of distinct action-orientations, which are likely to have an impact on development (Kalberg 1994: 61). As mentioned in chapter four, the European Union has proved to be a key player in this respect as well as, in the particular case of Germany, some political parties such as the Greens, a party born out of the spirit of the social movements from the 1960s onwards. Together they championed the ideals of female representation.

In the literature on *diversity* within police forces, one often encounters the call to compare the situation of police officers from post-migration backgrounds to that of female police officers who gradually joined—in West Germany—the forces from the 1970s onward (see Behr 2006; Dudek 2009; Franzke 1995; van Ewijk 2012). This plea reflects, it seems, more a claim to self-representation, a particular spirit of diversity, and the trajectories of the researchers uttering it than an empirical reality or research necessity.[21] From the analytical standpoint outlined in this chapter, that of a relationship between interests and ideas of a group of actors, the empirical question is not whether we should necessarily draw a parallel between women's issues and other minorities or whether minorities actually make a difference within police forces, but more importantly: *how the specialists— among whom women are well represented—have set the conditions, which made the assumption according to which one best represents one's interests, a successful claim.*

---

in den Gerichten des Bundes [*Bundesgleichstellungsgesetz*, BGleiG], 2001, Abschnitt (section) 4, § 16).

21 In the academic literature on the police, diversity is generally linked to gender, migration background, and sexual orientation (van Ewijk 2012). Although they matter, other possible minorities, the East Germans for instance (see Dudek and Raczynsky 2002; Glaeser 2000 as well as the second chapter of this book), are never mentioned in this respect.

4. REACTIONS TO MS. BERGER

Listening to Claudia Berger and being attentive to the kind of attention she was getting, I realized that a lot of sociologists are the inheritors and carriers of this spirit of diversity. At once it became clear to me that the specialists I was looking for in the police had been in fact present all along: it was a fellow sociologist, it was one of my colleagues.[22] As such, it is no coincidence if the young social science student who transcribed the interviews I conducted with Claudia Berger wrote to tell me that she really liked her. That being said, professional sociologists may not entirely agree with Ms. Berger's methods and discourse. The protagonist of this chapter adheres to feminism, though she is not too inclined toward theories and is more concerned with praxis. She is sensitive to discrimination, but does not criticize instruments we find in such areas as gender mainstreaming, mentoring, diversity management, and antidiscrimination. These instruments might appear to some sociologists somewhat mechanical, not theoretically grounded—an argument leveled by the police researcher against diversity management—, and cosmetic; fellow sociologists might want to argue that they depoliticize social movements' struggles and the call for structural changes in tackling social inequalities.

We may want to distance ourselves from Claudia Berger and diversity as a profession and vocation.[23] However, such attempts to criticize or reject her would only attest to the narcissism of small differences. For we share her value relation (*Wertbeziehung*) to the other ideal types, are sensitive to power structures and relations, and see discrimination where representatives of most types may not—or would deny as such. We are critical of the liberal variant of the principled type for not doing enough and for abstracting the character of the individual he promotes; the empathetic type appears to us as sympathetic and well intentioned, but naïve and paternalistic while

---

22 Note that, on the other hand, not all specialists are sociologists.
23 This idea is implied by Hannerz when he writes about those he refers to as interculturalists: "From an academic vantage point one may be critical of certain of the efforts—they may seem a bit trite, somewhat inclined to stereotyping, occasionally given to exaggerating cultural differences perhaps as a way of positioning the interculturalists themselves as an indispensable profession" (Hannerz 1999: 397).

opportunism is often deemed too thin. To the measure in which the questions we address in our work concern us as sociologists and flesh-and-blood persons, and as we maintain a strong value relation toward them, we too are more or less discreet characters in the sociological investigation. Omitting this dimension often leads to the blurring of the frontiers between research and advocacy.

Because we are to some extent specialists, we are—at least partly—blind to changes that have indeed taken place within the police forces and to groups of actors who have contributed to it and have grounded them in the welfare of fellow officers, the democratization of police forces, or the advancement of one's career. It is indeed symptomatic that books, which—after being critical of the police culture in several chapters—end up with the surprising conclusion that things have changed (see, for instance, Dudek's interesting book [2009: 259] as well as Behr's book discussed in the previous chapter [2010]). As we know, the relation between intention and consequences is, more often than not, a complicated and unpredictable business. When we concentrate too much on official discourses on diversity rather than practice, or on the motives invoked to the detriment of the consequences of action as a starting and ending point of our investigations, we run the risk of blinding ourselves to change and to the variety of motives underlying action—not mentioning the potential to explain an order.[24]

The attitude toward difference, which we specialists are used to or would like to see animate the organization, meets resistance within German police forces. Despite the prevailing discourse and the apparent immobility of formal criteria and institutions, change cannot be denied since Inspector Piontek's early days in Hamburg.[25] Evidence is, for example, that what started as the granting of a permission, an exception rule to the civil service law to hire nonationals—an exception confirming the rule of homogeneity

---

24 Even Criminal Inspector Schmitt, after telling me the anecdote about the demonstrators and the undercover cop, toned down the arguments she had first invoked. She conceded that things look different in practice, that it is often difficult, and sometimes impossible, to appoint police officers from post-migration backgrounds for specific tactical purposes.
25 Nikola Tietze calls "dynamic immobilism" this pattern of small and inconspicuous changes within stable social institutions which, she argues, is typical of Germany (2008: 237).

and first legitimated on utilitarian or pragmatic grounds—, has turned into the promotion of candidates from post-migration backgrounds and efforts to change the police as an organization. And although the specialists' spirit of diversity does not characterize the empathetic type, some variants of the principled type, and the opportunist type; the motives of the real police officers I described in the previous chapters behind them have sometimes changed. In their own way, some of them have become specialists, or active carriers of diversity. When they did, they had to experience first hand with an organization that is resistant to diversity as a profession and a vocation.

Let us return to the question raised at the outset of this chapter: are the social characteristics of the specialists, the ideas they carry, or both, to be imputed for their absence in police forces? More than the specialists' characteristics or the desired tempo of changes, it is their spirit of diversity and the individual autonomy the group claims that irritate most within police forces. The letter sent to the police president I mentioned in the opening of this chapter epitomizes this gesture of autonomy that causes such irritation. The individual of the police forces—whether man or woman, from post-migration backgrounds or not—is to a large part an abstract one, and the real one must have a "thick skin." In the last chapter of this book, I will return to this particular way to apprehend the individual when dealing with the police as a form of organization and its ethos, what observers and actors refer to as "cop culture."

5. Conclusion: Meeting Up Again in a Few Years

Claudia Berger's case points to particular actors, their values, and mutual irritations among those who contributed to, or commented on, the acknowledgement of difference within police forces. As such, it turned out to be the missing piece of the puzzle, which will be helpful in pointing to the characteristics of the "successful" carriers of diversity in the Germany police forces, the language they have at their disposal to talk about differences and the way they deal with it. After gradually putting "together out of the individual parts which are taken from historical reality to make it up" (Weber 2007 [1904/1905]: 13), in the final two chapters I will be able to describe the relation toward difference, the spirit of diversity prevailing within police forces, and to explain it by grounding it in particular motives, their historical and cultural context, as well as in the context of the German police forces. In so doing, I will point to a particular and contested way to deal with difference and to apprehend the individual.

Will diversity as a profession and vocation make its way through the police forces with the passing of time and the recruitment of more candidates from post-migration backgrounds? This question could be at the center of a follow-up event to the 2006 conference where I first met Claudia Berger. Who would we meet if we were to attend this conference? Because Inspector Bobkowski retired, we might become acquainted with his designated successor, a male police officer from a German background and, eventually, one of the political education teachers of Turkish background. Provided she finds the time, the Berlin delegation might be led by Brigitte Winter. A police officer who, like Inspector Piontek in Hamburg, organized discussion groups for officers from post-migration backgrounds in her beat, she was once approached by police officials to take charge of issues related to "diversity." Brigitte Winter has, in the meantime, been promoted to a high rank in the police hierarchy. As we know, Inspector Piontek changed jobs; Tamara Schwarz, a young female police officer, replaced him part-time. Her supervisor, a senior male officer, is likely to attend the event. Criminal Inspector's Schmitt's successors are also likely to be present since the police authorities of her federal state seem to judge such conferences important. Police researchers and a few specialists, or interculturalists, are likely to join police delegations as consultants, not as members of the forces, whether uniformed or civil.

What about Claudia Berger? She is still around. She advises the recruitment section at the police academy on projects conducted and mentors police students in the framework of the seminars she offers. Much of what she instigated (initiatives, instruments, courses) is still in place, emulated in other police departments, and recommended by new research teams (Leenen et al. 2011; Leenen and Groß 2007).[26] In 2009 she took part in a

---

26 Between 2009 and 2012, a group of researchers carried out, a study on intercultural qualification and promotion of cultural diversity in one federal state. *Interkulturelle Qualifizierung und Förderung kultureller Diversität in der Polizei NRW* (Leenen et al. 2011) recommends institutionalizing the idea of cul-

working group set up at the federal state level to further examine the recruitment of police officers from post-migration backgrounds, intercultural education, and antidiscrimination measures on the workplace aimed at employees from post-migration backgrounds, and the possibility of setting up an Internet platform on religious and ethnic communities in Germany. She still strives for change and does not shy away from provocation, although she is no more combative.

Would Claudia Berger go to such a conference? When I last met her at the end of 2009, she confided that she felt she has accomplished her work and was in search of taking on new challenges. Pouring herself tea, she said: "I fear a bit that when the topic 'intercultural competence' becomes so to speak a normal topic in the organization, well that I simply have to see to it... Yes, where is my place, then?" She added smiling: "What do I do now? (…). I get bored. That's a bit my problem. And which theme it could be, at the moment I really don't know yet. And which one could interest me, that's another question. Well, in this respect I'm a bit at a loss at the moment. I don't know whether you can understand that?"[27]

---

tural diversity in the police's personal selection, qualification, and promotion processes.

27 "*Ich habe so n bisschen die Befürchtung, wenn dieses Thema 'interkulturelle Kompetenz' sozusaguen als Alltagsthema in die Organisation übergeht, ja dass ich einfach gucken muss... Ja, wo ich dann bleibe. (...) Was mache ich jetzt? (...). Dann wird es für mich langweilig. Das ist so n bisschen mein Problem. Und welches ein neues Thema sein könnte, dass seh ich im Moment überhaupt noch nicht. Und welches mich dann interessieren könnte, das ist ja noch mal die andere Frage. Also insofern bin ich da jetzt im Moment auch so 'n bisschen ratlos. Ich weiß nicht, ob Sie das nachvollziehen können?*" (interview with CB, 18 December 2009).

III. A Three-Dimensional Picture

The Details and the Overall Picture

Reflecting on painting, art historian Daniel Arasse (2004) writes that if one looks at a picture long enough and lets one's gaze float, something stands out (*fait écart*) and interrogates the viewer. In his books, he argues for what he calls a "*histoire rapprochée du détail*," a close-up history of painting (Arasse 1996 [1992], also 2000, 2004). Instead of leveling out details that may seem to stand in the way of interpretation by making them "normal" or "banal," he suggests lingering on them. One's reaction to these details is often, he contends, a key for interpreting a picture.

While writing the previous chapters, I soon found out that delineating ideal types is not unlike painting. Like the painter drawing contours of what he sees—lines that do not exist in nature—the sociologist must describe what he observes, but was not *already* there, to explain it (Houle 1987: 85). Social reality is sometimes difficult to work with. In constructing, organizing, and describing my empirical material, details stood in the way. Beyond the initial irritations they provoked in the research, those details often proved to be starting points to outlining ideal types or ways leading to the recognition of difference within German police forces.

Starting with the portrait of one inspector, Dietmar Piontek, the police officer in charge of recruiting candidates from post-migration backgrounds in Hamburg, I outlined a first type, the empathetic one. The type was, it seemed, grounded in a Culture Protestant pastoral care of the soul. I was a little disconcerted. Was what I was seeing not an over interpretation on my part, a sociologist trained in the field of religion? No, it adequately described a possible motive and a way to deal with difference, albeit not the only one. In Berlin, I encountered Inspector Klaus Bobkowski, a political education teacher and lay historian. At that stage of the fieldwork, I had already conducted several interviews; what the Berlin inspector was saying seemed to not represent anything new. It was in line with what I was hearing in the police forces and resonated with the discourse that those I describe as specialists label as conservative and paternalistic. Yet, to my surprise, the inspector also referred to liberal figures of the Weimar Republic. This detail, which first puzzled me, later helped me to see that the motives underlying the inspector's action could not simply be superposed to the discourse frowned upon by the specialists; they pointed to another type, one devoted to a cause (*Dienst an der Sache*).

The encounter with Inspector Bobkowski was pivotal for the present research. From then on the research unfolded. I saw the types emerge and their contours appear with more precision. I could revisit and sharpen the empathetic type while watching as another type; the opportunist one, epitomized in Criminal Inspector Elke Schmitt (and its twin or mirror image) detached itself from the mass of empirical material. Another variant of the principled type emerged in the form of a group of specialists for whom diversity is both a profession and a vocation. This last figure was different than the previous ones: it sprung from an implicit comparison with Canada and a discourse on "diversity" one sometimes finds among academics. All along, I had expected to encounter this group of specialists within the forces, but it only materialized toward the end of the fieldwork just to disappear soon after. Claudia Berger, a former women's representative and a person who could be described as a specialist, did not stay long in the police forces.

Whereas I treated the ideal types in the previous chapters individually, and thus on equal grounds, the time has now come to assemble them together into a single and three-dimensional picture. In so doing, two details I had not noticed before catch my eye: the striking resemblance, or the common characteristics, of the actors appearing on the foreground of the picture, those whose motives and ideas stand in relation with the principles of police forces and its spirit, and the lasting impression that the picture has gone somewhat yellow before its time, that it looked outdated, even before it was finished. In this chapter, I dwell on these two details as a way to interpret the larger picture. The first detail brings out a characteristic but contested trait of the relation toward difference in the police forces. The second detail hints at a set of ideas that have preserved this trait in the specific context of the police forces while conferring it, from today's perspective, an outdated character. In the last section, I discuss two possible standpoints from which diversity can be examined within German police forces and how they influence the way we define, describe, and measure it as well as access change.

1. FIRST DETAIL: THE ACTORS' STRIKING RESEMBLANCE

All along the second part of the study, I was attentive to the different motives, which were characteristic of the ideal types: the care for the welfare of fellow officers, a sense of duty, or a contribution to the democratizing of the police, to educating or raising awareness, self-interest, or the will to advance one's career, professionalism, and social change. If one takes Claudia Berger as a counterpoint, Dietmar Piontek, Klaus Bobkowski and Elke Schmitt, those I had contrasted on the basis of the motives underlying their action, share striking similarities.

The people who contributed to the acknowledgement of difference were no outsiders to the police, at least not in the literal, or sociological, sense: they were police inspectors. As is usual in the forces, they had learned their new trade on the job. The officers were not managers by profession, as in the case of civil employees in charge of human resources or equal opportunity treatment programs, or as might be expected when glimpsing at the experiences of other countries or when perusing through the literature on "diversity." Nor were they experts holding a degree in intercultural management, intercultural communication, or industrial relations. They were all newcomers. Indeed, they were, for the most part, dilettantes. Perhaps this is no surprise for officers who are meant to change their field of activities in five-year-turns. With time, they often become self-made experts in their new field of activity. As I could witness following officers over time, their motives changed. What was a consequence of action had sometimes become something they bestowed with value. Drawing on a German expression, one could say that the officers who, as a result of their actions, contributed to the recognition of difference within the forces had sometimes literally "jumped over their own shadows."

Although most of the officers encountered had not all originally sought the acknowledgment or promotion of difference within the police forces, or even aspired to change the organization, they eventually contributed to it nonetheless (through the recruitment of candidates from post-migration backgrounds, publicity, in-house training, or the commemoration of the past); sometimes, they became mediators, border crossers, and even advocates of minorities. Against the commonly shared assumption, especially among those I referred to as specialists, that "certain issues are 'owned' by the groups that have a stake in them" (Joppke 2003: 5), the people I met often came to act as the official or unofficial representatives of members of ethnic (and religious) minorities. In contrast to similar initiatives in countries such as, say, Canada where women or people from post-migration backgrounds, or often both, have representation as members of the police force, the officers I met are not members of minorities; they were all ethnic Germans and, often times, male.

A Note on Representation ("Stellvertretung")

In suggesting a concept and a way to apprehend those who act as mediators or representatives, Johannes Weiß made me see this detail in a sharper light. In *Handeln und handeln lassen* (1998), the sociologist sets out to develop several ideas toward a sociology of representation. While the notion of representation is, he argues, central to politics, law, and theology, it is strikingly absent from sociology.[1] Yet, representation is, for him, nothing less than the missing link to the fundamental concepts of sociology.[2]

Weiß added a telling subtitle to his book, *Über Stellvertretung*. Unlike the English language, German distinguishes between *Stellvertretung* and *Repräsentation*. The former implies an *action* of an individual or group who speaks and acts on behalf of others. The latter necessarily connotes a degree of resemblance or correspondence between the representative and the represented, be it at the symbolic level or as a pure statistical mean

---

1 For an English text on the subject, see Weiß 1992; for references on the case of theology, see Bauke-Ruegg (2003).

2 For an exception, Weiß refers to Weber (1972 [1921]: 25, 1978a [1921]: 46-48) who briefly hints at the relation between representatives and represented from the angle of the accountability of action and its consequences (*Chancen und Konsequenzen*); and also to Simmel on the delegation of duties and responsibility to the group (1950 [1908]: 133-135).

(Weiß 1998: 189, footnote 71).[3] As the subtitle of his book hints at, Weiß favors *Stellvertretung* as a sociological concept, which he defines as follows: "By 'activity of representation' [*stellvertretendes Handeln*], we understand an activity (in the sense of recognition, decision, intervention, acting on or acting upon) of certain people (individuals or small authorized groups) to accomplish *on behalf of* individuals, groups, or so-called 'legal' persons or corporative actors" (1998: 18, I underline).[4] This choice of definition, as well as its wording, is not a trivial one: in defining representation as activity, Weiß thus inscribes it in the realm of empirical, or Weberian, sociology.

At the heart of intermediate social relations, the *Stellvertretung* embodies a third way between autonomy and heteronomy, between choosing for oneself (self-determination [*Selbstbestimmung*]), and a decision taken by a third party (*Fremdbestimmung*). Once one starts to think about representation from this angle, one sees it everywhere. Indeed, one can identify several manifestations of this type of activity and its bearers: as delegates, deputies, lawyers, guardians (*Vormünder*), middlemen, smugglers, proxies (Weiß 1998: 40). These figures all *mediate*, but they do not necessarily intend to *conciliate* as the word may otherwise suggest; the motives underlying their action can be manifold.

Weiß identifies three characteristics of the *Stellvertretung* (1998: 187): first, it refers to the activity of an authorized person or group who speaks on behalf of others whereby—and this is the second point—the represented carry the consequences of the representative's action. Weiß adds a third characteristic, which goes beyond the Weberian frame: the activity of representation is limited in time and in scope, its realm is circumscribed (1998: 16-17, 187).

---

3   From the 17th century on, representation means in English both to symbolize and to stand for. The uncertainty has, Raymond Williams comments, continued until today (1983 [1976]: 266-269).

4   "*Unter 'stellvertretendem Handeln' wird also ein Handeln (im weiteren Sinne: als Erkennen, Entscheiden und tätiges Eingreifen, als Tun und Erleiden) verstanden, welches von bestimmten Menschen (einzelnen Subjekte oder kleinen, handlungsfähigen Gruppen) im Namen anderer Subjekte, Individuen und Kollektive, aber auch sogenannter 'juristischer Personen' oder korporativer Akteure, vollzogen wird*" (Weiß 1998: 18).

Considering representation as an activity allows for a distancing of oneself from a common understanding of "representative," one widely shared among specialists. And because contemporary sociologies—most notably in its postcolonial (Spivak 1988) or feminist variants (Alcoff Martin 1995)—generally understand representation as *Repräsentation*, it also forces me to take a step back, to appreciate that *Repräsentation* is nothing natural while being, of course, aware of the sensibility toward issues of agency and advocacy these authors express. If I am indebted to Johannes Weiß for the first characteristic, I however question the second one: are, I wonder, the represented accountable for the action of the representatives? Do they typically carry the chances and consequences of action? This emphasis on the actors' imputability bears, it seems, the imprint of Weberian sociology whose origins are to be found in legal science and legal history (Turner and Factor 1994);[5] they might be here slightly displaced. After all, the police officers portrayed in this book who acted as representatives carried, at least at the moral level, the consequences of their action and the responsibility for it. The third aspect is the one that retains my attention the most. It points to a fiction (and not a reality), to a belief in the limited and circumscribed character that grounds representation as a type of activity. Underlying this characteristic is the assumption that speaking for, acting, and deciding on behalf of others is only acceptable as long as the represented cannot do it themselves; that they should do it themselves if they could (Weiß 1992; 1998: 18). Although heteronomy can of course be chosen, there is a tension inherent to this type of intermediate relation: one fears that it could be a threat to individual autonomy and could take on an authoritarian character if it were to become institutionalized (Weiß 1998: 187).

Understood as *Stellvertretung*, representation raises empirical questions, but also normative ones. As such, it is a border concept of sociology (Weiß 2006): it provides avenues for empirical sociology while raising a series of tensions. Indeed, as soon as one touches upon issues of integrity and identity of those who are represented, it raises a normative dimension—both for the actors under examination and the observers expressing a concern for

---

5   Incidentally, Weiß uses the term *Stellvertreter* and not *Vertreter*, thus privileging a legal connotation; perhaps unwittingly, he makes of the attorney the figure *par excellence* of this type of intermediate relation.

issues of agency and advocacy (Thériault and Bilge 2010: 12). In the previous chapters, I have mainly dealt with this dimension from the point of view of police officers, paying particular attention to the existential tensions, life contradictions, and dilemmas they were—freely to varying degrees—confronted with as a result of their action.[6]

In the next section, I turn to the police forces and examine them with the activity of representation in mind. I advance the following hypothesis: representation without resemblance (*Stellvertretung ohne Repräsentation*), the detail that had struck my attention and was shaped by the reading of Weiß' book, is a characteristic trait of the treatment of difference in German police forces. In other words, I argue that there is representation, but no mirror representation. Before attempting to place it in relationship to the police principles and organization, I first turn to some of the manifestations I encountered during fieldwork and then stage a fictional conversation between the persons portrayed thus far in the chapters to assess how police officers apprehend this particular type of activity.

1.1 A Specific Trait of the Relation Toward Difference...

Although I did not call it as such, I kept coming across the figure of the *Stellvertreter* while writing this book. It appeared under different guises.

With the passing of time Inspector Piontek became, as I showed in chapter two, the unofficial representative of the officers he had recruited. He counseled them and, although it was not part of his official mandate, he spoke and intervened on their behalf in cases of conflicts. This is rather peculiar as it goes against the principle according to which, in cases of conflict, an officer first talks to his or her immediate superior (*Dienstweg*).

Remember Inspector Bobkowski's and his colleagues' endeavors to commemorate Bernhard Weiß, an observant Jew who became deputy chief of the Berlin police forces in the 1920s? He too was such a representative. Uncompelled, the inspector had stressed that he did not want the help of the Jewish community so as to avoid, he had added, special treatment. The inspector's efforts constitute not only an example of treatment of difference,

---

6 An alternative would have been possible, that of a value discussion (Weber 1949 [1917]).

but also of a kind of representation without resemblance, even if of a posthumous kind. Because of a majority resolution in the district of Mitte to name streets only after women as long as women remained underrepresented, the plan to name a square or a street after Weiß failed. Police officials were annoyed to see their plan not realized. Reacting to the resolution and its implementation, they underlined the importance of Weiß as a democratic figure at the time of the Nazi regime and argued that the principle of equitable representation underlying the district's memory politics—which wording echoes the legislation on equal treatment of women and men—was not an absolute necessity (see Oloew 2006).

Aside from the inspectors presented in greater details in the chapters, I came across many other *Stellvertreter* specimens while researching the book: the person in charge of the *Clearingstelle* in Berlin mentioned in chapter three provides such an example. The *Clearingstelle* is an ombudsman or mediation office set up under the aegis of Inspector Bobkowski in 1993 to deal with complaints stemming from the migrant population involved in conflicts with the police.[7] The position is currently held by a male police officer from a German ethnic background. If I was at first somewhat irritated by the fact that a police officer represented the interests of non officers in conflicts with the police, this did not seem to be a contested matter—at least not in this case. There were counterexamples in other cities: in Frankfurt (Main) and Hanover, so-called mediators (*Mittler*) act as mediators between the police and the population they serve; these are civil employees from post-migration backgrounds (Leiprecht 2002: 38-44).

Another telling example of representation without resemblance would be the person in charge, between 1992 and 1996, of representing gay officers in Berlin (*Ansprechpartner für gleichgeschlechtliche Lebensweise*, formerly called *Schwulenbeauftragter*). A heterosexual man, he called himself a *Berufsschwuler*, a "gay by profession" (Uth 1996: 151). Although things have changed since then as openly gay officers now occupy this function in Berlin, in at least one other federal state, a heterosexual acts as a gay representative.

---

7   *Clearingstelle* is a neologism, which borrows from English, but relates to the German *klären* ("to clear up," "to settle"). There are other such offices in the police forces, for the youth or road accidents for instance.

As mentioned in the previous five, majority women have successfully claimed the idea according to which the interests of women are best represented by women themselves. The representation of women by women and the principle of equal representation are enshrined in equal treatment legislation at the state and federal levels (*Landesgleichstellungsgesetz* and *Allgemeines Gleichbehandlungsgesetz*); they have to be enforced in public administrations, the police forces included (Dudek 2009: 71). Next to the women's movement of the 1970s and 1980s, the claim to representation spread to other social movements. The literature on antidiscrimination shows that the principle tends to expand its logic to other groups and areas: such as ethnic, religious, and sexual identities (Calvès 2004). Of course, these claims do not equally materialize according to regional and national contexts. In German police forces, it formally applies to women—although young and old officers are represented in police unions and gay officers have some associations.

1.2 ... But a Contested One (A Fictional Conversation)

While I am writing these lines I think about the people I met in the forces while researching this book. Based on observations and questions I asked them (such as "who should, or would be likely to, replace you once you leave your job?" or: "who would be good candidates as recruits?"), I decided to convene a fictional conversation with them and talk about representation without resemblance. Thinking about what the actors see—or might see—as right, or contested, enables me to better grasp the meaning conferred on this particular type of activity and the legitimacy they bestowed onto it. Because the conversation also allows for distinguishing subjectively intended and objectively valid "meanings," it helps putting representation without resemblance in relation with the context and principles of police forces.

Barbara Thériault [sociologist]:
"What do you think about representation without resemblance?"

Dietmar Piontek [inspector described as empathetic]:
"Representation without resemblance you said, well yes... Yes, I represented the recruits... There was no alternative to this type of representation."

Inspector Piontek sees no injustice. He maintains the tension, the fiction of representation. He acts for the represented until they can stand for themselves. In 2004, he could not conceive minority representation. Before being autonomous, he believes all recruits need to be introduced in the forces. Recruits from post-migration backgrounds confirmed the need for such representation. They confided that they were sometimes not taken seriously when facing problems with colleagues, and had sought Piontek's help.[8]

Klaus Bobkowski [inspector described as committed to a cause]:
(matter-of-factly) "Representation is actually the normal mode of functioning within the police forces... It might be a problem for you, but not for the police. In the forces, the immediate superior acts as the representative; he is a police officer. There should be no special treatment, though one should look for another, be ware of upcoming problems."

Inspector Bobkowski does not see the activity of representation as problematic. After all, he is the one who put in place the *Clearingstelle*, the mediation office—led by a police officer—dealing with complaints stemming from the migrant population involved in conflicts with the police. That said, the inspector also tones down his claim. Before retiring, he made sure that two officers of Turkish origin joined the political education team and he mentioned that he would have liked to recruit a woman too; however, he added jokingly in his farewell address at his retirement party, "Women are too good and leave."

I turn to Elke Schmitt. I know that her office companion, a liaison officer for Muslim institutions (the so-called Islambeauftragten one encounters in the police forces), is not Muslim. I point to her companion's chair.

Barbara Thériault:
"Would it not be normal to choose Muslims for such a task?"

---

8 Participant observations, Hamburg Police Academy, 17 June 2004 and 23 November 2006.

Elke Schmitt [criminal inspector described as opportunist]:
"What do you mean?" (and after a while): "Yes, it could be neat."

The same question was posed in 2010 to liaison officers for Muslim institutions. When asked if Muslims should be appointed as liaison officers, the interlocutors often did not first understand the question. After a pause, they then generally agreed that it might indeed be a good thing. Like Criminal Inspector Schmitt, they did not express much concern for this issue. In August 2010, there were 5% of all liaison officers for Muslim institutions in her federal state who were from post-migration backgrounds among whom half were women. As one interview partner put it: "They are not used to this task."[9]

When Criminal Inspector Schmitt talked about being one of the first recruits to go straight to the investigation service after her training and about her mandate to recruit candidates from post-migration backgrounds and to incorporate them in the forces, she never mentioned being a woman nor the importance of being a woman for being appointed in charge of the strategic plan to increase the number of officers from post-migration backgrounds in the forces. For her, there seems to be no tension, no dilemma to the activity of representation.

Ms. Berger is getting nervous and impatient; she wants to talk.

Claudia Berger [former head of recruitment described as specialist]:
"The experience of being part of a minority is important, and good. One of the first things I did when I was appointed as head of recruitment was," she reminds us, "to create a group with women colleagues from post-migration backgrounds."

Claudia Berger expresses a clear position, one differing from the other discussion partners. She favors resembling representation. For her, it is the natural thing to do; it is not an issue that a minority experience makes a difference, and a positive one.

When she speaks, one notices that she masters what could be described as the official language of "diversity," words which usually (like gender mainstreaming, antidiscrimination, or intercultural training) fall clumsily from the mouths of some police officers or are accompanied by sarcasm

---

9   Interview with LC, 31 August 2010.

and a mocking tone (see also Wetterer on the use of the word "gender" [2002: 138]).

Barbara Thériault:
"If I may sum up, my dear conversation partners, I would say that the activity of representation (*stellvertretendes Handeln*) is a characteristic trait of the relation or attitude toward difference with the German police forces, though a contested one."

"(…) the idea of representation without resemblance is neither shocking nor a problem; it is, we could say, indifferent to police principles. However, it clashes with the spirit of diversity advocated by specialists like Claudia Berger for this type of representation tends to suppress difference. That said, not all police officers necessarily react to the idea of representation in the same manner. In fact, it is not excluded that Inspector Piontek experienced what was portrayed by his colleagues as a tragic faith—being sent back to patrol after being counselor for candidates of foreign origins for eleven years—precisely because he had, in part, adopted the spirit characteristics of specialists."

"When looking at phenomena such as representation, I try to be attentive to the complex relation between ideas, interest, and the ethos of a group, that's what I do. Of course, I know that they are other possible standpoints to gauge on diversity in the forces, which would accentuate other characteristics as essential. I will return to this point if you bear with me."

There is some agreement, but my conversation partners are not dissatisfied; they interrupt me. They want me to resolve the issue:

Elke Schmitt (annoyed, but still polite):
"Does it work or not? I mean, does one need to 'share the characteristics of the bearers of difference' as you put it? Which way works best to acknowledge and promote difference in the forces?"

Barbara Thériault (knowing that there is no way out, no possible retreat):
"There are several possible paths to acknowledge, talk about, or promote difference. It is possible to find an appropriate way within each of them. Many things work: it need not be the specialist's way, although it surely is an alternative."

"(...) You have shown me the tensions inherent to the different paths, and I thank you for that. I've mirrored them to you in a condensed form. The question is, now how much discrimination are you willing to tolerate? You don't like the word discrimination? O.K., let's put it this way: 'How thick must a police officers' skin be?' How much conflict is acceptable? And how much individual autonomy is wished for? It's a matter of choice. In the end, it's up to you to decide."

I stop, though I doubt my conversation partners are now satisfied with my answer.

There is evidence that representation without resemblance is indeed a characteristic trait of the treatment of difference in German police forces. Yet, there is also resistance, as voiced by Ms. Berger and also some police officers. Occasionally, police officers showed signs of uneasiness with regard to their competencies and the right to talk on behalf of others. For instance, when I asked a trade union representative who had organized seminars for police recruits and officers from post-migration backgrounds to meet me, he felt hesitant and asked me if he should bring a colleague, a woman of Turkish descent, along.[10] And when a journalist asked the representative for gay officers within the Berlin police forces if there was not something special about being a "gay by profession," he is reported to have answered by the negative: "After all, the foreigners' commissioner is not a Turkish woman, the drug advisor is no junky."[11] However, in the answer to the journalist who had presented him as a "former marathon runner and now trainer at a triathlon club who is not gay himself," the need to justify himself is palpable.

This uneasiness attests to a certain tension and to the partial institutionalization of the idea, or the spirit of diversity advocated by the specialists. To be sure, things might change in the future. Yet, seen from the special-

---

10 Interview with GM and TP, 12 June 2007.
11 *"Der frühere Marathonmann und heutige Trainer eines Lauf- und Triathlon-Klubs ist selbst nicht schwul. Schließlich sei die Ausländerbeauftragte keine Türkin, der Drogenbeauftragte kein Fixer"* (Hasselmann, Fred, "Heinz Uth, Schwulenbeauftragter bei der Polizei." *Berliner Zeitung*, 16 November 1995. URL: http://www.berlinonline.de/berliner-zeitung/archiv/.bin/dump.fcgi/1995/1116/politik/0110/index.html (accessed, 22 July 2011).

ists' standpoint, the idea of representation without resemblance is remarkably resistant to change. As it turns out, *stellvertretendes Handeln* bodes well with the belief in the neutrality of the civil servant (*Beamter*) and, as we have seen from the fictional conversation and the real interviews, is deemed normal by police officers. More than a necessity, the police are—as an organization—*indifferent* to the idea of representation without resemblance so dear to specialists.

2. SECOND DETAIL: THE WEIMAR CONNECTION

Next to Inspectors Piontek and Bobkowski, the person in charge of the Berlin *Clearingstelle*, and some representatives of gay police officers, I also came across another figure of representatives while researching this study, and that is when things took an interesting turn. Remember the liberal patrons of men such as Bernhard Weiß and other Jews who acted as their middlemen in the public service at the time of the Empire and the Weimar Republic (chapter three)? These men stemming from the educated liberal middle class embody another figure of the representative, an important one, one that I had not considered problematic.[12]

Whereas the liberal patrons or advocates of Jews at the end of the 19th century and the beginning of the 20th century did not strike me as unusual, the police officers I was observing presented an astonishingly outdated character. Where I expected to encounter specialists like Ms. Berger, inspectors were referring to Weimar. Contrasting these temporalities points once again to a value relation we (sociologists) entertain today toward difference and according to which this type of representation is problematic. This reaction does not mean that representation is *per se* impossible, or bad, but that it is contested. In the present context, and even when they promoted ideas similar to those of liberal men under Weimar, the police officers' liberal attitude is, today, conservative in outlook (see Elias 2001 [1929]). Perhaps the portrait, which can be drawn from the relation and treatment of difference within the police forces, might be qualified as liberal conservative. This is an idea I will explore in the next chapter as a

---

12 Representation for Jews—though not yet for women—was probably considered a pending necessity among Weimar liberals (see Geller 2006).

means to describe in greater details the particular spirit of diversity within the police forces.

I pause and think to myself: Could a German version of liberalism be the formalin that has preserved the idea of representation or *Stellvertretung*—and with it perhaps a certain spirit of diversity—intact? If this type of representation bodes well with the belief in the neutrality of the civil servant and the specific logic of this organization, it does not seem to be limited to the police forces. Indeed, it seems that this type of representation can be extended beyond the case of the police forces. What about the national and federal commissioners for the integration of immigrants, those whose official mandate is to represent nonnational residents and refugees (the former *Ausländerbeauftragten*, now called *Integrationsbeauftragten* [*Beauftragte der Bundesregierung für Migration, Flüchtlinge und Integration*])? In 2007, Maria Böhmer, the federal commissioner, announced a shift in politics: "We do not talk about migrants anymore," she said, "but we talk with them."[13] Although undeniable, this change also attests to continuity: as most of her counterparts at the state level and representatives in state institutions, Maria Böhmer is from a German ethnic background.[14]

In the next and last chapter, I deal in detail with the police as a peculiar form of organization, the status of the individual in it, and a German version of liberalism. As a way to conclude this chapter, let us reflect on two possible standpoints, or ways, from which the picture can be drawn and the way it impacts the ensuing description, measurement of diversity, and assessment of change within police forces.

---

13 "*Wir reden nicht mehr über die Migranten, sondern mit ihnen*" (Nationaler Integrationsplan). URL: http://www.bundesregierung.de/Webs/Breg/DE/Bundes regierung/BeauftragtefuerIntegration/NationalerIntegrationsplan/nationaler-intregrationsplan.html (accessed 5 September 2007).

14 In April 2010, I asked the commissioners of all German federal states whether they came from a post-migration background. Of the 16 representatives, only one answered with an affirmative, one hesitated, but finally said no. She possibly hinted at her Jewish background. Six representatives are women.

3. THE PICTURE AS A WHOLE

Closing up on details, I try to put in perspective my material and bring out a three-dimensional picture. What do the details tell us about the picture as a whole? What do we see when we look at it? The final picture one puts together—the people portrayed, their location, the sharpness of their contours—changes according to the standpoint one chooses to adopt, one that aims to measure "diversity" or to understand relations to difference through the construction of ideal types of the motives underlying action.

Standpoint 1. Most observers, among whom the police researchers were well represented, were first and foremost interested in the types of actors that were the most present in the field. Seen from this angle, the less committed type, the one characterized by opportunism and self-interest as a motive, appears in the foreground. If Criminal Inspector Elke Schmitt did not hold her position long in human resources, there were other people like her, as I could experience first hand during fieldwork and as I could read in the literature on "diversity" and difference and the police. Those who paint such a picture define diversity and measure its success by counting the numbers of recruits and police officers from post-migration backgrounds in the forces (Hunold, Klimke, Behr, Lautmann 2010) and, eventually, their level of retention and promotion (van Ewijk 2012). They examine official statements and goals; as a result, they are likely to point to modest changes and be rather critical of the meager numbers. Interestingly, the fact that they examine official statements and goals, the "concrete outcomes or indicators of performance against which outcomes can be measured" (Chan 1996: 125) contributes to the institutionalization of the criteria set by people who could be in part described as specialists. While the opportunist type is in the foreground of their picture, the principled (or liberal) and empathetic types might not be seen in their picture, or only in a blurred manner, for the path taken by the former might not be contemplated as an object related to "diversity" and the latter might not carry significant weight in their eyes.[15]

Standpoint 2. Refusing to define diversity from the outset, I drew another picture. I include measures and actors who are not always examined from the first standpoint. Indeed, these measures are not only limited to recruitment initiatives and practices, but are extended to counseling, intern

---

15 Interview with TE, 25 November 2009.

publicity, education, in-house training, and the commemoration of the past. I examine the motives underlying the work of those who have actually contributed to the acknowledgement of difference within the police forces. Attempting to *understand* through types, I accentuate the motives, which find echo in police forces and stand in relation with police principles and a particular spirit of diversity. From this standpoint, the three first ideal types (the empathetic, the principled—in its liberal form—, and the opportunist ones) are in the foreground of the picture while specialists stand in the background. Looking attentively, one notices that police researchers are not absent from the picture. Looking at the opportunist from some distance, one sees them sitting in one of the back corners.

The criteria to assess the types' empirical weight, to "measure their success," are different than those used to draw the first picture. One does not just look at the numbers of recruits and police officers from post-migration backgrounds selected, their retention, and promotion in the forces, but also at the capacity to explain the resistance to some changes and a particular spirit. One indicator is, for instance, the possibility to maintain one's job in the forces. Let us recall that Inspector Piontek was eleven years counselor for candidates of foreign origins before returning to a precinct and Inspector Bobkowski remained within the Political Education Unit until he retired, that is thirty-five years. Ms. Berger could not stay. That is not to say that she did not contribute to the acknowledgement of difference. She certainly did extend to some according to the criteria set by police researchers. As we have seen, the numbers of recruited officers from post-migration backgrounds in the federal states examined were similar. However, she was not allowed to continue her work.

Perhaps the encounter with Inspector Bobkowski turned out to be so important for the ideal types to unfold because it hinted at a narrative, which bodes well with the guiding principles of the police and another spirit of diversity. The fact that police officers did neither have much a vocabulary to talk about difference nor of an institutional frame to work with was an obstacle. Although often considered important, but too "thin" (Blom 2004), political education, a nonpartisan education, which emerged under Weimar Germany in the face of the different political forces in place and was revived after World War Two, proved to be one noticeable channel (*Weichensteller*) to talk about difference. Yet, this is only one side of the story: seen from the first standpoint, political education may also be considered a barrier to a spirit of diversity we, and the specialists, might want to come about.

The picture I drew from putting together the four ideal types together could be entitled, *Stellvertretung*. It pointed to one important, though contested, characteristic of the relation toward difference within German police forces. In the next and last chapter, I will return to the second detail, one I have only hinted at thus far: several actors (and myself included) made allusions to the past. These backward-looking connections will serve as a point of reference to describe and explain, as promised, the particular spirit of diversity within the German police forces.

Diversity. A Word With Qualities

As a way to conclude this study, I want to return to the second detail I had noticed when assembling the ideal types together: the outdated character of the picture, the impression that it went yellow before it was finished. It occurred to me that in the individual chapters I kept alluding to elements from the past: a Culture Protestant cure of the soul and the empathetic type, a liberal heritage and the type devoted to a principle; if the opportunist did not call to mind such references, a neo-Kantian twist was perceptible in its mirror image. If the first detail, the *Stellvertretung*—a specific though contested type of representation—, revealed itself through the gaze of the observer, this second detail was also pointed out by the inspectors accompanied and interviewed; they also made references to the past. Indeed, my informants sometimes couched their practices and discourse in experiences of the civil service under the Weimar Republic and their carriers. I might not have paid much more attention to this detail if it were not for an observation made by anthropologist Werner Schiffauer.

Writing on political culture in four different national contexts, Schiffauer mentions that there is something *bildungsbürgerlich* about boundary drawing and the relation toward ethnic and religious difference in Germany (1997a: 47). To describe this relation, he draws on the writings of Ernst Troeltsch (1997a: 46), an early 20th-century Protestant theologian and historian who, as it happens, was also a member of the *Bildungsbürgertum* himself, the educated middle class of that time. It is as though Schiffauer had seen the detail I later spotted while reading Troeltsch. Is that a mere coincidence or is this allusion to the *Bildungsbürgertum* instructive regarding the picture drawn?

References to the past were noticeable all along the study; yet, there is no straight line, no immediate causal relation, to be drawn between the 19th and 20th-century educated liberal middle class and today's police officers. Like me, the inspectors I interviewed could not point to direct connections between the two either. This was most telling in the case portrayed in chapter three. When, in the context of commemorating deputy chief of police Bernhard Weiß, Inspector Bobkowski makes attempts to draw a line between the intentions of Weiß' supporters and those of his fellow police officers, he feels uneasy and tries to evade my questions. Portraying the FDP as the natural successor of the DDP, Weiß' party—and, incidentally, the liberal party Ernst Troeltsch and Max Weber had cofounded at the time of the Weimar Republic—seemed somewhat clumsy. When presenting his work to police officials at the Police Federal Academy in Münster, another inspector, Dietmar Piontek, also couches his practices in the civil service under Weimar.[1] How do these entities intersect and interact?

Would the examination of these vague connections help us pinpoint the specificities, or particular spirit of diversity within the police forces? And if so, how? These are the questions at the centre of this chapter, which deals less with the actors than with the ideas prevailing within the German police forces and their specific *quality*. With an eye on my fieldwork, in the first part of this chapter, I describe aspects constitutive of the spirit of diversity within German police forces. And, in so doing, I cast light on what is, or appears to be, *bildungsbürgerlich* about them. In the second part of the chapter, by drawing on Georg Simmel and his definition of the secret society, I then attempt to account for the relation toward difference within police forces and a puzzling attitude I encountered. A key element in this account involves the delineation of a peculiar way to apprehend the individual.

1. (ANOTHER) SPIRIT OF DIVERSITY

1.1 Making Sense of Actions: Motives, Orders, and Legitimacy

At the outset of the "Basic Sociological Terms," Weber enjoins the reader to contemplate the task of sociology as the interpretive understanding of

---

1 Internal document, Hamburg (1999 [1997]).

social action—that is the discerning of motives—in order to *thereby* [*dadurch*] explain it.² For Weber, understanding and explaining belong to the same and only analytical movement, one that is best illustrated in his *Protestant Ethic* (Weber 2007 [1904/1905]). Isolating religious motives, he describes the spirit of modern capitalism while pointing to its origin. This spirit is the quality that characterizes modern capitalism, and that even after religious motives have, to a large extent, given way to instrumental ones. Once isolated, the motives underpinning action point to the particular spirit of what Weber calls an order, or patterned action. They provide the basis for a genetic model of explanation, one "with reference to certain important cultural significances (…) for modern culture" and to which they stand in adequate causal relation (Weber 1949 [1904]: 93-94; Turner and Factor 1994: 152).

In the "Protestant sects" (Weber 2001 [1906]), a text which could have been entitled *The Protestant Ethic "revisited,"* Weber does not look at religious motives and their transformation anymore; instead he is confronted with the multiplicity of motives grounding modern capitalism and its ethos at the beginning of the 20th century. Seen from this angle, the situation is not so clear anymore, the motives do not appear so sharply; however, the order is still well in place and has to a large extent maintained its quality. Faced with a plurality of motives, the sociologist pursues a different question, one that could be stated as this: How can an order exist in spite of diverging motives and beyond the erosion of its initial basis?

Thinking about Weber's approach and question with my fieldwork in mind, I first looked at an order, represented in initiatives that contributed to the acknowledgement of difference. This was my starting point. I then moved on to investigating the motives of the individuals carrying them out. I knew that beyond their apparent external resemblance, several motives could sustain an order (as it turned out in this case empathy, devotion to a principle, opportunism, or a negative reaction to opportunism); they need not contradict the existence of a common order, and they point to a specific quality. One example should suffice to make the possible plurality of motives evident. As we could see in the negative reactions expressed in carica-

---

2 The exact citation reads: "Sociology (…) is a science which attempts the interpretive understanding of social action in order thereby to arrive at a causal explanation of its course and effects" (Weber 1978a [1921]: 4).

tured references to the Dutch case (chapter four), most inspectors showed some degree of resistance toward management-induced measures. Yet those officers invoked different motives to ground their reaction: the necessity to care for individual fellow officers, assumed exceptions against the principle of equality expressed in the much repeated maxim, *kein extra-Würstchen*,[3] or the rejection of the use of people for instrumental purposes.

"By means of the idea of legitimacy," Albrow writes about Weber's answer to his own question—how can an order exist in spite of diverging motives)—, "he secured an intimate linkage, a loop back between motives and beliefs, providing the conceptual possibility for a common order to arise out of various and conflicting individual motivations, without ever postulating common will or attributing reality to collective ideas except as symbolic point of reference" (1990: 164). To that, I would add the following hypothesis: an order is likely to be strong, that is valid, if its motives remain vague and are subject to different interpretations.[4] Conversely, it is likely to be weak when the need to articulate the motives in greater detail surges; for once clearly defined, differences become manifest, which may divide and offer the basis on which criticism can be nurtured.

1.2 Specific Traits (Historical Individual)

With a group of specialists as a counterexample, I attempt to underline some aspects, which are characteristic of the spirit of diversity within the German police forces. I see three such aspects: a specific conception of culture, a belief in education, and a distinctive view of the individual.

The inspectors interviewed shared a diffuse, but common conception: they sought the development of a German, yet heterogeneous culture (see also Schiffauer 1997b: 153). This is an important feature of the spirit of diversity in the police forces. As I noted in chapter four, this conception is

---

3   "No special treatment" or, literally, "no extra sausage."
4   On a similar note, research on police occupational culture points to similar traits that, however, provoke different reactions to the same challenges. Loftus points out, "It would appear, then, that officers in Northville and Southville shared a related set of occupational norms, values and behaviour. It is important to note, however, that the substance of each theme had the potential to carry different meanings and emphasis" (2010b: 15).

also largely shared by police researchers in Germany, those concerned with reforming organizational practices, and those for whom culture is an important focus (see Behr 2006: 179-181; also Blom 2005: 29). Behr talks about the police's *elasticity* (2006: 174).[5] This conception favors conformity to the forces' principles, a conformity, which, in this ideal form, is opened to all through education. It is therefore not surprising that educational measures played such an important role in the fieldwork and in the literature. Herman Blom (2004), a police researcher writing on the situation of police officers from post-migration backgrounds in Germany and the Netherlands, stresses in this regard that seminars and educational measures are good, but he warily adds that they are not enough. At conferences I often heard police researchers bemoaning that educational measures are an alibi, a mere reflex response to criticism. If there is evidence of both arguments to be found, one can also observe that education is seen by the officers as a way to talk about difference and act in response to it.

Closely connected to the educational imperative is the responsibility conferred onto the individual. As Schiffauer (1997a: 47) noted, such a stake puts strains on the real, empirical, individual. And because the abstract character of the individual turns out to be an important characteristic, he or she must have, as goes the maxim, a "thick skin." Such an injunction shows the way through which the inherent tensions individuals face are internalized and dealt with, that is mostly at the personal level: enduring becomes a value in itself. The tensions may also be externalized through humor, or what P.A.J. Waddington calls the "canteen chatter." In listening to what the police officers say when they are in each other's company, to the heroic stories, which do not correspond to their daily experience, the police researcher points to the role of the canteen chatter as repair shop and a rheto-

---

5 Next to *Elastizität*, *Heterogeneität* is another word sometimes used in this context. As an example, one can think of the successor of the Max Planck Institute for history in Göttingen, which was first named *Max-Planck-Institut zur Erforschung multireligiöser und multiethnischer Heterogeneität* (The Max Planck Institute for the Study of Religious and Ethnic Heterogeneity) but, later, *Max-Planck-Institut zur Erforschung multireligiöser und multiethnischer Gesellschaften* (The Max Planck Institute for the Study of Religious and Ethnic Diversity).

ric "that gives meaning to experience and sustains occupational self-esteem" (Waddington 1999: 295; also Schwell 2008: 235-240).

2. SOMETHING *BILDUNGSBÜRGERLICH*

These traits—the ideal of culture with education at its core, and the strains put on the individual—could be referred to as the police's "existential code," one common to most ideal types outlined in this book and through which differences are looked at and acted upon. This corresponds to an earnest understanding of culture, an understanding also perceptible in expressions such as "devotion to the whole" (*Hingabe an das Ganze*) Schiffauer quotes from Troeltsch. In fact, in all representatives of the types except the specialists, the spirit of diversity is characterized by the palpable moral charge it conveys.

There is an air of *Bildungsbürgerlichkeit* about these traits. Once more, I ask myself the following question: is there merely an external resemblance, an accidental relation, between this particular form of liberalism and the spirit of diversity within German police forces? Is it a coincidence if Schiffauer noticed a similar detail while reading Troeltsch? I too made numerous references to Weber, one of Troeltsch's contemporaries, with whom I also engaged in dialogue. His work was the backdrop against which I examined the protagonists of the foregoing chapters. Arguably, this approach to the subject might reveal more about me, the interpreter, than the case itself. But used as an *instrument*, this dialogue might perhaps be one original aspect of the present study. In further defining the peculiarity of the spirit of diversity, this aspect might be worth developing in a more formal and explicit manner in future research.

With an eye on Weber, Troeltsch—to whom Georg Simmel as well as some of their contemporary literary counterparts are added—, we can observe what seems to be a *bildungsbürgerlich* character of the treatment of difference within police forces. Let us first have a look at their conception of culture, education, and the individual in their context. Writing at the end of the 19th century and the beginning of the 20th century, they operate within a particular context, German liberalism. They are its late representatives. Guenther Roth incidentally portrays Max Weber (1864-1920) as a belated liberal democrat of the 1848 revolution (cited in Breuer 2006: 1).

Although declining, this version of liberalism was nevertheless an important point of reference, a cosmos to which belonged both its supporters and its critics. Precisely because it did not appear self-evident anymore, its preservation became—to borrow Elias' words on the formation of worldviews—"a conscious program of an interested strata" (2001 [1929]: 220).

Thomas Mann was one of the social scientists' literary counterparts; he referred to himself as an "old-fashioned liberal" (2006 [1950]: 199). Because he provides us with an outline of the conception of German liberalism of the middle class, the writer's ideas can be brought to fruition for sociology.[6] In the following excursus, I take up his recollection of the last third of the 19th century as a standard to throw light on the liberal conception of culture, education, and the individual in the context of Germany.

2.1 On German Liberalism

Excursus: A Literary Account of the German Liberal Individual

Taking example on Goethe, Thomas Mann reflects in *My Times* upon his life and time on the occasion of his 75th anniversary; we are in 1950. With assurance, he reflects on the liberal and bourgeois era of his youth he feels very much attached to:

"(…) it is not a little thing to have lived in that last quarter of the nineteenth century—a grand century—the twilight of the bourgeois, the liberal age, to have breathed its air; it is, one is tempted to claim in his old-age assuredness, an educational advantage over those born into in the present dissolution, it is an endowment, a dowry, absent for those who come later, though they naturally do not know what they are missing" (Mann 2006 [1950]: 192).

Mann's individual is perceptible in the characters of his novels. He is a man whose ethos and life conduct is infused with a rigorous sense of duty and a strong work ethic, be he a businessman or even an artist (Mann 1970). Education and culture (*Bildung*) allows him to attain, in principle,

---

6 For a dialogue between social theorists and novelists, see Austin Harrington (2002, 2006), Harvey Goldman (1992), and Wolf Lepenies (1988: 299).

such a goal beyond social adscription—one could talk of an "unequally distributed possibility." On the political spectrum, he is a liberal, whose central values are individual freedom, and the ideal, or duty, of self-perfection; money is a token of his success. If based on self-interest, an action is abhorrent to his sense of duty. One could describe his worldview in the manner Albrow uses to depict Max Weber's: "any motive which led one to perform a duty for reasons other than simply the fulfillment of duty could only detract for the moral worth of the action" (Albrow 1990: 41). This individual is committed to his actions and feels a high degree of responsibility toward them.

These traits are anchored in Protestant life conducts and Kantian ethics, and are embodied in figures such as Mann's protagonists. He captures them from the standpoint of the twilight of a liberal age on the brink of decline; a standpoint that confers a kind of eschatological feel to some of his novels.

Let us take *Buddenbrooks* (Mann 1994 [1901]), the novelist's family chronicle spanning over three generations, as an example. While Johann Buddenbrook has a strong sense of duty and solid faith, his son Thomas, the "achievement-oriented moralist" (Lepenies 1988: 298), is increasingly confronted with the inconsistencies between the imperatives of the world he lives in and his inner life; plus, he feels as though he did not live up to his actions, as though he did not recognize himself in them. His own son, Hanno, does not try to confront the world; he flees by taking refuge in music. Reading Mann, one recognizes the three moments, the same that stimulate the play between intentions, consequences, and destiny in Weber's *Protestant Ethic*. The first moment is the rare articulation between intentions and consequences; the second moment corresponds to the chasm opening between the imperatives of the objective world and the will of the individual, one submitted to the world's functional imperatives; the third one is materialized in a search for sense, or its succedaneum (see Martuccelli 1999: 229-230).[7]

What happens when one places the two circles of people one over the other, here, the late 19th and early 20th-century members of the educated liberal

---

7   We also find these same movements in the three characters, and the three volumes, of Hermann Broch's trilogy *Sleepwalkers* (1978 [1930-1932]) or Joseph Roth's *Radetzky March* (2004 [1932]) and *The Emperor's Tomb* (2002 [1938]).

middle class and the police inspectors? There are, of course, numerous discrepancies between 21st century police inspectors and 19th century members of the *Bildungsbürgertum*—a chief one being the central value given to the *Bildung* itself; however, there are also some similarities between the two. Folding the circles crosswise, one over the other, in the manner of *histoire croisée* (Werner and Zimmermann 2006: 37), one sees the individual and its particular quality appear at their point of intersection. This conception of individuality is important because it points to tensions typical of the police forces as an organization while offering a language—both for the observers and the actors—for describing it.

If we can draw on novelists to delineate a particular conception of the individual, it is because the individual, and with it individuality, is a dual concept for social scientists; it is an analytical tool, but also a "theoretical conviction" (Martuccelli and de Singly 2009: 20). The theoretical conviction is linked to an existential dimension expressed, for instance, in Weber's concern for the paradoxical character of action and in the notion of fate—"the consequences of one's action, compared to one's intention [*Absicht*]" (["(...) *die Folge seines Handelns gegenüber seiner Absicht*"] 1988 [1920]: 524). We also find it in the ethics underlying his political writings and in his methodological texts. "Behind the particular 'action,' stands the human being," writes Weber (1949 [1917]: 38). If he needs to remind us, it is because the individual threatens to slip through the net of his ideal typical method. We also find it in Troeltsch's discussion on the particular and the general, which provides Schiffauer with the vocabulary to describe boundary drawing in contemporary Germany.

Like no other sociologists, it is however Georg Simmel who stresses the dual nature of the individual. Drawing on Nietzsche, he writes in his *Sociology*: "Mankind and societies are two different vantage points, as it were, from which the individual can be viewed" (1950a [1908]: 63). Mankind relates to an existential and qualitative dimension while societies relate to more mechanical and quantitative ones. Simmel's time clearly preferred mankind as a quality with the individual at its core: *Einzigkeit* (uniqueness), not *Einzelheit* (the average unit) or, translated to the object of my inquiry: uniqueness, not social difference. This notion runs through German sociological theories of the time.

In the next section, I will pay particular attention to Simmel because he provides a key to apprehend the individual in the specific context of the police forces. I will review his writings on the secret society (*geheime Gesellschaft*). Although not usually quoted in this context, Simmel's insights on the secret society can describe the police forces as organization and the fate of the individuals in them. In doing so, they help to solve a puzzling attitude that I was confronted with all along the process of researching the book: the constant appeal to a logic that seeks recognition while striving to confirm the principle of equality (*Gleichbehandlung*). This principle, I kept being told, constitutive of the police organization and did not fail to raise an impression Behr had hinted at and according to which officers—even the committed ones—did not fully endorse the change they were supposed to initiate.

3. SIMMEL, THE INDIVIDUAL, AND THE RELATION TOWARD DIFFERENCE IN THE FORCES

3.1 Individuation and De-Individuation

Simmel notes that society "(...) promotes a leveling of its members. It creates an average and makes it extremely difficult for its members to go beyond this average merely through the individual excellence in the quantity or quality of life" (1950a [1908]: 63). If leveling is inherent to sociation (*Vergesellschaftung*), it is most apparent in one particular form: the secret society.

Simmel contends that some secret organizations—his examples include the freemasonry, communal associations of medieval Germany, and criminal groups—can best be understood through the synthesis of two sets of reciprocal relations. Let us consider these sets of relations, which are characteristic of these societies: *equality versus hierarchy* and *the leveling and the magic character of secrecy*.

Secret societies are hierarchical and equal. Against possible expectations, Simmel observes that equality does not necessarily contradict hierarchy. "(...) Secret societies," he writes, "practice great relative equality among their members. This does not contradict the despotic character of their organization: in all kinds of other groups, too, despotism is correlated with the leveling of the ruled" (1950b [1908]: 374). The relation between hierarchy and equality often implies what the sociologist calls the leveling of the ruled, or: de-individualization. Simmel writes that "de-individualization is the sociological character which, in the individual member, corresponds to this centralistic subordination" (1950b [1908]: 372-373). In terms of the heightened measure of leveling of the individuality, or "de-selfing" (*Entselbstung*), Simmel sees in the secret society that which is also at the core of the total institution seminally described by Goffman (1961: 120-121).[8]

The outcome of the first set of relations directs our attention to a second set of relations: the one between leveling and the magic character of secrecy. The leveling of the individuality is countered by the almost magic character of secrecy: indeed, "the secret also operates as an adorning possession and value of the personality" (1950b [1908]: 337). Secrecy confers a unique character and, as such, separates from the larger group ("the secret embodies and intensifies such differentiation" [1950b (1908): 335]). Next to the "heightened measure of leveling of the individuality" that distinguishes the secret society the process of sociation in general, the secret also sets apart this particular form of society from other groups. The adornment is matched by individuation. Seen from this perspective, the secret society also produces individuation, it has the potential to enhance the individual. The secret is not a stigma but an adornment or, in Goffman's words, a favorable proactive status.[9] More than the content of the secret—which may

---

8   Although Goffman does note cite Simmel, his influence is palpable, notably in his stressing the impact of the total institution on the self.

9   In *Asylums* Goffman list of total institutions: among them are concentration camps, prisons, psychiatric hospitals, ships, monasteries, boarding schools, officer's schools. "Very often, entrance means for the recruit that he has taken on what might be called a proactive status: not only is his social position within the walls radically different from what was what it was on the outside but, as he comes to learn, if and when he gets out, his social position on the outside will never again be quite what is was prior to entrance. Where the proactive status is a relatively favorable one, as it is for those who graduate from officers' training schools, elite boarding schools, ranking monasteries, etc., then jubilant official reunions, announcing pride in one's 'school,' can be expected. When the proactive status is unfavorable, as it is for those who graduate from prisons or mental

or not exist—, it is its magic aura, the veil of mystery surrounding it that matter most. As Simmel writes: "Before the unknown, man's natural impulse to idealize and his natural fearfulness cooperate toward the same goal: to intensify the unknown through imagination, and to pay attention to it with an emphasis that is not usually accorded to patent reality" (Simmel 1950b [1908]: 333)." This magic aura is nurtured by the group and confers a unique character upon its individual members; as such, it tends to separate him or her from the larger group or society.

Figure 6: Simmel's Secret Society

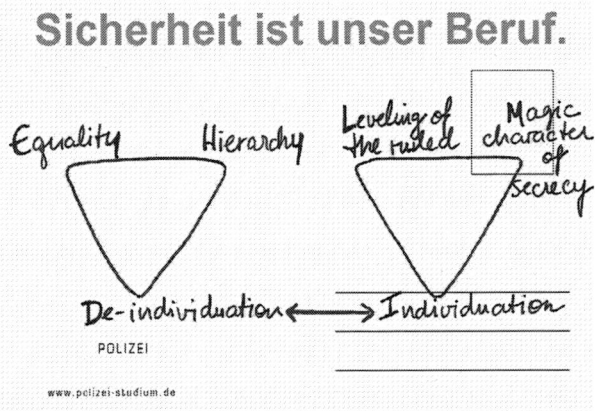

3.2 The Police as Secret Society

The movement, back and forth, between de-individualization and the valuation of the individual can be contemplated as the characteristic of the secret society.[10] In considering, on the one hand, police forces as organizations

---

> hospitals, we can employ the term 'stigmatization' and expect that the inmate may take an effort to conceal his past and try to 'pass'" (Goffman 1961: 72).

10 There are other possible readings. Looking at groups at different stages and in various surroundings, Hazelrigg (1969) concentrates on the protective function of secret for the group while Marx and Muschert (2009; 1981) stresses the con-

with their own culture and, on the other, police officers dealing with the acknowledgement or promotion of difference, in the following section, I argue that this movement corresponds, in large parts, to the status of the individual in police forces and accounts for the puzzling attitude I outlined above.

Police and Police Research

Like secret societies, police forces are characterized by a chain of commands, by the separation of an in-group from the larger group, and by an oath of allegiance sealing the entry into the group. More than external characteristics, it is, however, the movement between de-individualization and individualization that they set in motion that retains my attention. The police embody such a movement; they level the individual while differentiating and conferring value upon her or him. The police uniform contributes to it: as a mask and, at the same time, as an adornment; it levels those wearing it while conferring upon them a unique character and, as such, separating them from the larger group.

Looking at the forces through Simmel's lens, the secret society and the prism of relations characteristic to it both confirms and casts research findings on police occupational culture, or cop culture in a new light.

Cop Culture

With its syntheses and textbooks (Newburn 2005; Crank 2004 [1998]; Brodeur 2003) the sociology of the police is a well-constituted subfield of the discipline. Among its main concerns, is cop culture, which has found its way back into the forces as a somewhat catchy expression. In order to expose its features, let me briefly review two compelling and relatively recent accounts of the cop culture, those of P.A.J. Waddington and Bethan Loftus.

In describing police sub-culture, Waddington follows Robert Reiner (1992) and underlines a "sense of mission; the desire for action and excitement (...); an 'Us/Them' division of the social world with its in-

---

trol of information or knowledge (see also Hazelrigg 1969: 323). That being said, individualization remains a central category of Simmel's work (see, for instance, Müller 2012).

group isolation and solidarity on the other hand, and racist components on the other; its authoritarian conservatism; and its suspicion and cynicism" (1999: 287)—to which he adds a masculine ethos (1999: 296). In her book, *Police Culture in a Changing World*, Bethan Loftus (2010a: 3-20; also 2010b) revisits theories on police culture and stresses the features Waddington and others isolate to which she includes, following William A. Westley (1970), secrecy, silence, solidarity, and an extreme form of resistance to difference.

Waddington makes a distinction between what cops say—what he refers to as "canteen chatter"—and what their job is about and their actual behavior on the streets. What they say, he insists, does not explain policing; instead, "canteen chatter" is a response to the police role in society and the pressures impinging upon it; it is reassuring.[11] More than merely pointing to features or core aspects of cop culture, researchers link these to structural contingencies (the potential danger, the exercise of authority, and the efficiency requirement), to the ways in which cops cope with the police's *role* in society. Following Skolnick (1966), Waddington stresses the authority inherent to policing. He emphasizes that "the exercise of coercive authority over fellow citizen" (1999: 301) is specific of the police; it notably distinguishes it from the army (1999: 301). The consequence of policing fellow citizens, he contends, accounts for core aspects of the police sub-culture. In insisting on this role, Waddington also touches upon the problem of value relation and the relation between the cop and the sociologist I evoked in chapter one: because it polices fellow citizens, the police are an organization one only accepts grudgingly in liberal democracies (1999: 301-302).

Loftus is also concerned with the police's role and the pressures associated with it (2010a: xiv). Against voices that have in the last decades pointed at the erosion of heterogeneity of cop culture (for example: Chan 1996, 1997), she argues that cop culture has shown remarkable endurance. In spite of developments and police reforms (such as community policing, new recruitment practices, and increase scrutiny and account-

---

11 Waddington writes: "The very fact that police devote so much rhetorical effort to affirming what their daily experience denies should alert us to its ideological importance" (1999: 300).

> ability), which have been carried out since the first studies on police culture in the 1960s, she shows that the basic pressures associated with the police role have remained and sustained cop culture under the new conditions.

Although police researchers—bar a few exceptions—do not refer to the sociologist,[12] a Simmel-inspired account of the police forces tallies with their findings. Research on cop culture echoes the practice of relative equality among officers, their leveling, and their separateness from the rest of society. Drawing on Simmel, we can bring aspects to the fore, which are absent in the research on police culture. Even more so than typical traits of the forces as outlined by this strand of research and the role of the police in society, it points to reciprocal relations within one type of organization and the concomitant status they confer onto the individual. In bringing our attention to the multidirectional relations between uniqueness, equality, and de-individuation—or, stated the other way around: equality, de-individuation, and uniqueness—, Simmel offers in his virtuosis-like fashion, a way to grasp aspects of police work without leveling out or reducing the tensions and the contradictions inherent to them.[13] The sets of relations he points out shape the modulations of the police's existential code, or cop culture, in different contexts.

---

12 In some of his writings, Westley (1956: 254, 1970: 111-118) mentions Simmel in passing. Manning evokes the police as a semi-secret society, but does not elaborate on it (1974: 289).

13 Simmel's students recall that "just about the time when... one felt he had reached a conclusion, he had a way of raising his right arm and, with three fingers of his hand, turning the imaginary object so as to exhibit still another facet" (Wolff 1950: xvii). On a similar note, Kracauer writes: "Often Simmel must first completely pick to pieces the familiar, commonplace image of whatever object he is examining, so that the aspect it shares with other objects can come to the fore. What is always at stake for the thinker in this process is the liberation of the thing from its isolation. He turns it this way and that way, until we recognize in it the fulfillment of a lawfulness that is simultaneously embodied in many other places, and we can thereby weave it into an extensive net of relations" (1995 [1963]: 235).

The Puzzling Attitude

I like thinking about the police as a secret society. More than police culture, Simmel helps me grasping some of the things that puzzled me while doing my fieldwork and reading research on the police in Germany. In this book I presented several examples of a seemingly contradictory attitude exhibited by the officers in charge of ethnically-based recruitment, teaching, counseling, or commemorating the past. This attitude was manifest, for instance, in the several exceptions Criminal Inspector Schmitt and her colleagues foresaw while vehemently denying special treatment, or in the efforts to commemorate Bernhard Weiß, a former police deputy chief of police under the Weimar Republic, by naming a square in Berlin after him.

I remember Klaus Bobkowski referring to Bernhard Weiß not as a Jew, but as a police officer and an exceptional, "incomparable example" (*kein vergleichbares Vorbild*) by pointing to his courage against racist attacks. The inspector acknowledged Weiß being Jewish only to underscore that he should not be commemorated as such. The same arguments were to be found in letters written by the Police Historical Society to lobby city officials to rename the square. When the initiative failed to materialize, a disappointed Inspector Bobkowski felt compelled to point out that at no moment did the Police Historical Society either raise the argument or seek the help of the Berlin Jewish community, not wanting—these were his words—"any preferential group treatment." Inspector Bobkowski's unprompted comment intrigued me. He talked about Bernhard Weiß as representative of the police, as a proud Prussian democrat as well as Goebbels' unflagging opponent—and not for being Jewish. Yet it is hard to imagine that Weiß' confession had not played a role in the will to commemorate him. Would have the Berlin police honored him had he not been Jewish? After all, there were other personalities who could have been mentioned such as, say, Albert Grzesinski, the chief of the Berlin police under Weimar, a social democrat.

I kept encountering this attitude, exhibited by Inspector Bobkowski, in the German police forces in. It transcended different types of discourses and actors over time in the forces. Officers whose commitment toward the recognition of difference I was certain did not fail to stress the formal principle of equality. In contrast to references to the principle in cases where resistance to the initiatives aiming at promoting difference was most felt, it was for Inspector Bobkowski and some of his colleagues in Berlin and other federal states clearly not just an alibi. How can this puzzling attitude be accounted for?

While engaging our thinking in terms of relations, Simmel's secret society points to the fate of the individual within a particular type of organization; indeed, it brings to the fore *an individual who can be both held dear and equal in an organization that produces de-individuation, and individuation*. This particular understanding of the individual—being held dear and equal—is a key to understanding the resistance, the seemingly contradictory attitude toward difference I encountered in German police forces, and the reception made to the people who can aptly be described as specialists and their version of the spirit of diversity.

The research on cop culture—in Germany and elsewhere—portrays the police as traditional and conservative in outlook. If the present study does not contradict this claim (resistance to change was a recurring feature), it brings a new quality to it: compared to other national contexts implicit to this investigation, the specificity of the German police forces is what could be referred to as a liberal attitude. Such a "liberal" attitude is, I argue, a specific *quality*, a spirit of diversity, of the German police forces. This quality, it needs to be stressed, can take many forms, from cosmopolitan ones to racist ones, and its vocabulary can be sometimes used to justify both inclusion and exclusion.

4. Type of Causation

The described way to apprehend the individual bodes well with one of my types: the principled one and a German version of liberalism. In Weber's words, the two stand in adequate causal relation to each other (Weber 1949 [1904], Weber 1949 [1906]; Eberle 1999). The affinity between one type of organization, the police and its way to apprehend the individual, and one ideal type, the principled or liberal one, points to adequacy of meaning. Indeed, the study of the motives, or meaning, underlying the action of the carriers of diversity and the members of the *Bildungsbürgertum* points to a family resemblance, or elective affinities, between both.

But let us be clear: neither all ideal types nor all the persons they represented exhibited such a resemblance. For instance, those best described as opportunists, a type for which presence on the field was considerable, resemblances cannot be attributed. Yet, the German police researchers attest to this quality when they bemoan the overwhelming presence of opportunism. Because they often speak in a manner similar to the representatives of the principled or liberal type, the vocabulary used by the officers, who are against the initiatives that aim at acknowledging difference, show what could be referred to as an external resemblance.

When they champion ideas similar to those of liberal men under Weimar, the police officers are, today, conservative. From today's perspective, they indeed appear somewhat yellowed, outdated. Diversity, as understood by the specialists, did not correspond to the treatment of difference one can observe within the German police at the time of the fieldwork. Because we contemporary sociologists are likely to share, at least in part, the specialists' conception or spirit of diversity, police officers often offend our sensibilities and irritate us. Conversely, the claim toward individual autonomy characteristic of this spirit of diversity typically annoys police officers. Other concerns of the specialists are the real, empirical, individual and bolder changes. She or he is right to point to the problem and to the following argument: "The equal treatment of unequals does not eliminate inequality, but maintains it. We have to do with structurally-based inequality" (Wetterer 2002: 142).[14]

If police officers do not necessarily deny these concerns (and might call for more elasticity in the forces), they tend, as police research shows, to value the heroic attitude that is not foreign to the conception of man one finds in some of Ernst Troeltsch's, Georg Simmel's and Max Weber's writings.[15] If I would for my part argue for a less pathetic version of the individual than the one prevailing in their theories,[16] I concede that—in point-

---

14 "*Die Gleichbehandlung von Ungleichen baut Ungleichheit nicht ab, sondern schreibt sie fort. Mit strukturell angelegten Ungleichheitslagen haben wir es (...) zu tun*" (Wetterer 2002: 142).

15 As Harrington (2002) points out, had the sociologists lived longer, they might well have been the carriers of other ideas. Already a few years later, Robert Musil presents us with a much more ironic reading of social life. See also Siegfried Kracauer and his equally ironic views on the superseded idealist concepts haunting his contemporaries (1971 [1929]: 31).

16 See this trend in recent French sociology (Martuccelli and de Singly 2009; Martuccelli 2009).

ing to their heritage—I might have unwittingly rehabilitated the same police officers who often irritate us by conferring them with the aura of respectability that surrounds these liberal figures. And I guess the references to the past invoked by the police officers I interviewed aimed precisely at this, at a desire to legitimize their work through historical sanction. They found in the invoked references to the past acceptable vocabularies of motives and possible *Weichensteller* for change.

Appendix: Synoptic Table of the Ideal Types

Types	Motive	Consequences	Domains and carrier group	Cultural context	Means
Empathetic	Empathy - Welfare of others	Diversity (+, -)	Recruitment - Police officers	Culture Protestantism	Individual guidance
Principled	Cause (*Sache*) - Democratization - Responsibility, sense of duty	Diversity (+, -)	Education - Police officers	Liberalism	Education (individual)
Principled	Cause (*Sache*) - Diversity / change - Self-realization	Diversity (+, -)	Outside of police forces - Social scientists - Women / minorities	Social movements	Structural change (personal emancipation and group autonomy)
Opportunist	Self-interest - Career	Diversity (+, -)	Management (recruitment) - Police officers	"Cause devoid of substance"	Varied, pragmatic measures

Bibliography

Albert, Gert, Agathe Bienfait, Steffen Sigmund, and Claus Wendt. 2003. *Das Weber-Paradigma. Studien zur Weiterentwicklung von Max Webers Forschungsprogramm*. Tübingen: Mohr Siebeck.
Albrecht, Thomas. 1999. *Für eine wehrhafte Demokratie. Albert Grzesinski und die preußische Politik in der Weimarer Republik*. Bonn: Dietz.
Albrow, Martin. 1990. *Max Weber's Construction of Social Theory*. Basingstoke: Macmillan.
Alcoff Martin, Linda. 1995. "Who Can Speak? The Problem of Speaking for Others." Pp. 97-119 in *Who can Speak? Authority and Critique Identity*, edited by Judith Roof and Robyn Wiegman. Urbana: University of Illinois Press.
Andrew, Caroline. 2010. "Récit d'une recherche-action: la participation et le passage de frontières de femmes immigrantes à la Ville d'Ottawa." *Sociologie et sociétés* 42(1): 227-243.
Angress, Werner T. 1998. "Bernhard Weiß — A Jewish Public Servant in the Closing Years of the Weimar Republic." Pp. 49-63 in *Jüdisches Leben in der Weimarer Republik*, edited by Wolfgang Benz, Arnold Paucker, and Peter Pulzer. Tübingen: Mohr Siebeck.
Arasse, Daniel. 1996 [1992]. *Le détail. Pour une histoire rapprochée de la peinture*. Paris: Flammarion.
—. 2004. *Histoires de peintures*. Paris: Denoël.
Arjouni, Jakob. 1987. *Happy Birthday, Türke! Ein Kayankara-Roman*. Zürich: Diogenes.
Bauke-Ruegg, Jan. 2003. "Stellvertretung in der (modernen) Literatur?" *Neue Zeitschrift für systematische Theologie und Religionsphilosophie* 45(3): 361-377.
Beaman, Lori. 2008. "Defining Religion: The Promise and the Peril of Legal Interpretation." Pp. 192-216 in *Law and Religious Pluralism in Canada*, edited by Richard Moon. Vancouver: UBC Press.
Behr, Rafael. 2006. *Polizeikultur. Routine — Rituale — Reflexionen. Bausteine zu einer Theorie der Praxis der Polizei*. Wiesbaden: VS Verlag für Sozialwissenschaften.

—. 2008 [2000]. *Cop Culture — Der Alltag des Gewaltmonopols — Männlichkeit, Handlungsmuster und Kultur in der Polizei*. Wiesbaden: VS Verlag für Sozialwissenschaften.

—. 2010. "Licht und Schatten: 'Diversität' für die Polizei." Pp. 145-156 in *Fremde als Ordnungshüter*, edited by Daniela Hunold, Daniela Klimke, Rafael Behr, and Rüdiger Lautmann. Wiesbaden: VS Verlag für Sozialwissenschaften.

Bering, Dietz. 1991. *Kampf um Namen. Bernhard Weiß gegen Joseph Goebbels*. Stuttgart: Klett-Cotta.

—. 1992 [1987]. *The Stigma of Names: Antisemitism in German Daily Life, 1812-1933*. Cambridge: Polity Press.

Bertossi, Christophe. 2007. "Ethnicity, Islam, and Allegiances in the French Military." Pp. 193-216 in *European Anti-Discrimination and the Politics of Citizenship. Britain and France*, edited by Christophe Bertossi. Basingstoke: Macmillan Palgrave.

—. "French 'Muslim' Soldiers? Social Change and Pragmatism in a Military Institution." To be published in *European States and their Muslim Citizens: The Impact of Institutions on Perceptions and Boundaries*, edited by John Bowen, Christophe Bertossi, Jan Willem Duyvendak, and Mona Lena Krook. Cambridge: Cambridge University Press.

Beschorner, Thomas. 2002. *Ökonomie als Handlungstheorie. Evolutorische Ökonomik, verstehende Soziologie und Überlegungen zu einer neuen Unternehmensethik*. Marburg: Metropolis.

Bigo, Didier. 2000. "Liaison Officers in Europe. New Officers in the European Security Field." Pp. 65-99 in *Issues in Transnational Policing*, edited by James Sheptycki. London; New York: Routledge.

Bittner, Egon. 1990. *Aspects of Police Work*. Boston: Northeastern University Press.

Blom, Herman. 2004. "Empfehlungen in Bezug auf 'Managing Diversity' in Deutschland und den Niederlanden." Pp. 22-24 in *Interkulturelle Kompetenz in der Polizeiausbildung*, edited by Ausländerbeauftragte des Landes Brandenburg. Potsdam: Büro der Ausländerbeauftragten des Landes Brandenburg.

—. 2005. *Anders sein bei der Polizei in Deutschland. Zur Position von allochthonen Polizisten an ihrem Arbeitsplatz, vor dem Hintergrund ihrer Rolle als Minderheit und der Tatsache, dass sie als 'anders' wahrgenommen werden*. Frankfurt am Main: Verlag für Polizeiwissenschaft.

Bornewasser, Manfred. 2009. "Ethnische Vielfalt im eigenen Land: Eine nicht nur sprachliche Herausforderung im Innen- und Außenverhältnis der Polizei." Pp. 16-44 in *Polizei und Fremde-Fremde in der Polizei*, edited by Karlhans Liebl. Wiesbaden: VS Verlag für Sozialwissenschaften.

Bornewasser, Manfred, Roland Eckert, Helmut Willems, Klaus Ahlheim, and Bardo Heger. 1996. "Fremdenfeindlichkeit in der Polizei?" *PFA. Schriftenreihe der Polizei-Führungsakademie* (1/2).

Breuer, Stefan. 2006. *Max Webers tragische Soziologie. Aspekte und Perspektiven*. Tübingen: Mohr Siebeck.

Broch, Hermann. 1978 [1930-1932]. *Die Schlafwandler: eine Romantrilogie*. Frankfurt am Main: Suhrkamp.

Brodeur, Jean-Paul. 2003. *Les visages de la police: pratiques et perceptions*. Montréal: Presses de l'Université de Montréal.

Buse, Dieter K. 2008. "The 'Going' of the Third Reich. Recivilizing Germans through Political Education." *German Politics and Society* 26(1): 29-56.

Calvès, Gwénaële. 2004. *La discrimination positive*. Paris: PUF.

Campbell, Colin. 2006. "Do Today's Sociologists Really Appreciate Weber's Essay *The Protestant Ethic and the Spirit of Capitalism*?" *The Sociological Review* 54(2): 207-223.

Cashmore, Ellis. 2001. "The Experiences of Ethnic Minority Police Officers in Britain: Under-Recruitment and Racial Profiling in a Performance Culture." *Ethnic and Racial Studies* 24(4): 642-659.

Certeau de, Michel. 1998 [1980]. *The Practice of Everyday Life*. Minneapolis: University of Minnesota Press.

Chan, Janet. 1996. "Changing Police Culture." *British Journal of Criminology* 36(1): 109-134.

—. 1997. *Changing Police Culture: Policing in a Multicultural Society*. Cambridge: Cambridge University Press.

Colliot-Thélène, Catherine. 1990. *Max Weber et l'histoire*. Paris: Presses Universitaires de France.

Crank, John P. (2004 [1998]). *Understanding Police Culture*. Cincinnati, Anderson Publishing.

Despoix, Philippe. 1995. *Ethiques du désenchantement. Essais sur la modernité allemande au début du siècle*. Paris: L'Harmattan.

Disselkamp, Annette. 2012. "Le secret et la connaissance interpersonnelle: un fondement original du lien social." *Sociologie et sociétés* 44(2): 143-163.

Doytcheva, Milena and Denise Helly. 2011. "La discrimination et la pluralité culturelle. Des objects de rhétorique des années 2000 en France." *Journal of International Migration and Integration* 12(4): 391-409.

Drews, Bill (Ed.). 1921. *Politische Bildung. Wille / Wesen / Ziel / Weg. Sechs Reden, gehalten bei der Eröffnung der Deutschen Hochschule für Politik.* Berlin: Deutsche Verlagsgesellschaft für Politik und Geschichte.

Dubet, François. 2002. *Le déclin de l'institution.* Paris: Seuil.

Dudek, Sonja. 2009. *Diversity in Uniform? Geschlecht und Migrationshintergrund in der Berliner Schutzpolizei.* Wiesbaden: VS Verlag für Sozialwissenschaften.

Dudek, Sonja, and Katrin Raczynsky. 2002. *Konstruktion von Geschlecht in der Berliner Polizei.* Master Thesis (*Diplomarbeit*), Fachbereich Erziehungswissenschaft und Psychologie, Frei Universität Berlin.

Eberle, Thomas S. 1999. "Sinnadäquanz und Kausaladäquanz bei Max Weber und Alfred Schütz." Pp. 97-119 in *Hermetische Wissenssoziologie. Standpunkte zur Theorie der Interpretation*, edited by Ronald Hitzler, Jo Reichertz, and N. Schröer. Konstanz, UVK.

Elias, Norbert. 1978 [1970]. *What Is Sociology?* New York: Columbia University Press.

—. 1994 [1990]. *Reflections on a Life.* Cambridge: Polity Press.

—. 1998 [1989]. *Studien über die Deutschen. Machtkämpfe und Habitusentwicklung im 19. und 20. Jahrhundert.* Frankfurt am Main: Suhrkamp.

—. 2001 [1929]. "On the Sociology of German Anti-Semitism." *Journal of Classical Sociology* 1(2): 219-225.

Engler, Wolfgang. 1995. *Die ungewollte Moderne: Ost-West Passagen.* Frankfurt am Main: Suhrkamp.

Ertener, Orkun. 2007. *2007: KDD – Kriminaldauerdienst.* ZDF.

Ewijk van, Anne R. 2012. "Diversity within Police Forces in Europe: A Case for the Comprehensive View." *Policing* 6(1): 76-92.

Faist, Thomas. 2009. "Diversity – A New Mode of Incorporation?" *Ethnic and Racial Studies* 32(1): 171-190.

Foucault, Michel. 1978 [1976]. *The History of Sexuality. Volume 1: An Introduction.* New York: Pantheon Books.
—. 1994 [1974]. "La vérité et les formes juridiques." Pp. 538-647 in *Dits et écrits: 1954-1988,* edited by Daniel Defert, François Ewald, and Jacques Lagrange. Paris: Gallimard.
Franzke, Bettina. 1995. "Menschen ausländischer Herkunft im Polizeivollzugsdienst – Zur Situation in der Bundesrepublik Deutschland." Pp. 9-45 in *Polizei und ethnische Minderheiten — ethnische Minderheiten in der Polizei* (Schriftenreihe der Polizei-Führungsakademie). Münster: PFA.
—. 1999. *Polizisten und Polizistinnen ausländischer Herkunft. Eine Studie zur ethnisch-kulturellen Identität und beruflichen Sozialisation Erwachsener in einer Einwanderungsgesellschaft.* Bielefeld: Kleine Verlag.
Gauthier, Jérémie. 2011. "Des corps étrange(r)s dans la police? Les policiers minoritaires à Paris et à Berlin." *Sociologie du travail* 53(4): 460-477.
—. 2012. *Origines contrôlées. La police à l'épreuve de la question minoritaire à Paris et à Berlin.* Doctoral Thesis, Université de Versailles-Saint-Quentin-en-Yvelines; Max-Planck-Insitut für ausländisches und internationales Strafrecht, Albert-Ludwigs-Universität Freiburg.
Geller, Jay Howard. 2006. "Theodor Heuss and German Jewish Reconciliation after 1945." *German Politics and Society* 24(2): 1-22.
Gerhardt, Uta. 1986. "Verstehende Strukturanalyse. Die Konstruktion von Idealtypen als Analyseschritt bei der Auswertung qualitativer Forschungsmaterialien." Pp. 31-83 in *Sozialstruktur und soziale Typik,* edited by Hans-Georg Soeffner. Frankfurt am Main; New York: Campus.
—. 2001. *Idealtypus. Zur methodischen Begründung der modernen Soziologie.* Frankfurt am Main, Suhrkamp.
Glaeser, Andreas. 2000. *Divided in Unity. Identity, Germany, and the Berlin Police.* Chicago: The University of Chicago Press.
Glaser, Barney G. and Anselm L. Strauss. 2008 [1967]. *The Discovery of Grounded Theory: Strategies for Qualitative Research.* New Brunswick; London: Aldine Transaction.
Glees, Anthony. 1974. "Albert C. Grzesinski and the Politics of Prussia, 1926-1930." *The English Historical Review* 89(353): 814-834.

Goffman, Erving. 1961. *Asylums. Essays on the Social Situation of Mental Patients and Other Inmates.* New York: Anchor Books.
—. 1969 [1959]. *The Presentation of Self in Everyday Life.* London: The Penguin Press.
Goldman, Harvey. 1992. *Politics, Death, and the Devil. Self and Power in Max Weber and Thomas Mann.* Berkeley, Los Angeles, Oxford: University of California Press.
Gombrowicz, Witold. 1993. *Diary. Volume 3 (1961-1966).* Evanston, Illinois: Northwestern University Press.
Graf, Friedrich Wilhelm. 1984. "Kulturprotestantismus. Zur Begriffsgeschichte einer theologiepolitischen Chiffre." *Archiv für Begriffsgeschichte* 28: 214-286.
Grzesinski, Albert Carl. 1974 [1939]. *Inside Germany.* New York: AMS Press.
—. 2001 [1934]. *Im Kampf um die deutsche Republik: Erinnerungen eines Sozialdemokraten,* edited by Eberhard Kolb. München: R. Oldenbourg.
Habermas, Jürgen. 1998. "Struggles for Recognition in the Democratic Constitutional State." Pp. 203-236 in *The Inclusion of the Other: Studies in Political Theory,* edited by Jürgen Habermas, Ciaran Cronin, and Pablo De Greiff. Cambridge, Mass.: MIT Press.
Hahn, Alois. 1982. "Zur Soziologie der Beichte und anderer Formen institutionalisierter Bekenntnisse: Selbstthematisierung und Zivilisationsprozess." *Kölner Zeitschrift für Soziologie und Sozialpsychologie* 34(3): 407-434.
Hamburger, Ernest. 1968. *Juden im öffentlichen Leben Deutschlands. Regierungsmitglieder, Beamte und Parlamentarier in der monarchischen Zeit 1848-1918.* Tübingen: Mohr Siebeck.
Hamburger, Ernest, and Peter Pulzer. 1985. "Jews as Voters in the Weimar Republic." *Year Book of the Leo Baeck Institute* 30(1): 3-66.
Hannerz, Ulf. 1999. "Reflections on Varieties of Culturespeak." *European Journal of Cultural Studies* 2(3): 393-407.
Harrington, Austin. 2002. "Robert Musil and Classical Sociology." *Journal of Classical Sociology* 2(1): 59-76.
—. 2006. "Hermann Broch as a Reader of Max Weber: Protestantism, Rationalization and the 'Disintegration of Values'." *History of the Human Sciences* 19(4): 1-18.

Hazelrigg, Lawrence E. 1969. "A Reexamination of Simmel's 'The Secret and the Secret Society': Nive Propositions." *Social Forces* 47(3): 323-330.
Hébert, Kavin. 2006. *Karl Mannheim et la question des intellectuels durant la République de Weimar.* Doctoral Thesis, Département de sociologie, Université de Montréal.
Hennis, Wilhelm. 1987. *Max Webers Fragestellung. Studien zur Biographie des Werkes.* Tübingen: Mohr Siebeck.
Herzog, Todd. 2009. *Crime Stories. Criminalistic Fantasy and the Culture of Crisis in Weimar Germany.* New York: Berghahn Books.
Hess, John E. 1997. *Interviewing and Interrogation for Law Enforcement.* Cincinnati, OH: Anderson Pub. Co.
Hidas, Zoltán. 2004. *Entzauberte Geschichte. Max Weber und die Krise des Historismus.* Frankfurt am Main: Peter Lang.
Hill Collins, Patricia. 1999 [1991]. "Learning from the Outsider Within. The Sociological Significance of Black Feminist Thought." Pp. 155-178 in *Feminist Approaches to Theory and Methodology*, edited by Sharlene Hesse-Biber, Cristina Gilmartin, and Robin Lydenberg. Oxford: Oxford University Press.
Hofstede, Geert, and Gert Jan Hofstede (Eds.). 2006 [1980]. *Lokales Denken, globales Handeln: Interkulturelle Zusammenarbeit und globales Management.* Munich: DTV-Beck.
Holdaway, Simon, and Megan O'Neill. 2004. "The Development of Black Police Associations." *British Journal of Criminology* 44(6): 854-865.
Holdaway, Simon. 1991. *Recruiting a Multiracial Police Force.* London: HMSO Books.
Houle, Gilles. 1987. "Le sens commun comme forme de connaissance: de l'analyse clinique en sociologie." *Sociologie et sociétés* 19(2): 77-86.
Hunold, Daniela. 2008. *Migranten in der Polizei. Zwischen politischer Programmatik und Organisationswirklichkeit.* Frankfurt am Main: Verlag für Polizeiwissenschaft.
—. 2010. "Vom Promille zum Prozent. Der Bestand an Polizeibeamten mit migrantischem Hintergrund in den Bundesländern." Pp. 137-143 in *Fremde als Ordnungshüter*, edited by Daniela Hunold, Daniela Klimke, Rafael Behr, and Rüdiger Lautmann. Wiesbaden: VS Verlag für Sozialwissenschaften.

Hunold, Daniela, Daniela Klimke, Rafael Behr, and Rüdiger Lautmann. 2010. *Fremde als Ordnungshüter*. Wiesbaden: VS Verlag für Sozialwissenschaften.

Jacobsen, Astrid. 2009. "Was mach ich denn, wenn so'n Türke vor mir steht? Zur interkulturellen Qualifizierung der Polizei." Pp 91-102 in *Polizei und Fremde - Fremde in der Polizei*, edited by Karlhans Liebl. Wiesbaden: VS Verlag für Sozialwissenschaften.

Jameson, Fredric. 1973. "The Vanishing Mediator: Narrative Structure in Max Weber." *New German Critique* 1 (Winter): 52-89.

Jobard, Fabien. 2003. "Usages et ruses des temps. L'unification des polices berlinoises après 1989." *Revue française de science politique* 53(3): 351-381.

Joppke, Christian. 2003. "The Retreat of Multiculturalism in the Liberal State." Working paper #203. New York: Russel Sage Fondation.

Juteau-Lee, Danielle. 1983. "La production de l'ethnicité ou la part réelle de l'idéel." *Sociologie et sociétés* 15(2): 39-55.

Kalberg, Stephen. 1994. *Max Weber's Comparative-Historical Sociology*. Chicago: University of Chicago Press.

Kalinowski, Isabelle. 2005. "Un savant très politique." Pp. 191-240 in *La science, profession & vocation. Suivi de "Leçons wébériennes sur la science & la propagande,"* edited by Isabelle Kalinowski. Marseille: Agone.

Kant, Immanuel. 1990 [1785]. *Foundations of the Metaphysics of Morals*. New York: Macmillan.

Kaufmann, Jean-Claude. 2008 [1996]. *L'entretien compréhensif*. Paris: Armand Colin.

Kemple, Thomas. 2006. "Spirits of Capitalism: Weber, Franklin, and Luther on the Arts of Sociological Allegory." Paper presented at the Centre canadien d'études allemandes et européennes, 13 October 2006, Montreal.

Kerr, Philipp. 1993 [1989]. "March Violets." Pp. 1-246 in *Berlin Noir*. London: Penguin Books.

Klimke, Daniela. 2010. "Die Polizeiorganisation und ihre Migranten," Pp. 27-59 in *Fremde als Ordnungshüter*, edited by Daniela Hunold, Daniela Klimke, Rafael Behr, and Rüdiger Lautmann. Wiesbaden: VS Verlag für Sozialwissenschaften.

Kracauer, Siegfried. 1995 [1920]. "Georg Simmel." Pp. 97-119 in *The Mass Ornament*, edited by Thomas Y. Levin. Cambridge, MA; London, England: Harvard University Press: 225-257.

Krell, Gertraude, and Hartmut Wächter (Eds.). 2006. *Diversity Management: Impulse aus der Personalforschung*. München; Mering: Rainer Hampp Verlag.

Krell, Gertraude, Barbara Riedmüller, Barbara Sieben, and Dagmar Vinz (Eds.). 2007. *Diversity Studies. Grundlagen und disziplinäre Ansätze*. Frankfurt am Main: Campus.

Kumbier, Dagmar, and Friedemann Schulz von Thun (Eds.). 2006. *Interkulturelle Kommunikation: Methoden, Modelle, Beispiele*. Reinbek bei Hamburg: Rowohlt.

Kundera, Milan. 1988 [1986]. *The Art of the Novel*. London: Faber and Faber.

—. 1999 [1990]. *Immortality*. New York: Perennial Classics.

—. 2001 [1993]. *Testament Betrayed. An Essay in Nine Parts*. New York: Perennial.

Langewiesche, Dieter. 1993. *"Republik" und "Republikaner." Von der historischen Entwertung eines politischen Begriffs* Essen: Klartext.

—. 2000 [1988]. *Liberalism in Germany*. Princeton: Princeton University Press.

Latour, Bruno. "How to Think about Science." Radio interview, Canadian Broadcasting Corporation (CBC), 30 January 2009.

Lautmann, Rüdiger. 2010. "Wissen und Organisation. Erfahrungen mit dem Versuch, Forschung und Praxis miteinander zu verbinden." Pp. 99-135 in *Fremde als Ordnungshüter*, edited by Daniela Hunold, Daniela Klimke, Rafael Behr, and Rüdiger Lautmann. Wiesbaden: VS Verlag für Sozialwissenschaften.

Lavoie, Danya. 2006. *Les dirigeants du SPVM, les chercheurs et les policiers arabo-musulmans: une étude sur l'institutionnalisation de la "diversité"*. M.A. Thesis, Département de sociologie, Université de Montréal.

Leenen, Wolf Rainer, Alexander Scheitza, and Isabelle Klarenaar. 2011. "Die unterschätzte Herausforderung: Implementierung interkultureller Kompetenz in der Polizei." Pp. 31-61 in *Polizei & Psychologie*, edited by Clemens Lorei. Frankfurt am Main: Verlag für Polizeiwissenschaft.

Leenen, Wolf Rainer, and Andreas Groß. 2007. "Praxisforschung als interaktiver Prozess: Vermittlung interkultureller Kompetenz für die Polizei." Pp. 183-200 in *Grenzen. Differenzen. Übergänge: Spannungsfelder inter- und transkultureller Kommunikation*, edited by Antje Gunsenheimer. Bielefeld: transcript.

Lehmkuhl, Ursula, and Laurence McFalls. 2012. *Diversity. Mediating Difference in Transcultural Spaces*. Program of the International Research Training Group (IRTG), Universität Trier, Universität des Saarlandes and Université de Montréal.

Leiprecht, Rudolf. 2002. *Politiewerk in de multiculturele samenleving Duitsland / Polizeiarbeit in der Einwanderungsgesellschaft Deutschland*. Gravenhage: Elsevier Overheid.

Lepenies, Wolf. 1988. *Between Literature and Science: The Rise of Sociology*. Cambridge; New York; Paris: Cambridge University Press; Editions de la Maison des sciences de l'homme.

Liang, Hsi-Huey. 1970. *The Berlin Police Force in the Weimar Republic*. Berkeley: University of California Press.

Liebl, Karlhans. 2004. *Fehler und Lernkultur in der Polizei*. Frankfurt am Main: Verlag für Polizeiwissenschaft.

Loftus, Bethan. 2010a. *Police Culture in a Changing World*. Oxford: Oxford University Press.

—. 2010b. "Police Occupational Culture: Classic Themes, Altered Times." *Policing & Society* 20(1): 1-20.

Lutes, Jason. 2008 [2001]. *Berlin. City of Stones (Book One)*. Montreal: Drawn & Quaterly.

Mahlmann, Matthias. 2003. "Religious Tolerance, Pluralist Society and the Neutrality of the State: The Federal Constitutional Court's Decision in the *Headscarf Case*." *German Law Journal* 4(11): 1099-1116.

Manasse, Ernst Moritz. 1944. "Moral Principles and Alternatives in Max Weber and John Dewey. I." *The Journal of Philosophy* XLI(2): 29-48.

Mann, Thomas. 1970. *Tonio Kroger and Other Stories*. New York: Bantam Books.

—. 1994 [1901]. *Buddenbrooks. The Decline of a Family*. New York: Vintage Books.

—. 2006 [1950]. "My Times." *New England Review* 27(4): 190-203.

Mannheim, Karl. 1929. *Ideologie und Utopie*. Bonn: Cohen.

—. 1958 [1935]. *Mensch und Gesellschaft im Zeitalter des Umbaus*. Darmstadt: Gentner.
Manning, Peter K. 1974. "Police Lying." *Urban Life and Culture* 3(3): 283-306.
—. 2005. "The Police: Mandate, Strategies, and Appearances." Pp. 191-214 in *Policing: Key Readings*, edited by Tim Newburn. Cullompton: Willan Publishing.
Martuccelli, Danilo. 1999. *Sociologies de la modernité: l'itinéraire du XXe siècle*. Paris: Gallimard.
—. 2009. "Qu'est-ce qu'une sociologie de l'individu moderne? Pour quoi, pour qui, comment?" *Sociologie et sociétés* 39(2): 15-33.
—. 2010. *La société singulariste*. Paris, Armand Colin.
Martuccelli, Danilo, and François de Singly. 2009. *Les sociologies de l'individu*. Paris: Armand Colin.
Marx, Karl. 1965 [1867]. *Capital. A Critical Analysis of Capitalist Production* (volume 1). Moscow, Progress Publishers.
Mills, C. Wright. 1940. "Situated Action and the Vocabulary of Motives." *American Sociological Review* 46(5): 904-913.
Monjardet, Dominique. 2005. "Gibier de recherche, la police et le projet de connaissance." *Criminologie* 38(2): 13-37.
Murck, Manfred. 1996. "Zwischen Offenheit und Empörung." Pp. 5-7 in *Fremdenfeindlichkeit in der Polizei? Ergebnisse einer wissenschaftlichen Studie* (Schriftenreihe der Polizei-Führungsakademie). Münster: PFA.
Newburn, Tim (Ed.). 2005. *Policing: Key Readings*. Cullompton: Willan Publishing.
Nisbet, Robert A. 1976. *Sociology as an Art Form*. New York: Oxford University Press.
Oakes, Guy. 1987. "Max Weber and the Southwest German School: Remarks on the Genesis of the Concept of the Historical Individual." *International Journal of Politics, Culture, and Society* 1(1): 115-131.
Otto, Martin. 2003. "'Selbstverwaltung ist kein ein für allemal feststehender Begriff' — Zu den Veröffentlichungen von Bill Drews nach 1933." *Archiv für Polizeigeschichte* 14(1): 20-26.
Overesch, Manfred. 1992. "Die Einbürgerung Hitlers 1930." *Vierteljahrshefte für Zeitgeschichte* 40(4): 543-566.

Passeron, Jean-Claude. 1996. "Introduction." Pp. 1-49 in *Sociologie des religions* (Max Weber), edited by Jean-Pierre Grossein. Paris: Gallimard.

Pikart, Eberhard 1958. "Preußische Beamtenpolitik 1918-1933." *Vierteljahresheft für Zeitgeschichte* 6(2): 119-137.

Pulzer, Peter G. J. 1992. *Jews and the German State: The Political History of a Minority, 1848-1933*. Oxford, UK; Cambridge, Mass.: Blackwell.

Rehberg, Karl-Siegbert. 1994. "Institutionen als symbolische Ordnungen. Leitfragen und Grundkategorien zur Theorie und Analyse institutioneller Mechanismen." Pp. 47-84 in *Die Eigenart der Institutionen*, edited by Gerhard Göhler. Baden-Baden: Nomos.

—. 2004. "Handlungsbezogener Personalismus als Paradigma." *Berliner Journal für Soziologie* 14(4): 451-461.

Reiner, Robert. 2010 [2000]. *The Politics of the Police*. Oxford: Oxford University Press.

Reuss-Ianni, Elizabeth. 1983. *Two Cultures of Policing: Street Cops and Management Cops*. New Brunswick, (N.J.), Transaction Books.

Roth, Joseph. 2002 [1938]. *The Emperor's Tomb*. New York: Overlook.

—. 2004 [1932]. *Radetzky March*. New York: Overlook Press.

Rott, Joachim. 2008. *Bernhard Weiss. 1880 Berlin — 1951 London. Polizeivizepräsident in Berlin — Preussischer Jude — Kämpferischer Demokrat*. Berlin: Hentrich & Hentrich.

Sanders, William B. 1974. *The Sociologist as Detective. An Introduction to Research Methods*. New York: Praeger.

Saupe, Achim. 2009. *Der Historiker als Detektiv — der Detektiv als Historiker*. Bielefeld: transcript.

Schicht, Günter. 2007. *Menschenrechtsbildung für die Polizei*. Berlin: Deutsches Institut für Menschenrechte.

Schiffauer, Werner. 1997a. "Die *civil society* und der Fremde. Grenzmarkierung in vier politischen Kulturen." Pp. 35-49 in *Fremde in der Stadt*, edited by Werner Schiffauer. Frankfurt am Main: Suhrkamp.

—. 1997b. "Islam as a Civil Religion: Political Culture and the Organisation of Diversity in Germany." Pp. 147-166 in *The Politics of Multiculturalism in the New Europe: Racism, Identity, and Community*, edited by Tariq Modood and Pnina Werbner. London; New York: Zed Books.

—. 2006. "Verwaltete Sicherheit — Präventionspolitik und Integration." Pp. 113-163 in *Migrationsreport 2006. Fakten — Analysen — Perspek-*

tiven, edited by Michael Bommes and Werner Schiffauer. Frankfurt am Main; New York: Campus.
Schiffauer, Werner, Gerd Baumann, Riva Kastoryano, and Steven Vertovec. 2004 [2002]. *Civil Enculturation. Nation-State, School and Ethnic Difference in The Netherlands, Britain, Germany and France*. New York; Oxford: Berghahn.
Schluchter, Wolfgang. 1991a. *Religion und Lebensführung. Studien zu Max Webers Religions- und Herrschaftssoziologie*. Frankfurt am Main: Suhrkamp.
—. 1991b. "'Wirtschaft und Gesellschaft': Das Ende eines Mythos." Pp. 597-634 in *Religion und Lebensführung. Studien zu Max Webers Religions- und Herrschaftssoziologie*. Frankfurt am Main: Suhrkamp.
—. 1998. "Replik." Pp. 320-365 in *Verantwortliches Handeln in gesellschaftlichen Ordnungen: Beiträge zu Wolfgang Schluchters "Religion und Lebensführung"*, edited by Agathe Bienfait and Gerhard Wagner. Frankfurt am Main: Suhrkamp.
—. 1998 [1979]. *Die Entstehung des modernen Rationalismus. Eine Analyse von Max Webers Entwicklungsgeschichte des Okzidents*. Frankfurt am Main: Suhrkamp.
—. 2006. *Grundlegungen der Soziologie. Eine Theoriegeschichte in systematischer Absicht*. Tübingen: Mohr Siebeck.
Schneider, Hans, and Lusaper Witteck. 2009. "Polizei und Fremde — Künftig gemeinsam als Verbündete?!" Pp. 193-202 in *Polizei und Fremde-Fremde in der Polizei*, edited by Karlhans Liebl. Wiesbaden: VS Verlag für Sozialwissenschaften.
Schütz, Alfred. 1974 [1932]. *Der sinnhafte Aufbau der sozialen Welt*. Frankfurt am Main: Suhrkamp.
Schweer, Thomas, Hermann Strasser, and Steffen Zdun (Eds.). 2008. *"Das da draußen ist ein Zoo, und wir sind die Dompteure": Polizisten im Konflikt mit ethnischen Minderheiten und sozialen Randgruppen*. Wiesbaden: VS Verlag für Sozialwissenschaften.
Schwell, Alexandra. 2008. *Europa an der Oder. Die Konstruktion europäischer Sicherheit an der deutsch-polnischen Grenze*. Bielefeld: transcript.
Simmel, Georg. 1950 [1908]. *The Sociology of Georg Simmel*, edited by Kurt H. Wolff. Glencoe, Illinois: The Free Press.

—. 1950a [1908]. "Individual and Society in Eighteenth- and Nineteenth-Century Views of Life." Pp. 58-84 in *The Sociology of Georg Simmel*, edited by Kurt H. Wolff. Glencoe, Illinois: The Free Press.

—. 1950b [1908]. "The Secret and the Secret Society." Pp. 305-376 in *The Sociology of Georg Simmel*, edited by Kurt H. Wolff. Glencoe, Illinois: The Free Press.

—. 1971 [1907]. "Prostitution." Pp. 121-126 in *Georg Simmel On Individuality and Social Forms*, edited by Donald N Levine. Chicago: The University of Chicago Press.

—. 1984 [1921/1922]. "On Love (a Fragment)." Pp. 153-192 in *Georg Simmel, on Women, Sexuality, and Love*, edited by Guy Oakes. New Haven: Yale University Press.

Skolnick, Jerome H. 1966. *Justice without Trial: Law Enforcement in Democratic Society*. New York: Macmillan.

Skolnick, Jerome H., and David H. Bayley. 1988. *The New Blue Line: Police Innovation in Six American Cities*. New York; London: Free Press; Collier Macmillan Publishers.

Spivak, Gayatri C. 1988. "Can the Subaltern Speak?" Pp. 271-313 in *Marxism and the Interpretation of Culture*, edited by Cary Nelson and Lawrence Grossberg. Urbana: University of Illinois Press.

Sterzenbach, Gregor (forthcoming). *Interkulturelles Handeln zwischen Polizei und Fremden*. Münster: Waxmann.

Suchy, Barbara. 1983. "The Verein zur Abwehr des Antisemitismus (I). From its Beginnings to the First World War." *Year Book of the Leo Baeck Institute* 28(1): 205-239.

Sullivan, Roger, J. 1997 [1994]. *An Introduction to Kant's Ethics*. Cambridge: Cambridge University Press.

Thériault, Barbara. 2004. *'Conservative Revolutionaries': Protestant and Catholic Churches in Germany after Radical Political Change in the 1990s*. New York; Oxford: Berghahn Books.

—. 2005. "Ordres légitimes et légitimité des ordres: une approche 'wébérienne' des institutions." Pp. 175-186 in *La légitimité de l'État et du droit. Autour de Max Weber*, edited by Michel Coutu and Guy Rocher. Québec: Presses de l'Université Laval.

Thériault, Barbara, and Sirma Bilge. 2010. "Des passeurs aux frontières." *Sociologie et sociétés* 42(1): 9-15.

Thomas, Alexander. 2006. "Interkulturelle Handlungskompetenz — Schlüsselkompetenz für die moderne Arbeitswelt." *Arbeit* 15(2): 114-125.
Tietze, Nikola. 2001. *Islamische Identitäten. Formen muslimischer Religiosität junger Männer in Deutschland und Frankreich*. Hamburg: Hamburger Edition.
—. 2008. "La régulation institutionnelle de l'islam en Allemagne." Pp. 235-244 in *La laïcité en question. Religion, État et société en France et en Allemagne du 18e siècle à nos jours*, edited by Sylvie Le Grand. Université Paris X, Nanterre: Les Presses Universitaires du Septentrion.
Tížik, Miroslav. 2001. "La conversion comme sacralisation du monde." *Sociétés* 74(4): 81-91.
Topal, Murat. 2005. *Getürkte Fälle. Ein Cop packt aus!* Zyx Music (CD).
—. 2008. *Polizei für Anfänger: das ultimative Buch für Ordnungshüter, Gesetzesbrecher und sonstige Normalbürger*. Oldenburg: Lappan Verlag.
—. 2010. *Der Bülle von Kreuzberg: Aus dem Leben eines deutschtürkischen Polizisten*. Berlin: Ullstein Taschenbuchverlag.
Turner, Bryan S. 2007. "Foreword." Pp. ix-xiii in *Good Intentions: Max Weber and the Paradox of Unintended Consequences*, edited by Mohamed Cherkaoui. Oxford: Bardwell Press.
Turner, Stephen P., and Regis A. Factor. 1994. *Max Weber. The Lawyer as Social Thinker*. London; New York: Routledge.
Uth, Heinz. 1996. "Am Ende ein Kreuzl!? Fünf Jahre als Ansprechpartner für gleichgeschlechtliche Lebensweise bei der Berliner Polizei." Pp. 145-153 in *Schwule, Lesben, Polizei. Vom Zwangsverhältnis zur Zweck-Ehe?*, edited by Jens Dobler. Berlin: Verlag Rosa Winkel.
Waddington, P.A.J. 1999. "Police (Canteen) Sub-culture: An Appreciation." *British Journal of Criminology* 39(2): 287-309.
Weber, Max. 1949 [1904]. "'Objectivity' in Social Sciences and Social Policy." Pp. 50-112 in *The Methodology of Social Sciences*. New York: The Free Press.
—. 1949 [1906]. "Critical Studies in the Logic of the Cultural Science." Pp. 113-188 in *The Methodology of Social Sciences*. New York: The Free Press.

—. 1949 [1917]. "The Meaning of 'Ethical Neutrality' in Sociology and Economics." Pp. 1-47 in *The Methodology of Social Sciences*. New York: The Free Press.
—. 1978a [1921]. *Economy and Society. An Outline of Interpretive Sociology I*. Berkeley; Los Angeles: University of California Press.
—. 1978b [1921]. *Economy and Society. An Outline of Interpretive Sociology II*. Berkeley; Los Angeles: University of California Press.
—. 1972 [1921]. *Wirtschaft und Gesellschaft*. Tübingen: Mohr Siebeck.
—. 1988 [1920]. *Gesammelte Aufsätze zur Religionssoziologie I*. Tübingen: Mohr Siebeck.
—. 2001 [1906]. "The Protestant Sects and the Spirit of Capitalism." Pp. 127-147 in *The Protestant Ethic and the Spirit of Capitalism*, edited and translated by Stephen Kalberg. Los Angeles: Roxbury Publishing Company.
—. 2001 [1910]. "Weber's Second Reply to Rachfahl, 1910." Pp. 93-132 in *The Protestant Ethic Debate: Max Weber's Replies to His Critics, 1907-1910*, edited by David J. Chalcraft, Austin Harrington, and Mary Shields. Liverpool: Liverpool University Press.
—. 2004 [1917/1919]. *The Vocation Lectures*. Indianapolis; Cambridge: Hackett Publishing Company.
—. 2004 [1919]. "Politics as a Vocation." Pp. 32-94 in *The Vocation Lectures*. Indianapolis; Cambridge: Hackett Publishing Company.
—. 2007 [1904/1905]. *The Protestant Ethic and the Spirit of Capitalism*. London; New York: Routledge.
Weiß, Johannes. 1992. "Representative Culture and Cultural Representation." Pp. 121-144 in *Theory of Culture*, edited by Richard Münch and Neil J. Smelser. Berkeley; Los Angeles; Oxford: University of California Press.
—. 1998. *Handeln und handeln lassen: Über Stellvertretung*. Opladen: Westdeutscher Verlag.
—. 2001. "Über interkulturelle Vermittler." Pp. 79-88 in *Sinngeneratoren: Fremd- und Selbstthematisierung in soziologisch-historischer Perspektive*, edited by Cornelia Bohn, and Herbert Willems. Konstanz: UVK Verlagsgesellschaft.
—. 2006. "Grenzen der Stellvertretung." Pp. 313-324 in *Stellvertretung. Theologische, philosophische und kulturelle Aspekte*, edited by Chris-

tine Janowski, Bernd Janowski, and Hans P. Lichtenberger: Neukirchen- Vluyn.
Werner, Michael, and Bénédicte Zimmermann. 2006. "Beyond Comparison: *Histoire Croisée* and the Challenge of Reflexivity." *History and Theory* 45(1): 30-50.
Westley, William A. 1956. "Secrecy and the Police." *Social Forces* 34(3): 254-257.
—. 1970. *Violence and the Police: A Sociological Study of Law, Custom and Morality*. Cambridge, Mass.: MIT Press.
Wetterer, Angelika. 2002. "Strategien rhetorischer Modernisierung. Gender Mainstreaming, Managing Diversity und die Professionalisierung der Gender-Expertinnen." *Zeitschrift für Frauenforschung & Geschlechterstudien* 20(3): 129-148.
Widmaier, Benedikt. 1987. *Die Bundeszentrale für politische Bildung. Ein Beitrag zur Geschichte staatlicher politischer Bildung in der Bundesrepublik Deutschland*. Frankfurt am Main: Peter Lang.
Williams, Raymond. 1983 [1976]. "Representative." Pp. 266-269 in *Keywords. A Vocabulary of Culture and Society*. New York: Oxford University Press.
Wolff, Kurt H. (1950). "Introduction." *The Sociology of Georg Simmel*, edited by Kurt H. Wolff. Glencoe, Illinois: The Free Press, xvii-lxiv.
Zaimoglu, Feridun. 2003. *Leinwand*. Hamburg: Rotbuch Verlag.

Other documents:
Amnesty International. 2004. "Erneut im Fokus. Vorwürfe über polizeiliche Misshandlungen und den Einsatz unverhältnismäßiger Gewalt in Deutschland 2004." URL: http://www2.amnesty.de/internet/deall.nsf/windexde/LB2004001 (accessed 24 June 2006).
Antrag der Fraktion der FDP (Abgeordnetenhaus Berlin). 2004. *Bernhard Weiss zu Ehren* (Drucksache 15/2404). Berlin.
Bemmer, Ariane, "Frauen-Quote für den Stadtplan," *Der Tagesspiegel*, 28 June 2004.
Bürgerschaft der freien und Hansestadt Hamburg, *Mitteilung des Senats an die Bürgerschaft. Ausländische Polizisten für Hamburg* (Drucksache 15/177; 30.11.1993). Hamburg.

Bürgerschaft der freien und Hansestadt Hamburg, *Mitteilung des Senats an die Bürgerschaft. Ausländische Polizisten für Hamburg* (Drucksache 15/2883; 21.02.1995). Hamburg.

Bürgerschaft der freien und Hansestadt Hamburg, *Decree IM* (31.07.1996). Hamburg.

Dippel von, Alexander. "Raus aus den Schubladen! Diversity Management in öffentlichen Verwaltungen und die Einbeziehung von Intersektionalität." URL: http://www.migration-boell.de/web/diversity/48_2150.asp (accessed 14 September 2012).

Förderkreis Polizeihistorische Sammlung Berlin e.V. 2003. "Die Deutsche Einigung als Teil eines Integrationsprozesses auf dem Wege eines geeinten Europas." *Berliner Polizeihistoriker (3. Oktober 1990 — 10 Jahre danach)* 8: 13-15.

Hasselmann, Fred, "Heinz Uth, Schwulenbeauftragter bei der Polizei." *Berliner Zeitung*, 16 November 1995.

Junge Gruppe Berlin (Gewerkschaft der Polizei). 2006. "Einstellungspraxis für Bewerber/-Innen mit Migrationshintergrund. Rechtswidrig und diskriminierend." URL: http://www.gdp.de/gdp/gdpber.nsf/id/jg_presse_1 (accessed 24 June 2006).

N.N. 1997. *Konzeption zur Erhöhung des Anteils ausländischer Mitbürgerinnen / Mitbürger im Polizeidienst.*

N.N. 1999 [1997]. *Mitarbeiter ausländischer Herkunft im Polizeivollzugsdienst.* Conference at the Police Federal Academy, Münster.

N.N. 2004. *Einstellung von Polizeibeamten ausländischer Herkunft.* Internal document, Hamburg Police Academy.

N.N. 2006. "Streit um Polizei-Einstellung: Erste Klagen angekündigt. Abgelehnte deutsche Bewerber wollen gleiche Chancen wie ausländische Jobanwärter," *Berliner Morgenpost*, 14 February 2006.

N.N. 2006. "Ausbildungs-Aktion: Multikulti im Staatsdienst," *Hamburger Abendblatt*, 7 November 2006.

N.N. 2007. Internal document, Police Academy of Lower-Saxony.

N.N. 2008. "Brücke für Polizei und Muslime," *Islamische Zeitung*, 26 February 2008.

Oloew, Matthias, "Männer hinten anstellen," *Der Tagesspiegel*, 18 April 2006.

Letters
Schertz's letter to Galinski, 9 May 1989.
Letter of the president of the Police Historical Society to the city councilor responsible for construction, 27 September 2004.

Index

affirmative action, 69
Basic Law, 24; basic rights, 87, 88, 100, 101, 106, 107
Berlin Police Academy, 86, 87, 89, 90, 108; Police Department, 67, 83, 85, 89fn, 91, 95, 96; Police Museum, 35, 86, 91, 92fn, 96
Beruf, 139, 166
Bildungsbürgertum, 77, 98, 177, 185, 193; *bildungsbürgerlich*, 177, 178, 182
Canada, 30fn, 33, 35, 74, 77, 117fn, 136, 138, 139, 150, 160, 162
Britain, 117
causal 47, 49, 55, 98, 177, 179, 193
CDU, 65
Charter of diversity, 126, 143
chaplaincy, 34, 74, 77
citizenship, 24, 25, 65, 67, 68, 69, 70, 80
Clearingstelle, 90, 166, 168, 172
Conference of Ministers and Senators of the Interior, 24, 30, 64, 113

Culture-Protestantism, 77, 177
DDP, 93-99, 178
democratization, 84, 100, 106, 107, 109, 122, 148fn, 153, 197
discrimination, 83, 79, 81, 89, 95, 105, 107, 122; antidiscrimination, 94fn, 126, 140, 149, 150fn, 152, 156, 167, 169, 171
diversity management, 29, 112fn, 124, 125, 126-127, 129-137, 140, 149, 152; spirit of diversity, 17, 28, 40, 55, 123, 134, 136, 139, 149, 150-155, 170-182, 193, 194
Drews, Bill, 85, 93, 99, 100
duty, 55, 66, 78, 79, 106, 124, 133, 134, 138, 161, 183, 184, 197
elasticity, 181, 194
Elias, Norbert, 39, 54fn, 81, 92, 97, 131fn, 172, 183
empathy, 75, 76, 80, 81, 84, 100, 106, 179, 197

entry exams, 73, 78, 80, 90, 115, 147
European Union, 68, 70, 89, 127, 146, 151
FDP, 93, 94, 98, 178
firms, 126, 130
Federal Office for Migration and Refugees, 26
feminism, 152; feminist, 107, 164
Foreigners' Commissioner, 89, 171, 173
Frankfurt/Main, 90fn, 166
Friedrichstraße, 93
gay, 107, 139, 166, 167, 171, 172
gender, 29, 31fn, 126, 151, 152, 169, 170; gender mainstreaming 33, 137, 150
German Democratic Republic, 83, 132fn; East German, 83, 84, 151fn
German Federal Republic, 66, 85, 86, 94, 132fn
Goebbels, Joseph, 93, 94, 192
Grzesinski, Albert, 13, 96, 99, 100, 103, 192
Hamburg Police Department, 66, 68, 69, 70, 78; Police Academy, 64, 66, 68, 69, 72, 73, 82fn, 168fn
Hanover, 166
historical individual, 31, 180
human rights, 34, 82, 109
ideal types, 16, 18, 19, 31, 32, 37, 38, 39, 40, 50fn, 57, 75, 99fn, 123, 124, 134fn, 136, 144, 152, 159, 160, 161, 174, 175, 176, 177, 182, 193, 187
interculturalist, 137, 152fn, 155; interculturalism, 145
Jews, 88, 92, 93, 95, 98, 99, 100, 103, 108, 172; Jewish, 39, 67, 88, 103, 105, 108, 173fn, 192; Jewish community, 95, 166
Kant, Immanuel, 39, 46, 50, 53, 54, 57, 106fn, 111, 132-134, 136, 177, 184
Liberalism, 18, 39, 85, 136, 173, 182, 183, 193; liberal 43, 52, 54, 77, 85, 86, 93-106, 109, 131, 134, 146, 152, 160, 172-178, 183, 184, 185, 193, 194, 195
legitimacy, 41, 43, 47, 103, 167, 178, 180
Maastricht, 68
Mann, Thomas, 17, 133, 183-184
mentoring, 152, 156
middle class, 93, 95, 98, 172, 177, 178, 183, 185
Montreal, 15, 16, 17, 18, 23, 25, 26fn, 33, 34, 41, 63, 66, fn, 137fn
motives, 16, 31, 36-59, 63, 67, 72, 75, 76, 80, 86, 97, 98, 99, 104, 105, 106, 109, 112, 119, 122, 123, 124, 130, 131-140, 144, 153, 154, 155, 159, 160, 161, 163, 174, 175, 178, 179, 180, 184, 193, 195

Muslim, 72, 105, 116, 143, 168, 169
NGO, 35, 37, 88, 89, 101
oath, 66, 67, 92, 189
opportunism, 39, 112, 124, 133-136, 153, 174, 179, 194
PDS, 94
police culture, 27, 74, 125, 129, 130, 131, 153, 190, 191, 192; cop culture, 41, 125, 129, 131, 135, 154, 189-191, 193
Police Federal Academy, 113, 117fn, 178
political education, 34, 85-91, 97, 107, 108, 109, 134, 142, 144, 146, 155, 159, 168, 175
principle of equality, 24, 70, 77, 96, 97, 99, 121, 180, 186, 192
Protestant ethic, 31, 46fn, 47, 48, 50fn, 56, 58, 123, 139, 179, 184
quota, 117
Stellvertretung (representation), 40, 162-165, 173, 176, 177
racism, 30, 73, 79, 88, 113
recruitment, 24, 25, 27, 28, 29, 33, 34, 37fn, 39, 52, 60, 63-70, 84, 90, 91, 96, 100, 101, 104, 113-116, 119-127, 139-144, 147, 149, 155, 156, 162, 169, 174, 190, 192, 197
secret society, 178, 186-189, 191fn, 192, 193
Seelsorge, 74, 77, 79
Simmel, Georg, 28fn, 61, 75fn, 98fn, 133fn, 134, 136, 145fn, 164fn, 175, 182, 185-195
SPD, 65, 94, 99, 100

specialists, 18, 34, 39, 40, 136-140, 149-151, 152-155, 160, 162, 164, 170-176, 180, 182, 193, 194
suspicion, 41, 190
The Netherlands, 23, 39, 116-118, 126, 181
trade union, 34, 35, 75, 77, 100fn, 102, 120fn, 171
Troeltsch, Ernst, 177, 178, 182, 185, 194
Turkish, 13, 25fn, 36, 64, 65, 67, 68, 69, 70, 73, 80, 84fn, 90, 91, 99, 143, 155, 168, 171
unification (of Germany), 83fn, 92
university, 23, 42, 66fn, 144
"we-ideal," 39, 97
Weber, Max, 15, 16, 18, 31, 32, 35fn, 38-59, 75, 76, 79, 89, 98, 104, 106, 121-124, 133, 134fn, 138, 139, 146, 150, 154, 162fn, 163, 164, 165, 178, 179, 180, 182, 184, 185, 193, 194
Weimar, 29, 39, 67, 85, 87, 92-105, 132fn, 134, 160, 172, 175, 177, 178, 192, 194
Weiß, Bernhard, 13, 86, 91-101, 106, 108, 165, 166, 172, 178
women, 17, 33fn, 72, 94, 99, 107, 126, 142-151, 160, 162, 166, 167, 168, 169, 172fn, 173fn, 197

The Characters
Berger, Claudia, 17, 139-158, 160, 161, 169, 170, 171, 172, 175
Bobkowski, Klaus, 17, 18, 39, 59, 85-109, 131, 134, 135, 148, 155, 159, 160, 161, 165, 166, 168, 172, 175, 178, 192, 193
Piontek, Dieter, 17, 24, 39, 60, 63-84, 115, 121, 122fn, 128, 142, 143, 149, 153, 155, 159, 161, 165, 168, 170, 172, 175, 178
The police researcher, 125-136; 153, 181, 186
Schmitt, Elke, 17, 37fn, 111-125, 127, 128, 129fn, 131, 135, 136, 143, 153fn, 155, 160, 161, 168-170, 174, 192
Schwarz, Tamara, 17, 76, 78, 79, 80, 82, 84, 122fn, 155
Winter, Brigitte, 17, 77, 105, 28fn, 155
The sociologist, 31, 38-44, 47-57, 74, 75, 104, 105, 135, 139, 152, 153, 159, 167-171, 172, 190, 191, 194